Empower Your Kids

Empower Your Kids

A Professor's Guide to Make Learning Fun Every Day

*

Noah Charney

BLOOMSBURY ACADEMIC
NEW YORK • LONDON • OXFORD • NEW DELHI • SYDNEY

BLOOMSBURY ACADEMIC
Bloomsbury Publishing Inc, 1359 Broadway, New York, NY 10018, USA
Bloomsbury Publishing Plc, 50 Bedford Square, London, WC1B 3DP, UK
Bloomsbury Publishing Ireland, 29 Earlsfort Terrace, Dublin 2, D02 AY28, Ireland

BLOOMSBURY, BLOOMSBURY ACADEMIC and the Diana logo are trademarks of
Bloomsbury Publishing Plc

First published in the United States of America 2026

Copyright © Noah Charney, 2026

Cover images: Urška Charney

All rights reserved. No part of this publication may be: i) reproduced or transmitted in any form, electronic or mechanical, including photocopying, recording or by means of any information storage or retrieval system without prior permission in writing from the publishers; or ii) used or reproduced in any way for the training, development or operation of artificial intelligence (AI) technologies, including generative AI technologies. The rights holders expressly reserve this publication from the text and data mining exception as per Article 4(3) of the Digital Single Market Directive (EU) 2019/790.

Bloomsbury Publishing Inc does not have any control over, or responsibility for, any third-party websites referred to or in this book. All internet addresses given in this book were correct at the time of going to press. The author and publisher regret any inconvenience caused if addresses have changed or sites have ceased to exist, but can accept no responsibility for any such changes.

A catalog record for this book is available from the Library of Congress.

ISBN: HB: 979-8-8818-0307-0
ePDF: 979-8-8818-5627-4
eBook: 979-8-8818-0308-7

Typeset by Urška Charney
Printed and bound in the United States of America

All illustrations created by Urška, Izabella, and Eleonora Charney, used with permission.

For product safety related questions contact productsafety@bloomsbury.com.

To find out more about our authors and books visit www.bloomsbury.com and sign up for our newsletters.

To Carla M. Horwitz, Calvin Hill Daycare,
and the Foote School

Contents

	Introduction	ix
1	**The Lesson Game Approach**	1
	The Rules of the Lesson Game	1
2	**Your Utility Belt**	9
	Preview—Engage—Review	9
	The Superpower Toolbox	12
	The Magic of Fifteen Minutes (or Far Less)	20
3	**Empowering Parents**	25
	Dog vs. Baby	25
	Journaling Your Lesson Games and Superpowers	29
	Quantifying the Lesson Plan	31
	Four Ways to "Slow Down" Our Happy Memories with Our Children	32
	Totally Legit "Cheats"	36
4	**The Lesson Game in Practice**	39
	Leveling Up Your Superpowers	39
	A Superpowered Cooking Course at Home with Your Kids	41
	The Power of Make-Believe Roleplaying	47
	Outsourcing Lesson Games: Aunty Liisa's Guide to Science Lessonlets	48
	Art Museums with Children	54
	Cezanne and *Goodnight Moon*	57
5	**The Role of Screens in Learning**	61
	Use *Harry Potter* to Teach Your Kids: Turning Movies You'll Watch Anyway into a Fun Lesson Plan for Your Children	62
	Introduce Your Favorite Childhood Video Games and Cartoons to Your Kids	67

	How to Serve Your Kids a Slice of Nostalgia Through Film	69
	Superpower Your *Tomb Raider*:	
	Making Video Games Educational	74
6	**Novelty and the Power of Slowness and Boredom**	**79**
	The (Super)Power of Boredom:	
	Why Letting Your Kids Get Bored Is a Gift	79
	The Beauty of Silent Togetherness	81
	On Consistency and Novelty	83
	How to Travel with Your Children:	
	Tips for Car Rides, Holidays, and Virtual Travel	86
	A Way to Virtually "Travel" from Home	89
7	**Empowering Grandparents**	**93**
	Virtual Grandparenting 101	93
	Virtual Learning with Dr. Diane Joy "Nonna" Charney	95
	Virtual Reading with James "Greppen" Charney, MD	100
	The Superpower Reading Menu	103
	Nonna's Perspective on Empowering Your (Grand)Kids	107
	Greppen's Perspective on Empowering Kids	110
8	**Cultures of Education**	**123**
	Positive Parenting in Early Childhood Education	123
	Six Things an American Father Has Learned	
	from Raising Kids in Slovenia	128
	Tips for Multilingual Families or Learning New Languages	131
	Meditation and Mindfulness for Kids	134
	Applause for You, the Reader	137
9	**The Superpower Menu**	**139**
	Suggested Further Reading	221
	About the Author	223

Introduction

You would do anything for your kids, right? What if you could do everything for them, in less than fifteen minutes a day?

You can. You can give your kids superpowers. These superpowers come through a combination of knowledge and empowerment, which is the result of attention from you parents while you play games with your kids. The game happens to be built out of miniature lessons. Lessonlets, let's call them. You see, I'm a parent of two girls. I'm also a professor, and the two roles can overlap. My superpower is that I'm a dad who knows how to teach and to make the act of learning feel easy, painless, even fun. I practice with my kids every day.

The key to *Empower Your Kids* in seventy words or fewer? Here it comes:

Teach your kids a single new thing each day through Lesson Games, taking as little as a minute and no more than fifteen. Then, as a reward, engage in free play with them, doing whatever they want to do. The lessonlets are designed like a loose syllabus and presented with some professorial tricks to make them more fun and stick better.

First off: Congratulations! You are officially a wonderful, proactive, loving, thoughtful parent by virtue of the very fact that you've bought this book. You want the very best for your children and wish to cultivate a lifelong love of learning and the closest possible relationship with them. Bravo! I'm delighted to bring you these ideas and activities that my wife Urška and I have developed with our daughters, Eleonora and Izabella.

I regularly host events (in Slovenian, believe it or not), and one of them featured three early childhood specialists. While each approached advice for parents from a different perspective, they all agreed on one thing: the fifteen-minute rule. Every day, even if just for fifteen minutes, they suggested, parents should spend time playing with their kids, in whatever way the kids would like. If they want to play with Legos, great. Hide-and-seek? Super. Read a story or stare at the clouds? All good. Let the kids choose, and engage 100 percent, with no distractions. Just pure together-time. Those fifteen minutes of unadulterated adult-child interaction sometimes feel impossible for even the most well-meaning parents, who are used to doing things on the fly, juggling their attention, or urging their kids to do something that is the parents' choice of what to play, not the kids'.

The specialists insisted that this playtime be without any didactic elements. If you're playing with numbered blocks, parents shouldn't throw in "what number is this?" too much, or it feels like work to the kids. The pure bliss of parental together time doing what the kids want is a great gift for young children, who want only the love, comfort, and attention of their parents.

But as the discussion continued, I prodded a bit. Isn't it good to be a bit didactic? I'm a professor, so this comes naturally. I'm always looking for ways to teach my daughters, who were age five and seven when I had this discussion and wrote the first draft of this book, while we interact. They agreed that this was indeed a good approach, to develop an association with learning as part of parental play, but not at the sacrifice of the free play time, which is what young children crave most.

So, I proposed, what if I reserve at least fifteen minutes for free play, but I also set aside fifteen minutes a day for learning play time, for lesson games? This seemed a good solution to all, but I wanted to take it a step further. My professorial approach meant that I wanted to be structured, rather than random, in what I taught my girls. So, I developed an idea that I planned to execute and document in a series of articles that would then become a book.

This was a book I was supposed to write in, say, ten years, when my kids were teenagers and no longer focused on learning from their parents. The plan was to keep track of this Lesson Game idea of mine, which has been in place since my girls were three and five, and monitor it until they were around thirteen and fifteen. I would keep track of what I taught them, where I pulled lessons from and what went over well, to create a handbook that other parents might use as a template for their own Lesson Games tailored to their interests and those of their kids. It was going to be a retrospective book with lessons developing as my kids aged and their attention spans and levels of understanding grew.

But then Covid-19 arrived and suddenly the world stood still. Almost everyone, almost everywhere, was at home with their families for, at the time, who-knew-how-long.

Introduction xi

This was a dramatic and cataclysmic event, but that is not what this book is about. This book came so early because I was inspired by the solidarity that I saw, particularly on social media, which has long been bemoaned as a way that too many of us interact instead of doing so in person, and now has become the only way we can safely interact. So many sympathetic people were offering material designed to educate and entertain and help pass the time in a positive way.

That was the inspiration for my writing the book when I did. It first appeared as an article in the *Observer* entitled "An Art History Professor's Tips on Taking Your Kids on a World Tour—From Home." The article went viral and I got so much positive feedback that I decided to do my part in the solidarity of shared isolation time. Perhaps my ideas could inspire other parents?

Isolation Time did not change what I'd been doing and planned to do moving forward with my Lesson Games, and of course it works just as well during "normal times." I still use it today, long after the pandemic has ended. In fact, it's really designed to slip in as a hardly noticeable, but very powerful addition to everyday, normal life.

The idea is simple: Pick a lesson, small, miniature, large, complex, sometimes hardly a proper lesson at all—something gently educational, one new thing a day, that I will teach my kids. It can be longer than fifteen minutes. Usually it is much shorter—it's often been a sentence or two, taking a minute or so. Fifteen minutes seems to be a sweet spot as the general maximum for a few reasons: (a) It doesn't feel too daunting for parents. Any parents can say to themselves, "You know what, however busy I might be, I really can slice out fifteen minutes to be with my kids with 100 percent of my attention"; (b) it doesn't feel too daunting for children. Doing anything for fifteen minutes, even if it doesn't initially feel particularly exciting, is reasonable enough; and (c) it's all you need—sometimes much more than you need—to feel connected with and inspiring for your kids, to make you feel that you've given them a great, intangible gift each day, that you've shared special, precious time, and that you are helping them to develop in a positive way.

These are all the dreams of parents, but it's totally understandable if it can feel tricky to achieve. That's why a bit of guidance can help. The sort I offer here is not the least bit dogmatic and absolutist. There is no one right way to do this, or right thing to teach. This book simply uses my own experience to offer a soft template for parents to adopt and adapt however they see fit. The key is to make you and your children feel happy and fulfilled. Do whatever feels right and comfortable, and nothing that does not.

***

The final section of this book, the Superpower Menu, will be divided into units, as it would if I were planning a syllabus for a university course. But it will be flexible in terms of execution. For example, we'll have a cluster of lessons focused on cooking skills, but you should wait for the right moment to begin them, when your kids express interest. Maybe they see an episode of MasterChef Junior or the film *Ratatouille* and it gets the ball rolling. That's the time to ride the wave of interest that has come organically from your kids and pick the lesson cluster from the Superpower Menu that engages with the enthusiasm of the moment. There are 365 lessonlets featured in this book, but many of them are referenced in the main text, not exclusively in the Superpower Menu.

The activities should be tailored to the ability levels of your kids, but most of all they should tap into their interests. Over the course of a year, there will be material I'd like to cover, but I'll never force it. That defeats the point. I let my kids guide. Part of the Lesson Game is a chance to have more structured, productive interaction time that feels like play but with a purpose. It's an arsenal of options to choose from when the moment arises.

It should also never be instead of pure play—if you've only got fifteen minutes a day free with your children, then the priority goes to free playing, allowing the kids to choose how they'll spend their time with you. But given a bit more time, even just an extra fifteen minutes, we can strike the balance of doing one activity that the kids choose, and one that the grownups choose. The ideal routine is to follow a short Lesson Game with the reward of fifteen minutes of pure play.

A key is that this time, even a short time, is proactive and focused, that you are as close as possible to 100 percent mentally engaged with your kids when interacting. This means that the TV is not on in the background (though music is fine), and that your phone is nowhere within view (too

Introduction   xiii

many parents convince themselves they are playing, when in fact they're sitting next to their kids while browsing through their smartphones).

Much of the secret is in how you present learning to your children. Each new thing they learn gives your kids a "new superpower" (if they are younger and this feels like the right term) or it will "empower them" (if they are a bit older). You don't call this "study time" or "additional schooling" (ugh), but you *play* Lesson Games in order to give them superpowers. Have you ever met a kid who didn't want to play games and get superpowers?

Play to your strengths, comforts, and what your kids enjoy and show interest in. This is a template for you to run with however you see fit. I'm an art history professor living in the Slovenian Alps with daughters who speak Slovenian and English and have their own sets of interests and abilities, who have a toy silver rhinoceros named Albrecht Dürer and a real Peruvian Hairless dog named Hubert van Eyck. I'm guessing that does not describe a single one of you readers precisely (if it does, then we should probably go for a beer). Do what feels of greatest interest to you and your family.

It's early days, but when we are old(er), not only will we be able to look back and quantify and record what we did with our children, but the time we spent with them will feel longer, deeper, and richer for its diversity and the proactivity of the project. And conveying knowledge is empowering. Each new thing learned does feel, to younger children, like they are acquiring a superpower. Tie on your capes, because here we go.

***

I started writing this book during the self-isolation period in the spring of 2020, when we parents had our children at home full-time. At the time, I thought to myself, "Now, we can either count the days until it's over which, in retrospect, will make this time feel lost, or, as Muhammad Ali is credited with saying, instead we can make the days count." I decided to consider that time with my kids as a gift, a bonus bestowed upon us. Now that it has long since passed and "normal life" has resumed, I looked back on that isolation period with fondness for the togetherness it cultivated and with a sense that it was both rewarding and productive. That was a time when we had more time to be together, to engage.

During the pandemic, my daughters were five and seven years old. As I write, they are ten and twelve. As any parent can attest, those are very different eras in child development and interests. This book is still aimed at parents of children up to around age ten or so. For older kids, depending on the interests and circumstances of each child, a different level of intellectual activity, interests, and pursuits, one led more by the child than the parent, will come into play. I've added a chapter on engaging with slightly older children in the ways recommended in this book, because it is still relevant. The main difference is that kids ten and up are not as wide open to being introduced to whatever a parent comes up with, and are more likely to want to engage when given a choice, not told "this is what we're going to do."

Since I had the opportunity, rare for us authors, to revisit an older manuscript and see what I'd like to change, I was pleased to see that my answer was: very little. The original text and ideas have held up well over the years, as attested by my own parenting experience and in reports from the readers of the original version.

The difference now is that our time together is more limited, and therefore more precious. Our days are packed, the routine can drain us, and we feel like our energy is limited. We'd like to do so much more, but where is the time? Parents are already superheroes, balancing making a living with caring for a family, sacrificing so much of themselves in the process. That's true love: when your family's happiness and well-being are more important to you than your own.

The approach I've developed and use with my kids is entirely grounded in the understanding that, though parents may be superheroes, we're generally over-tired superheroes with limited stores of extra energy. We also already have rhythms and approaches to parenting that work for us. So there's no need to reinvent the wheel and turn things on their heads. That's not what this is about. This is about a small daily addition, a grace note, something that does not feel like any extra work, a minimal effort that produces a maximum reward. You'll feel great, more productive and effective as a parent, and you'll be gifting your children "superpowers" as I used to call it when speaking with my five- and seven-year-olds. Today, I would use the slightly more grownup but still accurate term *empowering*.

Worth a try, right?

Introduction

Even on a busy day, any of us can find fifteen minutes or less—sometimes much less—to be fully engaged with our kids, to teach and empower them. This book will show you how I've done it and will hopefully inspire you to either do the same or invent your own, personalized variation.

There is no one right way to approach this. No one knows how to raise your kids better than you do. Consider this a set of ideas and inspirations for you to try out, riff off of, or make your own.

You can instill in your children a love of learning and even a supply of superpowers, all while having fun with them and sharing special, memorable moments.

Let's *Empower Your Kids* by playing the Lesson Game.

1 The Lesson Game Approach

This chapter introduces how the Lesson Game works. It's the primary tool and takeaway that I'd like you to integrate into your lives to whatever extent feels right. It's important to me, whether I'm teaching or parenting, that what I suggest is flexible and not in any way absolutist. You know best what will work for you and your family. But if this sounds good, there are myriad ways to apply it and level up your dynamic with your kids and their enthusiasm for learning.

The Rules of the Lesson Game

These learning activities have no set rules, per se, but are more like guidelines on how to keep the experience positive, enthusiastic, casual, and unforced. That goes both ways: don't force your kids and don't force yourselves, as parents.

I have a very mild obsessive streak in me that keeps me productive, but I can see how it could tip into compulsive behavior that would slow me down. For instance, I cannot check email without responding immediately to everything in my inbox. Not to do so, to put off responding, makes me nervous. This is why I check email only once a week (I get a lot of emails commenting with enthusiastic curiosity about the line at the bottom of my email template apologizing for my slow replies). I map out projects and work packages in my weekly planner notebook and have empty squares next to each. I cannot bring myself to turn the page to the next week unless the squares are checked off, meaning I've done what I portioned myself to do that week (there's a chapter in this book about how these eccentricities have actually made me more productive, and you're welcome to borrow them).

I mention these quirks because you need to know what works best for you, to make teaching your kids feel manageable and never like work.

You've already got enough work at, well, at your work. Home time should feel relaxing and fun whenever possible. So, knowing myself, I do not map out what I want to accomplish with my kids week to week, much less day to day. That would make me nervous and prompt me to push the kids to fulfill specific lessons, when in fact I want to allow them to guide what we learn about together. For this reason, I prefer to keep a long master list—the Superpower Menu, which is at the back of this book—in which I put all the ideas I get for mini lessons, our lessonlets, and then I usually don't even refer to it. I like to know that it's there, but I do not want to feel chained to its content, and least of all to a certain order. I only find myself referring to it when I can't think of anything off the top of my head, and I'll dip into the list for inspiration. I'll also use it to try to find cross-referencing lessons, one that would logically and inspirationally follow another, and string them together.

For example, I watched the classic film *Bedknobs and Broomsticks* with my girls. They loved it, especially the "substitutiary locomotion" song and the great battle scene at the end when the friendly witch (played by a young Angela Lansbury) successfully animates a museum full of suits of armor which proceed to chase an invading Nazi squadron from a seaside English town. It's a magical moment (literally and figuratively) and the girls were totally into it. This led me to play the Lesson Game in a number of directions inspired by what they were interested in.

- We talked about how to say "substitutiary locomotion" in a less fancy way ("replacing movement"), and why a "locomotive" is an older word for a train.
- The film features a variety of British accents including London Cockney, a polite "received pronunciation," and a sort of gangster slang. We talked about various accents in English, which ones they find more difficult to understand, and which ones they could imitate.
- We talked about the suits of armor from various time periods and then browsed through a book we have of arms and armor. We looked at horse armor, described what it felt like to wear armor, how it was put on.
- The "substitutiary locomotion" spell can make inanimate objects move around on their own, as the good witch explains in the film. We talked about the difference between animate and inanimate objects. I listed things and asked my girls to tell me if they were animate or inanimate: a fish, a shoe, our dog, a hot dog, a suit of armor, a knight in armor,

a photograph of a knight in armor. I was trying to be tricky, because once I saw that they grasped that animate objects were living and capable of movement, I pulled a fast one asking about a photograph of something that is animate (the photograph being inanimate). I also played with words to be tricky and playful (our dog is animate, a hot dog is inanimate).

- The film has some silly Nazi bad guys (not the scary kind) but we talked a bit about who they were, why they spoke German, and that there had been a war a long time ago—Second World War history lite—to gently inform but not overcomplicate or upset a five-year-old.
- There's a great scene on Portobello Road in London, where the characters search for the second half of a torn book of magic. I lived in London and had been there many times, so I told them about the antiques market there, we watched a walkthrough video of the market and I asked what they would be interested in looking for if they were there.
- The film has a scene in which the children list their favorite foods, and the list sounds intriguing but confusing to non-British kids: bubble and squeak, sausage and mash, toad in the hole. So we looked up what these dishes were and cooked some for ourselves.

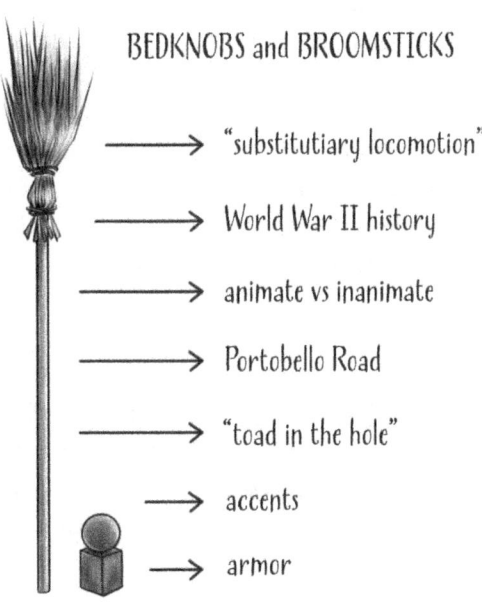

Those are seven mini-lessons (which we'll call "lessonlets" because the word "lesson" unfortunately has the connotation of work) that emerged from the fun of watching one film. Suddenly you've got your whole week's worth of Lesson Games laid out for you in one go. On the first night, you watch the movie together and talk about it afterward, reviewing what you saw and what stood out. Then each of the following six days, you pick one of the lessonlets above to play with together. There could be infinitely more of them, but this is to give an example of how a web of ideas can emerge from each activity.

Each of these lessonlets gives your kids a new power. Some of these powers are as simple as learning a new word. But don't for a moment think that learning a new word is anything short of a powerful tool. Think how impressed your seven-year-old's teacher would be if she throws in the words "substitutiary" and "locomotion" in conversation. Each new word opens up a window in your child's imagination palace, letting in light and allowing them to see out in a way they never could before they learned that word. The world around them becomes fractionally clearer. The next time they encounter the word they will not glaze over and ignore it but *understand* it. The various accents that they hear in different films will not just be funny ways people talk but will carry meaning and help identify where the speaker comes from.

What's your newest superpower, you might ask your kids after each lessonlet: "I cut vegetables with a knife. I can build a snow man. I can count to ten in Chinese. I can whistle. I can play foosball. I know what "locomotion" means. I know the capital of America. I know the world's fastest fish. I know why the sky is blue. I can eat brussels sprouts" (I'm looking at you, bubble and squeak—and for most kids, eating brussels sprouts voluntarily qualifies as a superpower).

***

Let's review the basic "rules" of the Lesson Game. At this point I'm already repeating some of the keys to *Empower Your Kids*, and there's a reason I'm doing so—repetition is part of my professor bag of tricks to help students (or, in this case, you guys) memorize concepts without having to study or work at it.

Each day we teach a different, single thing. Not even a lesson, just a fact, a how-to, a new word. It shouldn't feel like a lesson. It should feel like deep interaction with a didactic purpose, and it can be as short as is necessary to convey the idea and be sure that your kids grasp it. Watching things can also count, as long as what is watched is selected with purpose, if we parents really watch with our kids (not using the screen as a chance to catch up on emails while the kids are distracted), and if we talk to our kids about what we are seeing. I'm a fan of anything with a story or learning behind it, so feature films, TV shows, documentaries are all good. YouTube clips can also qualify, if we select what we see there (for instance, that's how I introduced my daughters to the Marx Brothers: by finding highlight clips). Just about anything goes, and there is no absolute right and wrong—it is for each parent to feel out what suits best, and what works with their kids, at their age and interest and application levels.

These lessons should be limited to fifteen minutes in most cases, and since my daughters are so young, they are often far shorter—as little as a minute or two. There can be exceptions (such as watching a documentary), but it is key to (a) keep it short and punchy; (b) stop while it's still fun, so the educational element doesn't feel tiresome or overlong; and (c) practice what scientists called "reductionism," boiling down even complex ideas into the simplest possible format, to make them easier to understand, teach, and remember. This is the TED format—any idea can and should be able to be conveyed clearly and simply in fifteen minutes. It really works, especially for younger children whose attention spans are less developed. It is also important that this project, these lessons, should not feel like "work" to the parents. It should not be a chore, but instead something to look forward to. Fifteen minutes a day feels doable to anyone, and it's a big first step to hear an idea that appeals and say, "Yeah, I can actually do that." It's like reading recipes in a cookbook—some recipes sound and look great, but you scan the ingredients list (oh, man, I don't have half of these things) and the number and complexity of the steps, and you shut it out as a possibility. "I'd love to eat this, but only if someone else made it for me" or maybe "Ah, I'll have to save this one for a rainy day," and then it never happens. But those recipes that sound and look great, and for which you can access all the ingredients—and they sound particularly easy to put together, easier than you would've thought? Those are the ones we go for with enthusiasm.

The lessons can be planned ahead, but loosely and in a grab-bag fashion. I've come up with scores of ideas for you, but you should feel free to skip those that don't suit, add whatever you like, focus on what you and your kids are into, the specialties that you have (which will surely differ from what I feel most adept at doing), and what you choose on which day should never feel forced and rigid. It's actually best to let your kids choose from a "menu" of options you offer. This is particularly the case as children get older. They want to feel that they're choosing their own adventure.

That said, there can be a superstructure in mind for the lessons. We professors are used to making strict syllabi for our courses and designing individual lessons and semester-long courses in a tactical way that will maximize the benefit to the students, building layers of knowledge. We won't get that complicated, but the basic principles of planning ahead and looking at how a series of very short lessons can be linked together into a larger lesson, or a thematic period of time, is in place. For instance, you might have ten ideas for individual lessons about natural history, or even about dinosaurs. Rather than scatter these around a period of two months, randomly throwing them in, it is more useful to establish a Dinosaur Week and have the lesson each day of that week be on the same theme. Then you'll look back and think, "Yeah, we covered dinosaurs," and your kids will feel empowered because they didn't just learn ten things, they now know ten things about dinosaurs that they didn't know before.

Empower Your Kids encourages what I call Lesson Games for a reason. Everyone likes games. Lessons? Depends who you ask. What you propose should be treated as a game. It should never be forced. Don't feel like doing it now? No problem. It should have no required location, no "school room," but be completely flexible and portable. Driving around? Go ahead and play. In the bathtub? Go ahead and play. Note that I use the word "play." We want to support entirely positive associations with learning. Learning should be fun. We should learn through games that we play. For young children, this is key to encouraging them to want to learn things from moment to moment and to develop in them a long-term love for learning.

We tend to engage in activities with our children that are random—we watch whatever is on TV or tickles our fancy when browsing Netflix, we plan whatever games our children want or what we think of on the fly. This is fine, but the same level of engagement can be had with a more structured approach to together time. Rather than seeing which wildlife documentary is on Animal Planet that day, instead we can choose to work our way through a series of documentaries in a logical order—one week focusing on the arctic world, for example, another week on insects.

Lessons should be followed by short quizzes, which may amount to just simple "what did we learn today?" dialogues with your children. This has a purpose of reinforcing what was learned, fixing both the event and the lesson's content in the memory. At the end of the day, I like to talk through what I did with my kids through the day. We played tag, we ate stir-fry, we read a chapter of *Harry Potter*, we watched an episode of *Trollhunters*, we cleaned up your bedrooms. It helps to make each day feel fuller and richer, and it helps your kids remember their lessons. That's why teachers assign tests—to encourage the repetition of ideas so they are better retained. And a student who can teach a new idea to others is a student who truly grasps the idea. So, this summary of what we learned can ideally take the form of: "Okay, today we learned how to yo-yo. Now can you teach me how to yo-yo, the way I taught you?" When kids feel that they can now teach something to others, they really "own" it, with a sense of pride and a greater likelihood that the idea will be retained.

***

These are just a few of the ideas we'll present in this book. We will flesh them out in more detail and then offer up all sorts of possible lessons for you to try out. But remember that this is a soft template—what you choose to do with your kids and when is entirely up to you, and no one knows what will suit you or your children better than you do.

2 Your Utility Belt

When I was in elementary school, I knew exactly what subjects were to be taught each year, and I couldn't wait to get to them. This was particularly true for history class: The Revolutionary War, the Middle Ages, ancient Egypt. Each unit was something to look forward to. Maybe I was extra nerdy, that I got pleasure in anticipation of learning, but even if there was something I dreaded (I'm terrible at hard science and couldn't stand chemistry class) I still found it helpful to know what was coming, to preview what I would engage with. It helped me set boundaries and expectations. I use this when teaching. If I start a lecture stating, "Today, we will cover four paintings that started artistic revolutions," then my students can prepare mentally to absorb that information. Four feels feasible, not endless. This approach is far more satisfying and digestible than my saying "Today, we will cover some paintings that started artistic revolutions." How many? Two? Two hundred? It helps to know what will come, what to expect.

Preview–Engage–Review

Preview. This is the Preview element to my recommendation for how to present lessonlets. You can do this long before you start the Lesson Game, or just before. For instance, during the week you might say, "This weekend we're going to go to the woods and learn how to navigate with a compass," triggering anticipation of something that sounds fun. Then, or in addition, on the day you can say, "Now we're off for an adventure in the woods, where we'll learn how to navigate with a compass. If you ever get lost, you'll always be able to find your way."

I like to whet appetites by describing learning as acquiring a superpower. We're in the superhero phase (my five-year-old was totally into Wonder Woman—at least during the week I wrote this chapter). I grew up with a cheesy poster in my bedroom, featuring Superman with the dynamically drawn phrase "Knowledge is real power" echoing behind him. I guess this rubbed off. This idea began with my kids when encouraging them about getting vaccinated. "If you get a vaccine, then you have a superpower that you are invincible against this particular illness." It went over well.

But knowledge *is* like a superpower. If you have a compass and get lost you really can find your way. If you learn to tell time suddenly you can know what time it is and read clocks and watches. If you learn to make cookies, then anytime you want cookies, voilà, you can make them! Learn to do a somersault and, abracadabra, you're a ninja. For those parents of my generation, you'll fondly remember the miraculous cult that was *The Matrix*. I was a student in London when it came out and it totally blew my mind. I still recall fondly the idea that you can "upload" knowledge via a plug in your brain and, in seconds, you can "know Kung Fu." If only we were able to upload knowledge so immediately (it's probably not far off), but for now, learning things is as close as we get to uploading knowledge. I'm not talking about study-for-exam knowledge, memorizing dates of famous battles or physics equations. That comes later and, honestly, it isn't always fun. I'm talking about very basic bits of information that feel like great leaps forward to small children. The leap from "my parents have to cut everything for me because knives are too dangerous" to learning basic knife skills by training on cooked carrots with a butter knife is huge. Suddenly your four-year-old feels like "I can use a knife" which morphs into "I can cook" and is triply-empowering: (1) It feels great to have accomplished something new that perhaps felt out of reach, if it had been considered at all; (2) it feels good that parents entrusted a child with something previously forbidden or unimagined; and (3) the child has the fruit of this knowledge for life—he or she can now, in this case, use a knife to cut things and begin cooking.

Engage. You know that annoying person in a movie theater who talks throughout the film? That's me when I'm watching something with my kids as part of our Lesson Game. If they or we are watching something just for fun, then I'm appropriately quiet. But when it's part of the Lesson Game, constant proactive engagement is a big part of the learning experience. This is true watching anything or engaged in an activity, when reading or doing crafts. I'll be peppering my kids with questions about what they see, what they find interesting, what they like, and more: Would you try that? Which is the nicest in your opinion? Do you recognize anything we see? I want my kids to ask relevant questions—the more the better. Questions that distract and are not relevant, a popular children's tactic, are to be deflected, but any question, no matter how basic, is a good one if it is well motivated. And I want them to get used to answering questions, even if they seem too simple. Just "What do you like about this?" is enough. Asking questions prompts children to think more deeply and broadly about what they are doing. It removes the risk of drifting minds or doing something on automatic pilot. It keeps the activity fresh and keeps the kids on their toes.

If I see that there's something that they're not sure about, perhaps a word that they don't understand, I'll always pause whatever we're doing and take the opportunity to explain it. But I first ask them if they can tell me what it means. Since being able to explain or teach something to someone else is the mark of truly grasping an idea, it is empowering for children to "teach" their parents (even if the parents already know what they are being taught). So whatever we're doing during a Lesson Game, we're doing in a stop-and-start fashion, with plenty of dialogue and Q&A throughout.

It goes without saying that parental engagement (at least one parent—the other can be napping) is key during these few minutes of Lesson Gaming. That means no multitasking, no smartphones in hand, no half-doing your tax return. You request 100 percent engagement from your kids and offer them the same in return. This is focused, shared time. Total engagement, even if it's just for those few minutes a day. Five minutes of total engagement is far more valuable to your children than two hours of passive sharing of space, while they watch *Frozen* for the forty-seventh time and you check email while playing Scrabble and watching the Mavs game.

Review. I like to tell my university students that, if they pay attention during my lectures, then they should not have to study for my exams. (By extension, I warn them that the exams will show me who was paying attention and who wasn't.) I teach in such a way that I try to repeat key points enough that the students memorize them organically. The key to this is review, repetition, and having the student explain and teach the material back to the teacher. It's the same with Lesson Games with young children. After we finish a lessonlet, I'll repeat what we did, or ask my kids to summarize what we just learned. Then, often when I'm tucking my kids in at bedtime, I'll summarize all the things we did that day that felt special. "Today, I really liked making apple pie with you, and playing freeze tag, and learning to yo-yo." Then I'll preview the next day, if I'm organized enough to have something planned (which is not often, but it's good in theory):

"Tomorrow, you can choose between learning a yo-yo trick or learning to do a cartwheel."

This is the Preview – Engage – Review cycle that works well in university classes and for Lesson Games with kids at home.

The Superpower Toolbox

The Lesson Game is designed to require no purchases on the part of parents. Many of the ideas for activities involve using material available for free online, but I must write that they are available at the time of writing (with the understanding that the online world can change and the specific URLs and precision of the content may shift by the time you read this, in which case I'd encourage you to seek out something similar on your own). YouTube is an infinite source of material (much of it of little educational or real value, but there are innumerable gems in the mix). When I reference films, I leave it to you to decide how you access them, but also encourage you to think flexibly. If I say that the animated film *Antz* can be a point of departure to talk about how ant colonies work, understand that, if you can't find *Antz*, then another cartoon or even documentary can be just as good an entry point to the theme.

There are a lot of ways to teach, but one of the best and easiest is to dip into books, especially illustrated encyclopedias or compendia. These are naturally subdivided into "bite-sized" entries, each of which takes just a few minutes to read with your kids. When I teach (at University of Ljubljana, for The Smithsonian, for Yale, for the National Gallery—regardless of the age of my audience), I use a preview-engage-review approach, and it's the same at home. I talk about what we are going to learn to whet the appetite. While reading I stop frequently to ask questions, clarify, be sure they understand. And when we're done, for the rest of the day and that week, I'll circle back to ask questions about what we learned or repeat the information, so it naturally, organically, is committed to memory.

You can do this with any books you happen to have at home or take out of the library. You can use online sources, but this doesn't have the same feeling of tangible engagement—the screen in some way "separates" you from your kids in a way that the printed page does not. So opt for real books when you can. What follows is my subjective list of ideal keystone books that I have found incredibly useful and well worth owning. My kids and I go back to them often and for many lessons. If you're open to adding to your library, these are some strong choices that will, single-handedly, provide hundreds of lessonlets. Most are compendia, or visual encyclopedias. Each one offers ready-made lessons on every page.

DK Smithsonian Picturepedia: An Encyclopedia on Every Page (DK)

This wonderful picture book is a perfect accompaniment to playing the Lesson Game. Each double-page spread is packed with photographs grouped by theme: gems, occupations, foods, mammals, tools, and so on. There are didactic illustrations but what is most fun for kids is just browsing. Open any double page spread and just talk through what you see there, and you've fulfilled your lessonlet for the day. The visual nature makes it easier for kids to memorize. I like to let my kids point to which paragraph of didactic material they want me to read in which order, to give them the power to choose.

5 Language Visual Dictionary (DK)

DK is great when it comes to picture-first compendia, and this series is particularly satisfying. The standard version is an encyclopedia of pictures of objects and words but with the twist that each word is presented by a picture and the word translated into five languages: English, German, Spanish, French, and Italian. Teaching your young kids a second language is a powerful and practical way to play the Lesson Game, and this is a great way to start. Or, if you have bilingual children, as I do, then this also suits as we use it to develop a third language (German), or to play The Translation Game, in which we try to stump each other by asking for translations of words between our two household languages, Slovenian and English. If you have bilingual kids, then you may find specialized versions of this book featuring English, German, French, Italian, plus your local language (our edition has the fifth language as Slovenian).

***The Way Things Work* by David Macaulay (HMH Books)**
This is a classic (and there's a recently updated and expanded edition), with beautiful cutaway drawings that illustrate how mechanical and building projects function. It's ideal for enthusiastic young engineers.

Any Illustrated Encyclopedias: of Animals, of Dinosaurs, and Beyond
There are so many to choose from. Those by National Geographic and DK Smithsonian are excellent. The key is having plenty of good pictures and concise didactic material. This is more about browsing, less about reading.

***Encyclopedia of Things That Never Were* by Robert Ingpen and Michael Page (Viking)**
It's great to have a heavily illustrated book of fairytales at hand. Those by the Brothers Grimm (Hansel and Gretel, Rumpelstiltskin, Rapunzel, The Frog Prince), Hans Christian Andersen (The Little Mermaid, The Princess and the Pea, The Emperor's New Clothes, The Ugly Duckling, The Snow Queen—which inspired *Frozen*), and by Charles Perrault (Sleeping Beauty, Little Red Riding Hood, Cinderella, Puss in Boots, Mother Goose) are the big three, the originators of so many of the classics (and so many Disney movies). The less text and more illustrations per page, the more absorbing it will be for younger children. So, while I recommend illustrated compendia of such stories (reading each fairytale offers a ready-made lessonlet), *Encyclopedia of Things That Never Were* is a gorgeously illustrated collection of mythological and fairytale creatures and characters, with their stories and origins summarized in brief. I used to adore browsing this book. It's out of print now, but if you can find a used copy, it's well worth it.

***The Book* and *The Black Book of Inventions* by Hungry Minds**
The Book is an extensively illustrated oversized tome that was the second-most-successful Kickstarter project in history. It functions like an encyclopedia of everything one needs to know about civilization. I was so taken with it that I contacted the team behind it, Hungry Minds, and soon we planned a follow-up book together, one that I would write, called *The Black Book of Inventions*. These are great for kids since they are illustration-heavy, but with educational how-things-work illustrations, and a modest amount of text that concisely emphasizes why something is important and how it functions.

Any Illustrated Collection of Myths and Biblical Stories
Myths and Bible stories are the foundation tales of culture. Developing an understanding of them, recognizing references to them, can go a long way toward helping students interpret culture later on. I probably shouldn't be admitting this, but when I was a student, I was able to proactively participate in loads of class discussions about books I had not actually read, because I was versed in the core tales that are so frequently referred to in literature, art, theater, and film. There is a set pool of stories from which so much subsequent culture draws: the Bible, Greek and Roman mythology, fables and fairytales, etcetera. Then, if we're getting into the Renaissance, we can add Greek philosophy and drama, Ovid's poetry, Dante, and Jacobus da Voragine's biographies of saints, but those you needn't worry about when you're talking to a five-year-old. The point is that early exposure to these stories is not only fun and interesting for kids but will later be useful. One's religion and level of faith are not necessarily relevant to introducing these stories for what they are: keystone tales upon which so much later culture was built. If your family is religious, then you can present them in that context. If not, then you can present them simply as stories for now. The more illustrations (ideally one per page), the better for younger children.

D'Aulaires' Book of Greek Myths
This is the one I grew up with, but any collection of ancient myths (Greek just happen to be among the most popular) with lovely illustrations offers a great source of stories that are not just entertaining but are building blocks of world culture, constantly referred to in later traditions, religion, literature, art, and more. Thus, developing a recognition of some key stories will provide just that—keys to unlocking material later on. You might consider the audiobook version of this collection, which is particularly rich and engaging, with myths read by film stars including Sidney Poitier, Paul Newman, Matthew Broderick, and Kathleen Turner.

The Slavic Myths **by Noah Charney and Svetlana Slapšak**
If I may include another of my own books, this is part of the Myths series from Thames & Hudson, each of which is beautifully bound and illustrated. Ours happens to be about Slavic mythology (werewolves, vampires, Baba Yaga), but you can opt for whichever mythologies are of interest. Ours takes a distinct approach, retelling eight myths followed by essays about the

myths and Slavic mythology more generally. My older daughter, Eleonora, picked the book up because it was so beautiful as an object. I figured she'd maybe read the retellings of the myths themselves, but then she read the essays, too.

Audio Recordings as Your Ally
Don't be shy or consider it a cop-out to locate good professional readers of stories and let them do the storytelling for you. It's best for you to read to your children, especially the first time they encounter a story. That dynamic of cuddling, reading and being read to is special and bonding. But you might not feel like rereading the same story for the umpteenth time, and audio recordings of stories are perfect for car rides. There are various good storytelling podcasts, but it's tough to beat top-level audiobooks read by actors, many of whom specialize in reading, interpreting characters with different voices, and producing an entirely deeper experience.

Finally, You'll Need a Screen with Internet Access
Do not recoil in horror! I'm one of those parents who think that screen time should be selective and minimized. But it can be wonderful, useful, informative, and a powerful, gentle tool for good, so it is too often dismissed out of hand as the hallmark of "lazy" parents. It needn't be.

Nothing stirs debate quite like how much, and how early, parents should use screens to entertain their kids. Tablets, TVs, computers, smartphones—any way that moving images are consumed via screen falls into this category. I am not here to pass judgment, but I have some observations and thoughts relevant to the Lesson Game, because many of the ideas in the Lesson Game involve or begin with screen time.

While the temptation will often be to resort to moving images on screens, because frankly they are more immediately engaging to children, I encourage resistance. Use them, by all means, but save them, parcel them out. Imagination lies dormant when movies and cartoons do the work of imagining for you. Audio consumption of stories and being read to or reading books develops a child's imagination far better and more proactively. Use screen time in moderation, in controlled ways and as a reward in short bursts.

In moderation. I've seen that my kids would not be happy or function well if they just watched TV all day. They have an attention span of roughly two hours (a bit more than a feature film) during which they're really enjoying themselves and focused. If they go on to a second feature film, they start to get antsy. They climb on the couch, kick each other, hang upside down from an easy chair. They get aggressive because they are half-bored, half-distracted by the engagement on-screen. This is good for no one. A single feature film is plenty for any given day. If they are allowed to watch just a single episode of a cartoon (we Charneys are huge *Scooby-Doo* fans, the classic episodes from the 1970s and 1980s) then they feel just as rewarded and happy as when they are allowed to watch three episodes, or a feature film.

In controlled ways. Temper expectations by telling kids ahead of time what to expect—children (and dogs, incidentally) thrive on consistency and boundaries and act up when rules and expectations surprise them or defy expectations (this is discussed further in its own chapter). Browsing for entertainment has its time and place, but that should mostly be reserved for the parents. Kids can have their minds melt with all the possibilities of enticing programs on Netflix, for instance. There was a time when there was just one channel showing Saturday morning cartoons, and so that was what I used to watch with delight and without any sense of deprivation. The philosopher, Renata Salecl, has a brilliant book called *The Tyranny of Choice*, which describes how the abundance of options in capitalist society seems empowering, but actually can feel oppressive and make us nervous. Same thing with too many options for activities, cartoons, movies, and so on. When my kids browse for what to watch, they get so absorbed in the flipping and variety of options that they can never settle on anything and wind up arguing. They seem far happier when given a single "curated" option, or a small menu ("you can choose from these three films").

When we open up YouTube, the software throws at us all sorts of material that is more distraction than anything else. I like a good "silly kitten" video as much as the next guy (well, maybe a little less), but there's a time and a place for videos like that. I prefer to open YouTube when there is something specific that I already know I'm looking for. A walk-through video of an aquarium, for instance, or a POV rollercoaster ride. My girls will squeal with delight at seeing other options appear on-screen ("Lego princess assembly!") but I remain stalwart and muscle through to the predetermined target. Otherwise the floodgates are open. When the video we were after for our lessonlet has ended, I turn off YouTube before it starts making those suggestions for other videos it thinks I will like. YouTube can be like the supermarket trap written about in Emile Zola's nineteenth-century novel, *Ladies' Paradise*. You go into a store with a set, concise shopping list. You want to get in and get out. But the strategy of the store is to keep the goods you want apart from one another, so you have to pass, ogle and desire other things along the way, things you didn't think you wanted, and probably don't actually need. The path is strewn with temptation. But do your best to keep focused.

As a reward. Let kids' choice screen time be the reward, not the expectation. Look, I totally understand that setting up kids with screen-based entertainment, whether video games or cartoons or films, not only makes them happy but also gives parents a well-deserved break to go do whatever we parents need to do (including doing nothing at all, which is a vastly underrated practice). But use screen time to your advantage. If kids expect screen time, then they come to demand it as their right. Not giving it to them becomes a punishment, and they get grumpy if denied what they feel is "rightfully" theirs. This benefits no one. Though this is not a direct analogy, relationships with family pets can run in parallel. Do you give your dog treats whenever the dog wants one? If you did, then you'd have an overweight dog who would be controlling you, bossing you around, enlisting you as its servant. You want to give your dog treats, but trainers recommend that this be done in moderation, as a reward, and when you feel it's right to give your dog a treat. This is best done when your dog has done something to "earn" it. You might do some exercises with them, a form of training, and reward correct behavior with the treat as positive reinforcement. This is a good idea with kids and screen time, as well.

If your kids have been extra good and well behaved, then volunteer screen time as a reward. If they empty the dishwasher, take out the garbage, do their homework without complaining, help clean, etcetera, then reward such desirable behavior with positive reinforcement. Screen time is to kids what treats are to pets. The key is to let screen time be beneficial to parents as well as kids. Dose it out, reward with it, make sure it is not the baseline expectation. More screen time makes it feel less valuable. Less is more. Offer it when you need some time to yourself or when your kids have done something particularly reward-worthy.

When it is given as a reward, make sure to let the kids choose what they'd like. The caveat is that they should not just browse and browse.

They should tell you what they'd like and then you help them find it, or you can give them a limited menu of options. You can make these options connect to your Lesson Game plan. For instance, if you were just doing a lesson about dinosaurs, you might say, "Okay, you did so well today, you can watch a cartoon, but it should be a cartoon featuring dinosaurs. So, you can choose from *Ice Age 3: Dawn of the Dinosaurs*, *The Good Dinosaur*, or *Lego Jurassic Park*."

***

If you're ready to get started with your kids and jump into the Lesson Game, then go for it. No need to read all of this book before you fire it up. You can skip to the Superpower Menu at the back of this book anytime. (Hint: There are lessonlets located throughout the main text of the book, like the seven we mentioned based on watching *Bedknobs and Broomsticks*, so keep an eye out for them as we go—there are 365 total in this book, a combination of those mentioned in this main text and the rest of them in the Superpower Menu.) Otherwise, read on to look in more depth at some of the ideas at play here, where they come from, and why they work so well.

The Magic of Fifteen Minutes (or Far Less)

There are a lot of books and programs out there that use minutes in the title. It has been demonstrated by various studies in advertising that people find titles with numbers more appealing ("9 Discount Holidays," "33 Rules for the Art World," "Five Easy Steps to Rock-Hard Abs") because our expectations are defined, boundaries set in terms that we feel we can reasonably grasp. Each year I teach a one-day workshop for the London School of Public Relations on writing for PR and advertising, and this is a key lesson.

The best-known product of the "fifteen-minute school" is TED and its infectious, wonderful brand of peppy talks. It has become a household name by focusing on short, engaging presentations of single big ideas. I've done a few TED talks, and a TED Ed animated video, and they really do make an art form out of being concise. The talks are around fifteen minutes each (the official maximum length is eighteen minutes), and their point is that fifteen minutes should be all you need to make a really strong argument and convey a single powerful idea. As a professor used to forty-five-minute lectures or (heaven forbid) ninety-minute slots, I know that longer talks do not necessarily make for better ones. We tend to fill the time with additional examples when one or three would suffice and get more theoretical, include more history, and essentially expand upon the core idea. That can be fine, but a mark of a great mind, great writer, great teacher is being able to simplify and convey even the most complex ideas in the simplest, clearest, and most concise way. People simply learn and remember better what they learned this way. And that is talking about adults who are interested enough to voluntarily click on a TED talk on a subject that sparks their curiosity. When it comes to children, very young children, the timeframe must be reduced to accommodate attention spans.

I toyed with subtitling this book *A Professor's Guide to Teaching Children Everything in as Little as One Minute a Day*, but that sounded like too much of a promise. It would have quickly raised my inner skeptic. Fifteen minutes a day feels more reasonable as a daily commitment and time in which something could properly be taught. But to be honest, it is very rare that I spend more than a few minutes per Lesson Game with my girls. There are plenty of lessonlets that are sorted in a minute or two. And that's fine. Everything counts.

Choosing precisely fifteen minutes is not as important as choosing an amount of time that feels totally doable, an entirely reasonable commitment per day. You may have noted the shrinking timelines for popular cooking shows. We've gone from Julia Child encouraging four-hour, fiddly (but wonderful) recipes to cookbooks and shows that expect an hour's prep time. Now the time frame is shrinking even more. Jamie Oliver had a series of thirty-minute dishes, then he had fifteen-minute dishes. Gordon Ramsay has "Ramsay in 10." What's much more important is daily (or near daily) consistency—it's very important that you, as a parent, do not stress about this (and if you miss a day or ten, it "ain't no thang"). The length of time playing Lesson Games will depend on many factors: your schedule, the age and attention spans of your kids, your energy, and the content of that day's Lesson Game. Remember, each lessonlet gives your kids a new superpower as long as they have learned something new by playing. That superpower can take fifteen minutes to absorb, or two, or an hour—it's still a new superpower, an understanding that they did not have a few minutes before and now will carry with them forever. So don't sweat the details.

I'll have batches of days when I basically forget my own plans and do not play Lesson Games, or do not do so consciously—I've grown so used to the habit of interacting with my kids by asking questions and pointing out things and offering up lessonlets that I do it subconsciously. There are also days when I throw in a whole bunch because it just feels organic. On Easter, we talked about why people celebrate the holiday.

Me: "Well, there's a book called the Bible that tells about Jesus's life and adventures and the good things he did. And in it there are stories that he could walk on water. That was one of his powers. Do you think it would be cool to walk on water?"

Eleonora: "I can only swim in water. And snorkel."
Me: "The story goes that he was able to walk on top of the water, as if it were land. Pretty cool, huh?"
Eleonora: "Like a lizard."
Me: "Huh?"
Eleonora: "A lizard. *Kuščar*." (My kids translate words between Slovenian and English for me if I don't seem to follow their line of thought).

Me: "Oh yeah, of course. We saw it in a BBC documentary. That's called a Jesus Lizard. Can you guess why?"

Eleonora: "Because it can walk on water like Jesus. Come on, Dad. But the *kuščar* was more running on the water." (We get a lot of Slovenian words mixed in with English and vice versa in this age.)

Me (after quickly googling): "It's also called a common basilisk. Which movie had a basilisk monster in it?"

Eleonora: "One of the *Harry Potter* ones."

Me: "In that movie, the basilisk could turn people into stone just by looking at it."

Eleonora (ignoring my comment): "What other superpowers did Jesus have?"

Me: "He was able to heal people who were sick just by touching them."

Eleonora: "We could use one of those."

Me: "One of what?"

Eleonora: "A Jesus."

That was a good line, considering this dialogue took place on Easter 2020, during Corona Time. As I look back, there was one main instigator lesson that kicked things off. It's always good to let life or perhaps the calendar offer up ideas for what to cover. Since it was Easter, we talked about the holiday. (It goes without saying that every family should explain things as they feel is appropriate. If my family were religious, then our presentation of Easter would have a different flavor to it. Each parent will know what is best for them and their kids.) That led to a series of sub-lessonlets: Jesus's superpowers, and what we call Jesus's followers (Christians). I made no effort to keep the dialogue focused. I let Eleonora guide it wherever she had interest. She remembered having seen a documentary about lizards that can walk on water and made the association, so we shifted to a lessonlet about Jesus Lizards. I may be a professor but I'm constantly googling things I'm not sure about (which is most things), and there's no shame in doing so. Then I tried to be more professor-y (but still fun) as Google told me the proper name of the lizard: basilisk. Which, for people like me, who grew up playing Dungeons & Dragons, I associate with the mythical monster that a younger generation encountered in the second *Harry Potter* book and movie. But while I figured that association would be a cool one, as Eleonora loved the films (and we just started reading the illustrated novels), she didn't go for it. A swing and miss, but no problem, because she circled back with what interested her more: Jesus's other superpowers.

That real-life sample dialogue took about five to seven minutes. I was cooking Dutch baby pancakes at the time, and it came up organically. Within those, say, seven minutes there were five or more lessonlets—facts or ideas that were conveyed. One round of the Lesson Game with at least five lessonlets in it, each one offering a new superpower in miniature. Any one of the lessonlets "counts," and you should be totally satisfied if you have a day in which you slip in just one of them, and it takes about a minute. Give yourself a high-five for efforts and successes, regardless of the extent and duration.

3 Empowering Parents

This book is as much about empowering parents as helping parents to empower kids. The focus of this chapter is on how parents can feel that they are maximizing quality time (and the later memories of it) with their kids. But to kick things off, there's a short story about how I revved myself up for having children to begin with by having . . . a hairless dog.

Dog vs. Baby

I never fantasized about having a baby. I thought that I would like to have one, at some point, but it never preoccupied me—to be honest, I never really thought about it. On the other hand, I'd always been obsessed with having a dog, considering a canine companion in many ways preferable to, if not superior to, a kid. When it came time for me to have a human baby, it was my experience with the four-legged variety that truly prepared me for fatherhood.

When I was in my twenties, roving Europe as a nomadic, and single, doctoral student, I yearned for one of three things: an apartment of my own, a wife, or a dog. I didn't particularly care in what order these came, nor did I dream more about one than the others. During my solitary nights living in various cities (Venice, Ljubljana, Cambridge, Florence, Rome), curled on the couch with the two stalwart friends that have made every dorm room and garret feel like home (my hookah and white Christmas lights with which I deck out my living space), I would research dog breeds, consider the characteristics of the ideal future Mrs. Charney, and sketch interior designs for imaginary apartments. On the wife front, my only certainty was that I wanted to marry a European, thereby fully adopting the Continental lifestyle that I've always loved, and with which I've always felt most at home. As for dog breeds, living largely in Italy, where you can bring a dog with you absolutely everywhere, I wanted a companion small enough to sit on my lap on train trips and crouch beneath my table at cafes. On the apartment front, I maintained a fantasy about buying a deconsecrated church and converting it into a hipster home, one great space with only the bedroom and bathroom tucked into the sacristy. This was before I knew the dread of heating bills.

It doesn't take a psychoanalyst to realize what I was after in my single days: stability. Between a home, a wife, and a dog, I was looking for something constant in my otherwise voluntarily itinerant existence. A baby didn't even crack the top three on my wish list; perhaps because I'm a guy, perhaps because babies are the opposite of stable. In the best possible way, they turn your life upside down.

I wound up with the wife first and, from that moment on, I stopped yearning for the apartment or the dog. But my wife knew that I'd long wished for a dog, and she bought me one for my thirtieth birthday. She searched across Europe for a particular breed that satisfied our combined needs, in the dog department: small enough to carry, and no shedding. I've always liked dogs that are so ugly they're cute (here's to you, French bulldogs and pugs), but these shed. Not partial to poodles, we settled on a wonderfully exotic breed, one of the oldest in the world, and one guaranteed to draw the lenses of Japanese tourists, who happily ignore the Doge's Palace and the Colosseum, in favor of swarming our little Peruvian Hairless.

As I sit and write this, Hubert van Eyck is wrapped completely in a blue fleece blanket, cradled in my lap, making a satisfied sighing noise. He loves to have his head covered in a blanket, which I suppose I would too, if I had to walk around naked all day long.

Hubert van Eyck (Eyck for short) is my now fifteen-year-old Peruvian Inca Orchid, a.k.a. Peruvian Hairless—an extremely rare breed of dog, of which only around one thousand are known to be household pets outside of Peru. In summer, he is the color of overripe eggplant, but now he is pale, slate gray. His skin is completely hairless, aside from a patch of short, spiky red hair between his oversized desert fox ears, tufts of longer red hair between his webbed toes, and a tiny blond sprout on his right butt cheek. His skin feels like a baby elephant's and, depending on whom you ask, he resembles a young deer, a kangaroo, or a bat—anything but a dog. In truth he looks more canine than the crushed-face pug or the mop-end Lhasa Apso. He has an elegant bearing, large dark inquisitive eyes and, until a recent surgery, a pair of shiny balls that swung like Christmas tree ornaments when he walked. Without fur, all of Eyck's parts are in full view.

Being hairless, he loves to cuddle, and is always on my lap. This is exactly what I wanted in a dog or, as cynics might chortle, a wife. My wife also generously allowed me to name him after the mysterious brother of the famous Renaissance painter, Jan van Eyck, about whom I was writing a book when the puppy came into our life. He is my surrogate child, pampered and catered to, snuggled and goo-goo-ga-ga-ed, my little buddy and constant companion.

I can see why the ancient Incas used these dogs as bed-warmers. If I lie on the couch and throw a blanket over my legs, Eyck will have dashed under it and assumed a comfortable position before the blanket has floated into place. The Incas also used these dogs in religious rituals, and believed that the heat emanating from their body had healing properties. When he snuggles me, I certainly feel better about the world.

With a wife and a dog, I no longer feel the need to own my own apartment. I have the stability of two living creatures upon whom I can pour my love and cuddles. But not long ago, a third—and then a fourth came along.

Until I had the wife, a stable presence in my life and someone with whom I wanted to engage in the adventure of child-rearing, I didn't realize just how important having a baby was to me. Perhaps this is just male biology. If asked, I would have said that I wanted one, but the feeling was not the sort of knot in my stomach that I know my wife felt, until the moment she held our baby in her arms. When we were slow to conceive, however, the feeling rose in me. This might have been a case of reverse psychology, wanting what nature tells you that you cannot have. Conceive we did, the old-fashioned way, but it was still not until my child was born that I realized what all the fuss is about.

Now that I have both a hairless dog plus two young daughters, I have noted many parallels between a beloved dog and a baby.

For childless individuals and families, a dog provides a child stand-in, a loving, loyal, dependent creature to snuggle and care for. Folks without a dog think dog-obsessed pet owners are weird, speaking endlessly about their pets, just as people without babies can't imagine how anyone could talk for hours about diapers, strollers, and drool. Having experienced both worlds, two-legged and four, I understand how both nestle into places in their parents' hearts. And for me, the pseudo-child helped prepare me for the real one. The fact that I "trained" in how to care for a living creature for three years with my dog has been vital to my ability to care for my kids.

Before Eyck came into my life, I never had to take care of anything, or anyone, but myself (and I wasn't great at that, either). With Eyck and with the kids, I've had to wake in the night to attend to gastrointestinal needs. As a tiny puppy, Eyck had to be taken outside twice each night to answer the call of the wild, and when my kids were babies they needed to be fed and changed at about the same intervals. When Eyck had an upset stomach, I had to clean up after him, snapping into action without grimaces or evasion, although I am the squeamish sort. When my kids produced projectile bodily fluids on a semi-regular basis, I likewise needed to spring into cleaning mode, with no time for delay. Gathering and disposing of Eyck's "business" has never been the best part of my day, but I learned not to overthink it and just do what needs to be done. This was extremely helpful as a preparation for diaper duty. Rather than running for the hills when my kids fart, I'm quite used to it, because Eyck is a particularly flatulent sort of dog.

The greatest reward of all is, of course, the cuddles, and there the lap dog and a newborn baby run neck and neck. Eyck is a world-class snuggler, but babies quickly catch up, converting over-the-shoulder burping sessions into neck hugs, and looking irredeemably cute at just about all times.

It's not a competition, though childless pet owners and petless parents each think the other group is weird. A lover of both, I know that babies win out in the long run. What it comes down to is that Eyck will forever remain a largely mute, four-legged, four-year-old. He can be eloquent with his looks, his whines, his body language, but I can't reason with him. I can watch baseball with him, but can't talk baseball with him. Conversations are largely one-sided: I run ideas about my latest book by him, discussing the influence of Vasari's 1550 edition of *Lives of the Artists* on the development and spread of Mannerism in central Italy, and he licks my feet. My kids' responses to such discussions were along similar lines for a time, but they grow ever more interactive, responsive, opinionated, empowered, *human*. The dog and children all need me, and I need them. But my children change every month, will learn cumulatively, will remember, will reminisce, will ride on my shoulders, will ask me why the sky is blue (I'll have to look that one up), will hug me on their graduation, will dance with me on their

Empowering Parents

wedding days, will greet me with their own children and, the fates willing, will be there for me in my old age, the way I have been here for them since their first days on earth.

Dog versus baby? It's a close race, and they are the two best things a guy could wish for. But the kid's gonna win every time. Unless I want my feet licked, in which case the dog is definitely preferable.

Journaling Your Lesson Games and Superpowers

Part of the overall concept of *Empower Your Kids* is quantifying activities and successes. There's a chapter on this, and on the benefits of doing so in order to "stretch" the memories for us parents of our time with our kids. A big part of this is journaling throughout the process. This is a gift for you, as parents, as much as a record for your kids. This is how I do it, but of course you should use a method that feels right for you and, most of all, is easy for you to do, so it doesn't feel like too much work. This could be digital (a journaling app, an Excel file) or analog (a written diary). I tried to use a written diary but found that I wasn't doing it consistently enough and I also liked the searchability of a digital approach. But a daily planner is fine, an actual wall calendar (remember those?), whatever you like.

I use a free smartphone app that works pretty well. There are many options for journaling apps, but I've been using Journal It!

I use the app at its most basic level. I make sure to open a new entry every day that I do a Lesson Game with my kids (which is most days, but as we'll make clear, it's no problem at all to miss days, even many days—go easy on yourself).

First, I add a new entry, just one for the day. I try to take at least one photo of what we've done that day (sometimes just the fruit of our labor, like a drawing, sometimes a picture of the girls engaged in an activity; it varies). In addition to one or more photos, I add just a shorthand summary of what we did: which lessonlet and what cultural consumption that was new or special. I don't add in that we watched *Frozen* for the 137th time, but I would add it if we watched it for the first time, and I would add a note if it was the first time that the girls sang along with the correct lyrics to "Let It Go." If they ate something new, I'd add that. If we went somewhere distinctive, sure. My main goal is to include the activity we did and what we learned, what new superpower or level of a superpower was acquired that day. And that's it. Simple and quick. It takes a total of maybe half a minute.

Here are some examples (the lessonlets are in bold, just for illustrative purposes):

- June 14, 2020: **learned about coats-of-arms**, looked up Hogwarts coats-of-arms, copied their favorite (B Slytherin, Eleonora Gryffindor)
- June 15, 2020: **level up—made our own Charney family coat-of-arms**
- June 26, 2020: Visited Great-Grandma Tonchka, helped rake hay for cows (**talked about what and how cows eat**), picked raspberries (red and yellow)
- June 30, 2020: Girls picked a painting from a Van Gogh book and we all did a version of it, **learned about Van Gogh** (term *impasto* to describe splotchy paint Van Gogh used, cutting off his ear), listening to ABBA, watched *Mamma Mia!*
- July 1, 2020: Read *If I Ran the Zoo* by Dr. Seuss, then designed our own zoo and made up Dr. Seuss-y animals, **learned about what zoos are for and how they are designed and run.**
- July 17, 2020: Made egg-in-a-peg for breakfast with the girls flipping the bread (cut a hole in a slice of bread, sauté it in butter in a pan, crack an egg into the hole, then flip it to cook the other side). Did a virtual online tour of the tomb of pharaoh Ramses VI, the girls controlling it, and **talked about mummies, hieroglyphics as an ancient Egyptian written language, Egyptian gods with animal heads**, and linked it to their play of the Egypt section of *Tomb Raider*. Watched *Pirates of Penzance* and the girls memorized the first line of "It Really Doesn't Matter," one of the patter songs in it.

That last one is an example of me being a bit fancier and more extensive. How much you write and what photos (or even videos) you upload to the journal is all up to you. The goal is twofold: (1) for both you and your kids to feel a sense of progress, and (2) for us parents to be able to look back and recall what we've done with our kids, if and when we choose to.

Quantifying the Lesson Plan

This idea of every little lesson "counting" is an important one and brings us to the "quantified self" element of this project. Keeping track of what you do, the effort you put in, what you teach your kids and how, helps in a number of ways. The biggest plus is psychological.

I use my daily planner and a journaling smartphone app to keep very basic, sketchy notes about what my wife and I do with our kids each day, as noted above. For the sake of reinforcement, I'll repeat some of the ideas here (the Preview-Engage-Review system works for us grownups, too). I include anything that felt unusual, special, out of the ordinary. We played freeze tag several times a day in our garden during our isolation period, and I only kept track of that the first few times. Now it is no longer noteworthy. We've made Eggs and Soldiers for breakfast often now, so I only noted it the first time. Firsts are the most precious to remember, so that is normally what I include. For long-term and to help in writing this book, I keep track of the lessonlets, and I also try to list what sort of cultural consumption we cover. This means the list includes first times watching, reading, visiting, playing, listening, eating, etcetera. So I've included the first time we watched the Disney movie *Sleeping Beauty* (until my daughters became obsessed with the villain, Maleficent, and so I've not bothered with the next forty-seven times they watched it). The first time we read a whole novel together (*My Father's Dragon* by Ruth Stiles Gannett), the first time we visited an aquarium, we first time we played charades, the first time we listened to "Army of Me" by Bjork (their favorite, but mostly because they first encountered it as part of a badass video tie-in with the action movie, *Suckerpunch*), the first time they ate a Dutch baby pancake . . . .

This listing process allows you to track what is learned, when and how, but that is really the least of it (unless you're into the quantified self, in which case, enjoy!). To be honest, I almost never refer back to these lists—aside from when writing this book. But I like the idea that I *could*. To know that I could is a powerful force. If my daughters, for some strange reason, want to know the first time they ate calzone, fondly remembering it when they are, I don't know, thirty years old, I can tell them. Will that happen? Of course not. But I like the idea that I have the information in the safe. If I did not keep track of it as I went, then it would be all but impossible to retrace and fill out their histories of firsts in retrospect. I have a list of, yes, *every* film they've ever watched. It is largely useless but makes me feel good to have it. It also takes no time at all, just jotting down a single word or phrase once a day, often when I'm waiting for coffee to percolate or answering the, uh, "call of the wild" or some other "lost" time slot that would otherwise be spent spacing out or refreshing my feed in hopes of new news about my Boston Red Sox.

The idea that I *could* pull up this charted history of my children is comforting to me. I might not ever do it, but to know that I could feel good.

Four Ways to "Slow Down" Our Happy Memories with Our Children

We've all had that feeling that childhood passes by too quickly. We parents wake up one day and our kids no longer want to play with us, and we can feel that our recollection of this golden time of endearing neediness has slipped away. Well, what if there were a way to work against this feeling? To make the memory of our children's childhood feel slower, broader, deeper, richer? A quick dip into the history of memory, of mnemonic techniques, can offer a guide as to how.

The Memory Palace technique was once taught as part of higher education. Famous practitioners could memorize entire books and epic poems, which was a useful practice prior to computers and prior to the proliferation of inexpensive books. A scholar or monk might have access to a rare book only once in his lifetime, and perhaps just for a few days, and so the ability to quickly memorize as much as possible was a huge plus. Perhaps the best-known memory master was the Dominican monk, philosopher and mathematician, Giordano Bruno, who traveled the courts of Europe in the second half of the sixteenth century, teaching memorization techniques. A Jesuit priest, Matteo Ricci, brought the technique to China around the same time.

The basic principle is this: We humans remember things better if they are, well, memorable. This seems so obvious that you'd think it's a typo, but what this means is that normal, everyday, repeated activities, sites, practices are easily forgotten, or rather they all meld into one continuous memory.

What stands out are the weird moments, the surreal ones, the ones full of heightened emotion (joy, laughter, sadness, jealousy, anger). With this in mind, memory champions (and this exists—if you're curious to learn more, I recommend Joshua Foer's *Moonwalking with Einstein*) practice the ancient Memory Palace technique. They imagine an architectural space—it could be your home, or an imaginary and ever-expandable palace. Then when they wish to commit something to memory, for example the number pi, they do two things.

First, they imagine walking through the Memory Palace and affixing the memory to a specific location. For example, if I were to use my own home, I might fix the number pi to the wall just inside the main door and to the left, where we hang our keys. That way, whenever I wish to remember it, I imagine moving through the space until I reach the location where I "fixed" the memory. This is useful when you have to remember things in a particular order.

That "fixed" memory is then associated with something silly, weird or surreal. Pi starts with 3.14159, so we create a weird and therefore distinctive, *memorable*, image to associate with it. We humans are visual storytellers, so we'll remember an anecdote better than an abstract idea. Maybe "3." could be converted into a "three-pointer" in basketball? How about this: "Three-pointers were shot by 14 15-year-old number 9s." Visualization is important: take a memory and convert it into a mini-film that runs in your mind. I picture fourteen number 9s with little legs, like cartoon characters, but adolescents (15-year-olds) so maybe they've got pimples and backward baseball caps, and they're shooting three-pointers on a basketball court while eating slices of pie. That might be the memorization plan to remember that pi is 3.14159.

This two-minute summary of a very complex and elaborate technique is only for illustrative purposes to make the point that we remember what is weird, surreal, distinctive far better than what is normal for us. So, as parents, trying to do things with our kids that are not everyday, that are unusual, that are new, both in terms of what we're doing and in terms of where we're doing it, will make our memories of experiences richer, deeper and, well, more memorable.

It's more about the diversity of interactions. We tend to get lazy and engage in the same things every week, sometimes every evening. Our kids enjoy them, they are easy to slip into, so why change? Consider the message of Milan Kundera's novel *Slowness*, one based on many a psychological study: We remember things that are unusual, distinctive, out of the ordinary as if they are highlighted, standing out, whereas quotidian matters feel like one long continuum when we think back on them. Knowing that a time will come, all too soon, when my kids will want as little to do with me as possible, it's an ideal time to stock up on memories and experiences and have a richer well upon which to draw later. Here's something of a recap, a review of what we've presented thus far, with some additions.

1. **Keep Track of Firsts**. The key to expanding the sense of richness and breadth of our interactions with our kids is by quantifying and recording what we do with them. Keeping track of what you do, the effort you put in, what you teach your kids and how, when they have firsts (first time watching *Mary Poppins*, first time whistling, first time eating curry and so on) helps in a number of ways. The biggest plus is psychological. As noted, I use a daily planner and a journaling smartphone app to keep very basic, sketched-out notes about what my wife and I do with our kids each day. I include anything that felt unusual, special, out of the ordinary.

2. **Diversify What You Do with Your Kids and Where You Do It**. Expanding our memory of our children's youth is more about the diversity of interactions and their locations, and about recording them (in a journal, app, through video and photos, and so on) than anything else. We tend to get lazy and engage in the same things every week, sometimes every evening. A Peppa Pig episode on the couch before bed. Pancakes for breakfast on lazy Sunday mornings. Our kids enjoy these habits; they are easy to slip into, so why change? The "why change" question is answered by a look at how we remember. We remember things that are unusual, distinctive, out of the ordinary, as if they are highlighted, standing out, whereas quotidian matters feel like one long continuum when we think back on them.

3. **Changing Locations Helps Us Remember Activities**. We also remember things we did in diverse, new places better than places we spend a lot of time. Even if we do something we love, for instance biking with our kids on a favorite path in the woods near our home, if we do the same thing one hundred times, in our memory those hundred times will merge into one pleasant recollection. If we go to one hundred different

locations, each one will settle into our memory more distinctly, because it was new.

4. **Borrow the Ancient "Memory Palace" Technique and Focus on the Weird.** Here's that technique we just introduced. You'd probably remember the time you were out fishing and a trout jumped out of the river and into your boat, right? Well, if that happened every time you went fishing it wouldn't be noteworthy, would it? Seek out new, different, surreal, silly, weird activities and moments, and they'll be treasured in your memory, and your child's, much more vividly than anything "normal."

If we can expand, deepen and "slow down" our happy memories with our children, then that is a gift for parents when our kids get older.

The quantified self is also useful for us, as parents and teachers. At the end of summer, for example, you can look back and see what you covered with your children and feel a real sense of accomplishment if you've listed what you've done. It feels better to see the list and say, "Wow, we covered thirty lessons this month, including a special Dinosaur Week," rather than know, in a more passive way, that you covered thirty random things.

Totally Legit "Cheats"

Can't think of a good lessonlet one day? Or, like, five days? Me neither. It happens to us all, and that's fine and normal. The Lesson Game should feel easy, smooth, organic and fun, both for you and for your kids. Totally don't sweat it. And you can totally "cheat." Cheats aren't really cheating. You are still doing all the prescribed things: engaging with your kids, teaching them something, doing the preview-engage-review pattern, giving them their superpower of the day. You're just letting some external source carry the majority of the load.

I do this all the time, and it sometimes works even better than when my wife and I try to teach something. The thing is, and I'm sure you've noted this, kids and their parents have a very different dynamic than kids and teachers or kids and strangers with a level of authority. Our own kids twist us around their little fingers, and misbehave or behave differently, at home, in ways they never would at school. They're so comfortable with their parents, which is good, but it means that there's a dynamic that does not lend itself as well to learning.

Hence to bring in some backup is often a better way. A buddy of mine tried to teach his sons to tie their shoes. He tried different approaches, but they just weren't getting it. He was getting frustrated, the kids were, too, and feeling bad because they felt like they were "failing" their dad. It was getting messy. Then he found a YouTube video of some stranger teaching kids to tie their shoes. He set up the video and said, "Here you go, learn it!" then left the room. By the time he came back to check on them, they were both tying their shoes like pros. Calling in a ringer is sometimes just the thing. YouTube is full of time wasters but is also full of good stuff. A whole world of generous strangers has spent time preparing quality content that they uploaded for us to watch for free. This is a good thing. Take advantage of it.

I had a parallel experience to my buddy's with teaching my girls to read an analog clock. I set up the "carrot": When they can consistently read analog watch faces, we will buy them their first watches. They were into it, but our attempts at explaining how to read a clock were not going anywhere. I, at least, found it much harder to explain than I anticipated, because there are a number of factors that aren't at first logical: dividing a day into 24, an hour and a minute into 60. "Why aren't there ten hours a day," my kid asked. "There should be," I replied, "but I'm not sure who to talk to about changing the system." Then you've got the AM/PM thing, but we live in Europe so we've got the "military time" thing. "If the hour hand is pointing at 2, why do you say it's 1400?" "Good question, you just do, okay!" And so on.

So I turned to YouTube. There are a lot of short videos, both cartoons and real people, explaining how to read a clock. We watched several. What was interesting is that each one approached teaching this seemingly basic lesson in a different way. It *is* hard to explain, with a number of conceptual layers. But there was benefit in a third party teaching it, to outsourcing the Lesson Game. The kids associate watching things with fun free time, so they're into anything on YouTube, which checks the "game" box. And actually, the diversity of approaches to teaching the same content is useful. The kids are exposed to several presentations of the concept, giving them the repetition that helps solidify a lesson and the different ways of teaching it in each video, one approach of which might click better with your kid than another.

So, YouTube instructional videos are a good cheat that isn't actually cheating. Another is to call in a relative or a friend (we call all our close friends "uncle" and "aunt," so we've got an extended sort-of-family) and see if they would take a turn at teaching something. This could be by video or video call, or it could be in person. Anyone but a parent is often in a better position to hold a kid's attention and command enough authority to draw focus and a desire to please. Phone a friend if you've got one willing and able. You can have a little exchange program. For instance, I could offer to teach about art and history to the kids of my friends, and I might ask them to teach things I'm terrible at (I'm looking at you, math and science).

If you're short of ideas on what to present in the lessonlet of any given day, don't sweat it. That's what books are for. Particularly encyclopedias, dictionaries and atlases. It's good to keep some on your shelves. If I'm uninspired one day (and that happens often), I'll just say "Okay girls, open up the animal encyclopedia and pick any entry that looks interesting." And we read that together. Bam, Mr. Encyclopedia has provided our lessonlet for us. You can take it one step more professor-ish and work your way through one type of animal at a time. Say you'll work your way through entries on big cats before you jump to another type of animal. Read one entry, which takes just a few minutes, or more if they seem into it. Done and dusted.

Pick a page in the *Picturepedia*. Or open an atlas and pick a country to learn its location and a few facts about it. "Visit" it with Google Earth and explore. That's a totally legit lesson. Let them choose a recipe in a cookbook and make it together. Find a picture that they like and have them (and you along with them) draw it. An art lessonlet, sorted! Open a dictionary (I grew up with the *Sesame Street Dictionary* which contains very cute cartoons and kid-friendly definitions of thousands of words) and let their superpower of the day be understanding a new word. Then try to use the word as often as possible over the next few days, and encourage them to use it, too. Each time they use it properly in a sentence, they get a reward.

In summary, it's totally fine to cheat, because you're not actually cheating. You're still doing everything right, in the Lesson Game and as engaged, loving parents.

4 The Lesson Game in Practice

This chapter looks at applying the Lesson Game, its lessonlets and level-ups and superpowers, in practice. We examine a variety of types of activity from which lessonlets can be drawn and new superpowers acquired: watching movies, playing video games, reading, drawing, cooking, visiting museums, and beyond. For each we offer some specific examples based on our experience with our own kids but, as it is throughout this book, there are no required activities, so you should take all of these examples as an idea to try or a template that will allow you to adapt the concept to your own preferences.

Leveling Up Your Superpowers

We've talked about laying out each new activity as acquiring a new "superpower." It's always best to start with the most basic level of whatever you are presenting so that there is a feeling of empowerment on your kids' part that they can really do/understand/grasp/enjoy this activity. It is a step toward positive reinforcement. Something too difficult too early will put them off and can frustrate us parents (if we feel that they should really be able to do it already, as we sometimes have an over-optimistic idea of what our kids can do or will like to do). You should select the introductory level of any experience that will be feasible for your kids with a reasonable amount of effort.

Take, for example, telling the time. Though it may be tempting to begin with an analog clock or watch, a digital one will be far easier and result in a quicker feeling of progress. As long as they know how to read numbers, they can give this a shot. What's tough conceptually is the idea that time telling is divided into sixties and twenty-fours. Logic wants us to divide into tens and hundreds. But sixty seconds to a minute and sixty minutes to an hour it is. Then we have twenty-four hours in a day. These numbers make telling time a step more complex conceptually. Consider making the most basic level just to write out (perhaps with colors for each hour) a twenty-four-hour clock. Military time (or European time) is a step easier than the a.m./p.m. system. Therefore, take two drawings of a clock and color them in wedges for each hour, like a pie. Twelve to one might be purple, one to two might be green, etc. One clock is for daytime, one for nighttime. You might add a drawing of what you normally do in each hour. Maybe 1 p.m. to 2 p.m. during the day is lunchtime. Maybe 8 p.m. to 9 p.m. at night is getting ready for bed, and 9 p.m. at night until 7 a.m. in the morning is asleep time. That could be the introductory level, one lessonlet.

You can then "level up" by taking the same concept, the same overall lesson, and making the next level a step more complicated. This leveling up should take place on a different day. One victory is plenty for one day. Level 2 might be looking at a digital clock and telling which hour it is. Leave it at that. Another victory. Then level 3 could be the same for an analog clock, which has to be "read" in a more complex way than just reading a number on a digital clock. Level 4 could be adding in minutes on a digital clock. Level 5 could be the same on an analog clock. Level 6 might be using terms like "quarter past" and "quarter to" and "half past." Add in "noon" and "midnight," which will be additional vocabulary words that duplicate saying "at twelve." Level 7 might be a quiz: draw out a number of analog and digital clocks and ask your kids to read them. Level 8 could be a connect-the-clocks with drawings of activities (they have to draw a line between 1 and 2 in the daytime and a sketch of eating lunch). Level 9 might be reading an analog clock or watch with no numbers on its face.

If it seems appropriate, integrate rewards for success. Moving a level up should feel like a reward in itself, but it doesn't hurt to offer an M&M for each correct answer, for example. And, if they reach level 10, maybe you will buy them their first (very basic) watch?

How you level up lessonlets is up to you, but you can use this example as a template to apply elsewhere. You also might have kids who begin at a higher level than the most basic one. You might, then, start at level 5 if your kids can already handle telling time with a digital clock.

It's up to us parents to make sure children recognize that they are taking small steps, and that cutting cooked carrots with a butter knife does not mean that they can suddenly spatchcock a guinea hen with a kitchen knife, but you get the point. That is why we have the level-up system when

The Lesson Game in Practice

your kids are developing skills that will necessarily grow incrementally. Learning to doggy paddle and float in a pool might be the starting level of an accomplishment. Swimming ten yards might be the next level up. Swimming the width of a pool is level 3, while swimming the length might be level 4. Level 5 is for swimming while getting your face wet, 6 for swimming with a proper freestyle stroke, 7 for adding breaststroke, 8 for backstroke and 9 for doing ten laps in a row. You needn't be so rigid or have so many steps, and you should feel free to design the increments based on what feels feasible for your kids and then what feels like the next feasible goal that is still a pride-inducing stride forward.

In the Superpower Menu at the back, we've prepared suggestions for the basic level of a lessonlet, plus one or more ideas for leveling up. But remember, throughout this book, that I'm not here to tell you exactly how to do things or what to do or when. This is all about presenting parents with a conceptual framework through which to create their own Lesson Games that will suit them and their children.

A Superpowered Cooking Course at Home with Your Kids

We all need to eat, but we're used to feeding our kids, laying out a spread, then cleaning up after them. Because we all need to eat, and cook for ourselves sooner or later, it stands to reason that teaching kids to cook early will unlock many good things. Kids are more likely to try new flavors, dishes, or "funny looking" ingredients (I'm looking at you, beets) if they were involved in preparing a meal with them. This can be as simple as basic knife skills, beginning with a butter knife slicing boiled carrots, or proper MasterChef Junior training. There are cookbooks aimed at kids, with the photographed step-by-step approach particularly appealing and easy to follow. As our kids got older, we asked them to cook us one meal a week. But while they were still five and seven, I began the project to not just cook with my daughters, but to teach them cooking skills and theory in a curated way.

This meant that we developed knife skills step by step, beginning with slicing boiled carrots, then bananas, and on to using sharp knives on boiled chicken. We learned flavors by playing games like blind tasting various fruits and guessing what they were, and combining various flavors (cinnamon and vanilla, strawberry and chocolate) to see which worked best together. Most parents will cook or bake with their kids, and that's great. But we can "level up" the experience by being just a bit more organized and calculated in what we cook, in what order, and how.

Let's take a look at how this approach to not just cooking with kids but teaching our kids cooking theory and kitchen skills looks in practice.

We parents tend to engage in activities with our kids at random. When the moment arises, when we need to bake some bread, when it's rainy out and we're looking for something to do, then we go for it. This is fine and normal, and even a coordinated engagement of teaching kids to cook shouldn't feel like work (or in their case, like school) but should feel like playtime. That means that I avoid saying "every other day at 10 a.m. is baking time!" I let it flow and feel loose. But I do have a master plan drawn up, a sort of flexible syllabus of recipes I've come across that are linked to practicing specific kitchen techniques. I have them arranged by levels, from easiest to those requiring more skill, so my kids can "level up" to borrow the gaming term. I'll include a number of examples here.

This cooking "syllabus" isn't the least bit rigid. It's meant to be a grab bag of recipes I'd enjoy trying with my girls and that suit their current ability level and understanding. Making it once means that I don't have to think twice or look anything up when a good moment arises to, say, bake oatmeal cookies. I also know that, if my kids have gotten quite good at slicing hot dogs, then we can try leveling up to slicing poached chicken, so that each round in the kitchen feels like they're making progress in learning skills, not just preparing a meal or snack.

Let's look at knife skills. We began with plastic knives, the sort that wouldn't even cut you if you tried. These are good for figuring out how knives should be held, and the sawing versus chopping motions. To begin with, I boiled whole carrots until they were soft, and then made a game of my kids chopping and sawing them into bite-sized bits. First, they held them in place with their hands, but then we leveled up to their using a plastic fork to steady the carrots, as grownups would. The next step was to slice boiled hot dogs, which have more of a resistant texture, and to use metal knives, but still not the sharp ones. Poached chicken has still more textural complexity, so that was the third level. Then we introduced serrated knives and, under supervision of course, we cut first soft brioche and then sandwich bread. We haven't gotten to crusty loaves or steak or anything like that, but that's still to come. Each parent will know best the capabilities of their kids at any age or moment, so consider these just suggestions to take or leave as you like.

When it comes to baking, we began with the very simplest approach: store-bought cookie dough that you just slice, lay on a baking sheet and bake. This is the most passive type of baking but still engages with the process, gives the chance to explain that heat transforms the ingredients into plump and edible delights, and makes the kids feel that they're an active participant in preparing food, not just opening a package and eating. Level two was the world's simplest cookies: those with just two ingredients. There are a few variations, but one is just pureed banana and oats. Mix them together to form a dough, lay them on a baking sheet and bake at 190° Celsius until they are cookie-like (about twelve minutes. Another is just peanut butter and a sweet syrup (like maple syrup or date syrup). This doesn't get any easier but it still qualifies as mixing raw materials and baking them. Then sugar cookies can be level three: butter, flour, egg, vanilla extract, baking powder and baking soda, a touch of salt and sugar. From there you can explore more elaborate recipes: chocolate chip, oatmeal raisin, but still within the cookie continuum. You want to make things that your kids will be delighted to eat. They'll get a feeling of empowerment with each level up, and you can try some genuinely complex recipes, like the completely wonderful but elaborate "crack pie" cookies of the legendary sweet chef, Christina Tosi.

This general approach can be applied to all aspects of cooking. Knife skills, sautéing, soups, cookies, bread, cakes, muffins, pasta, you name it. The principle is to gather recipes ahead of time and divide them into categories and then levels of complexity. Keep moving your kids up levels as you go, and relish the feeling of engagement with them, their empowerment in acquiring new "superpowers" of cooking, and the delicious fruits of your labors, which can be eaten at the end!

I don't like following recipes. It's something about being told what to do. Look, I know that I'm being told what to do by a trained professional who has tested countless variations of a recipe and offers me the best and easiest option. Nah, not for me. I like to look at the pictures, get inspiration, half-follow the recipe, then wing it. Do I really need to get out my electric mixer (I'm already picturing the subsequent additional cleaning required)? Must I separate the yolk from the white? Come on, they're both going into the bowl later anyway? That sort of thing. I own just a few cookbooks, mostly gifts.

I do, however, enjoy looking at and even reading cookbooks. And this is something that I can do with kids. They are meant to provide inspiration as much as instruction.

I ordered a bunch of cookbooks, inspired by the Netflix series, *Ugly Delicious*, in which American chef and leader of the Momofuku restaurant empire, David Chang, hangs out with other chefs and celebrities and speaks, heartfully and honestly and without pretension, about foods that he loves and knows not enough about. I love the show and love Chang and think his restaurants sound amazing, which is also odd since I've never eaten in any of them. I'm a big fan based on how good his food looks and sounds. Not tweezer-foam-abstract expressionism good-looking, but I want to dive headfirst into this bowl that's finger-licking good-looking. It was after his episode on tacos that I clicked "place order" and the cookbooks winged their way toward me.

When they arrived, I did something I imagine few people associate with cookbooks. I *read* them. I read each one, cover to cover, pouring through as if they were novels. I've helped write a cookbook and my wife translated one, so I know a perhaps surprising statistic: some 80 percent of cookbook buyers do not use the recipes. They buy cookbooks for inspiration, to browse the pictures, because they're fans of the author. Now, cookbooks sell well, always. Turns out that most people buy cookbooks for everything but the recipes. But they buy cookbooks, nonetheless.

Which means that I'm in good company. Heck, the fact that I eventually got around to cooking from them, too, means I'm in the elite minority 20 percent!

The cookbooks I ordered included two David Chang offspring: *Momofuku* and *Lucky Peach's 101 Easy Asian Recipes*. The latter was written by Chang's business partner in the short-lived but wonderfully quirky *Lucky Peach* magazine, Peter Meehan, who is my new bro crush. Look, as a professional writer I know how hard it is to (a) actually make a reader laugh, and (b) write in interesting, fresh ways about food. Meehan does both. I literally laughed aloud many times while reading his short texts accompanying those Asian recipes. Then I read the text to my wife, with difficulty, as I kept cracking up. This is very hard to accomplish. Hat's off to you, Mr. Meehan. For some reason, being at home, particularly in the Slovenian Alps (where Alpine food is readily available, but Asian is not), I get cravings for Korean food and tacos. Being able to cook at home what you crave and can't get is sort of like a magic trick, and these cookbooks (particularly the *Lucky Peach*) allowed this, with wonderful élan and without worrying about authenticity, full of shortcuts when you can't get ingredients. And I love shortcuts.

I also hit up Enrique Olvera's *Tu Casa Mi Casa* (Mexican home cooking), published by Phaidon, *Feasts* by Sabrina Ghayour (various Arabic home cooking), Anita Sumer's *Sourdoughmania* (sourdough baking from Central Europe), Nadine Levy Redzepi's *Downtime* (Danish home cooking), and *Zahav* by Michael Solomonov (Israeli home cooking). *Zahav*, in particular, did what I want cookbooks to do—tell me the story of the food, through the voice of the chef, to teach me about an exotic world through food that, if I'm feeling plucky, I can prepare myself. The recipes are the least of it.

There is a comfort in cooking, and therefore a comfort in cookbooks. We all love food and we love our families. During this time when we feel at risk and isolated, one of the best gifts we can offer our family is to cook them delicious things that perhaps take a bit more effort.

My reaction, to my own surprise, has been to dive into cooking and actually follow recipes. I try to do as much as I can with the kids. Izabella is into baking, so we've made walnut brownies from Nadine Levy Redzepi, and sourdough bread from Anita Sumer. Eleonora wanted fried chicken, and we've tried Redzepi's recipe, as well as one from *Lucky Peach* and from *Momofuku*. I made "mall chicken" from *Lucky Peach* because I miss the totally inauthentic General Tso's Chicken of my Chinese takeout youth, which Slovenian Chinese restaurants do not make and have never heard of. I made lacquered whole roast chicken Lucky Peach style, then made their fried rice out of the leftover and made Enrique Olvera's chicken soup out of the carcass—very satisfying to get three meals out of one chicken. And I've been repeatedly making a hybrid of Christina Tosi's "crack pie" crossed with Redzepi's chocolate chip cookie recipes that, well, someone should put in a cookbook.

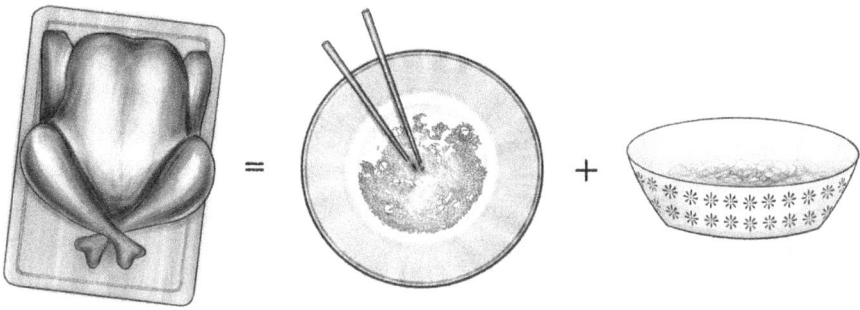

The Power of Make-Believe Roleplaying

Somewhere, sitting on an old-fashioned VHS video cassette, is a clip from a local television commercial promoting my hometown, New Haven, Connecticut (in the US), starring me and my father at the local Children's Museum. It was filmed at an old fire station converted into a play center, with interactive exhibits for parents and young children. This was back in the 1980s, where I was growing up in the United States. I can't remember why, but my father and I were invited to play while being filmed for this commercial. It was my first television appearance (not the last—I still do TV hosting a few times a year, usually for Discovery or History channels). And my parents used to love to show their friends this short clip (and show my future girlfriends—they had fun embarrassing me). I must have been about four, and I was putting various hats on my father, then dressing up as a doctor or as a fireman and sliding down a firepole or pretending to cook in a toy kitchen.

This sort of play offers a special type of interaction between parents and children and a journey into the imagination for children playing with each other. It transports children magically to a variety of different environments where their imagination can unfold. Best of all, it is entirely analog: There are no screens and no video games and no smartphones and no televisions. All that digital stuff can be wonderful, but even video games are a more mentally passive form of entertainment. The screen entertains you, and your focus is on whatever it chooses to show you. Screen-less engagement is far more stimulating for the imagination and for bonding, among children or between parents and their kids. There is nothing better than playing dress up and make believe, pretending that you are characters or heroes.

Too often, these days, we parents feel that children are not allowed to get bored. That we must provide them with entertainment at all times and, when we cannot do so, we should plug them into a device or set them up with a movie. But a little bit of boredom forces us to use our own imagination to entertain ourselves. This is hugely beneficial and stimulating. In the right environment, with a lot of inspiring tools and toys and spaces at your disposal, it is impossible to get bored, and the imagination is stimulated in myriad ways.

This is what was so great about children's museums, and you can surely find some wherever you are based. Children's museums are places where children and parents can spend hours immersed in their imagination, enjoying each other's company in the most direct, memorable and beneficial way. That direct bonding time, engaged in imaginative play, is hugely valuable. Every minute spent in direct, proactive interaction with your kids is a minute that is far more valuable than an hour of passive interaction that you might spend sitting together watching TV, but each in your own head space. Direct immersion in imaginative play is what bonds children with each other and bonds parents with children.

You do not need to go somewhere to engage in make-believe, role-playing fun. When you embody someone else, a character, a hero, a villain, a professional, someone from a film, whatever it may be—and when you act out that role alongside your child—it's a unique sort of play and bonding. You disappear through a portal to another dimension and synchronize your imaginations to visualize what each other sees before you. That dragon you both must fight, the fire you must both extinguish, the wild stallion you must ride. It's a similar bonding to taking a road trip with your grownup friends—travel, shared experiences. The only difference is that the travel and shared experiences are imaginary, but the bond is the same. So don't be shy about role-playing. The more you get into the groove, the more delighted your kids will be.

Outsourcing Lesson Games: Aunty Liisa's Guide to Science Lessonlets

We all have our specialties. My brain works in some useful ways, but it goes on strike when numbers, logic or science are required of it. I can screw in most types of lightbulbs, but that's about as handy as I get. I can do basic algebra, but any sort of math has always been an uphill battle. Logic is, to me, illogical. So I am in awe of friends who are handy, logical, and good at math and science.

Since we all have our strengths and weaknesses, there's a natural tendency to want to focus on the strengths and flee in the face of the weaknesses. This is not the best approach, especially when it comes to offering our kids a broad spectrum of experiences to cultivate a variety of skills. This is why it can be good to outsource certain experiences, lessons and activities that we parents might not be so good at.

Outsourcing is most obviously in play whenever we send our kids to school. We're expecting that the teachers there will do the teaching for us, and they do so. We can outsource to tutorial videos. This approach shouldn't be done all the time, because then the bonding opportunity and creation of memories is lost, but it's a strong option when we run into a roadblock or wish to teach something that feels beyond us.

Documentaries are also a great way to outsource. David Attenborough goes to all sorts of places we cannot, and gets footage of animals we certainly cannot, and so we're happy to let him provide some lessons about exotic fauna. I'm not the least survivalist-ish and so Bear Grylls and Ed Stafford provide fascinating tips in fields I could never hope to approach.

We inevitably borrow ideas for activities and lessonlets from other sources than our own wholesale invention, which is totally fine and to be expected. When it comes to science lessonlets, I'm at a loss because I know so little about science. This means that I'm delighted to find great sources, like the James Dyson Foundation Challenge Cards, available for free, containing forty fun at-home experiments to do with your kids to teach them scientific concepts. This fits perfectly within the Lesson Game format, as each takes fifteen minutes or less. Borrowing the idea for a project from another source is perfectly viable and recommended.

We can also outsource by calling upon the talents and attention of friends and family. Outsourcing does not provide the parent-child bonding experience but does provide bonding between our kids and the friends and family members we enlist. This is why, when it comes to science, I was delighted to ask for help from "Aunty" Liisa van Vliet, a biochemist at Cambridge, whom I met when studying there and who is a good friend. She offered us three "Superpower Science Lessons" that we include here. When you're outsourcing lessonlets, you can either ask for the lesson outline and then take on the role of leading it with your kids yourself or, if you're feeling hi-tech, you can arrange for your "Aunty" to lead it via Facetime or Skype, or wait until they come for a visit.

Here is what Aunty Liisa suggested.

Red Cabbage as a pH Indicator

The purple color in red cabbage contains a dye (anthocyanin) that changes color when it is mixed with acids or bases. The dye or pigment turns red in acidic environments (when the pH, the acidity level, is less than 7) or green/blue in a basic (alkaline) environment (when the pH is more than 7). To conduct this simple experiment at home, you'll need:

- a few glasses
- four red cabbage leaves and water (distilled water is best)
- a blender
- a sieve, cheese cloth, a tea towel, or a coffee filter
- a funnel
- a variety of solutions with different pHs, possibly: water, vinegar, baking powder mixed with water, bleach, lemonade, sugar mixed with water, household ammonia, washing powder mixed with water

Instructions

1. Blitz the red cabbage leaves and water in a blender or mixed
2. Pour this solution into a glass. This gives you a purple liquid as your pH indicating solution.
3. Prepare separate glasses each with a different solution in it (i.e., vinegar in one glass, baking soda water in another, etc.)
4. Add small amounts of the purple solution to each sample glass
5. Put the solutions in order by pH from acid to basic
6. Extra: mix a bit of strong acid (red) into a basic solution and see if you can make it purple (a neutral pH) again

The Lesson Game in Practice

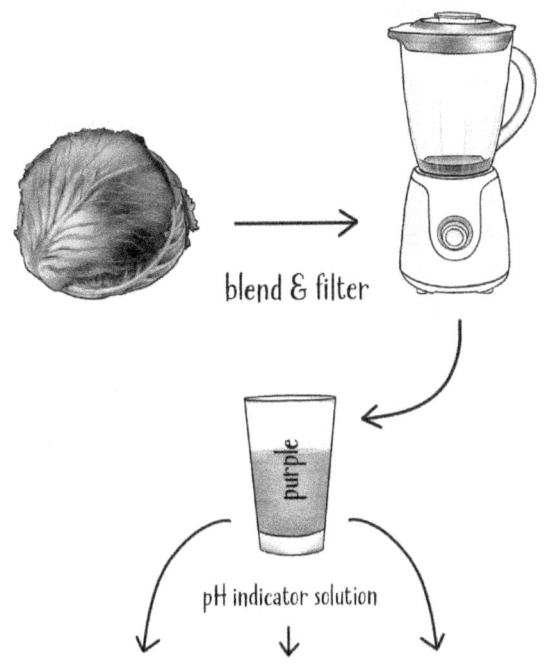

blend & filter

pH indicator solution

add the purple pH-indicating solution to each glass

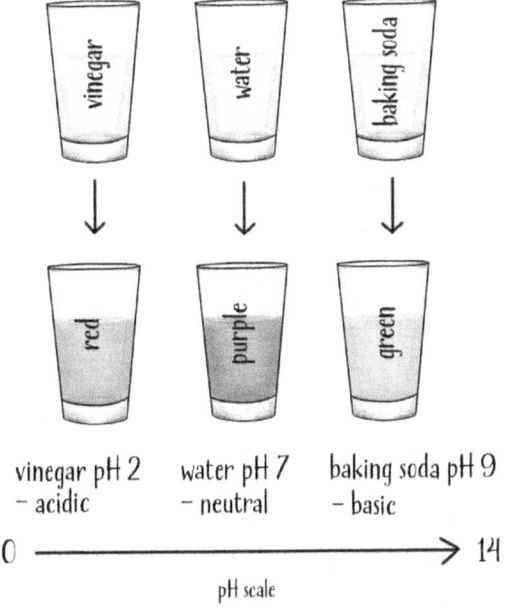

vinegar pH 2 — acidic water pH 7 — neutral baking soda pH 9 — basic

0 ⟶ 14

pH scale

Why Is Baking Soda a Raising Agent?

Here is a second, easy, at-home experiment you can conduct. It pairs well with baking, so you can see the effect of baking soda in action and practically applied. You'll need:

- baking soda
- vinegar or lemon juice
- a glass or small bottle
- food dye (optional, if you want to make it pretty)
- also optional: a candle

Instructions

1. Light the candle (if using one)
2. Add 25 mL of vinegar to a glass
3. Add a bit of water and optional food coloring
4. Add 1 tsp of baking soda to the glass
5. Watch the bubbles foam
6. Put the glass near the lit candle. The CO_2 escaping from the glass should extinguish the candle

Extra credit

1. Take a small plastic bottle
2. Mix baking soda, a bit of water, and red food dye in the bottle
3. Decorate the bottle, leaving the opening free to make it look like a volcano
4. When ready, add the vinegar

This shows how gas (CO_2) is produced when baking soda combines with something acidic. It's probably the most famous simple science class experiment. The CO_2 starves th-e candle of oxygen and so the flame goes out. Fire needs fuel, and that fuel is heat and oxygen. Think about how the baking soda, mixed with something acidic, made the liquid bubble and foam. This works in baking. If you bake a cake using a recipe that calls for baking soda and something acidic, like buttermilk, the bubbling and foaming transfers into the cake dough and make it rise and get all nice and fluffy.

Making Ice Cream Like the Victorians

For a final home science experiment, you can make ice cream the way it was done in Victorian-era England. You'll need:

- a bowl
- a large bag of ice
- 1 cup of rock salt
- 1 tsp vanilla extract
- ¼ cup of sugar
- milk and/or cream
- a large Ziplock bag and a smaller Ziplock bag
- gloves or a kitchen towel
- optional: add chocolate chips or swap out the milk for chocolate milk

Instructions

1. In a bowl, mix ¼ cup of sugar plus ½ cup of milk plus ½ cup of cream (or 1 cup of milk) plus the vanilla extract
2. Pour the ice cream mixture into the smaller Ziplock bag, then close it properly, trying to push out the air
3. In the larger Ziplock bag, add 2–3 cups of crushed ice or ice cubes so that it fills half the bag, then add 1 cup of salt
4. Place the "ice cream" mix smaller bag inside the larger bag and seal them both tightly
5. Shake and roll the ice bag around for 5–10 minutes until the mixture in the inner bag becomes ice cream. Don't forget to protect your hands, as it will be ice cold!

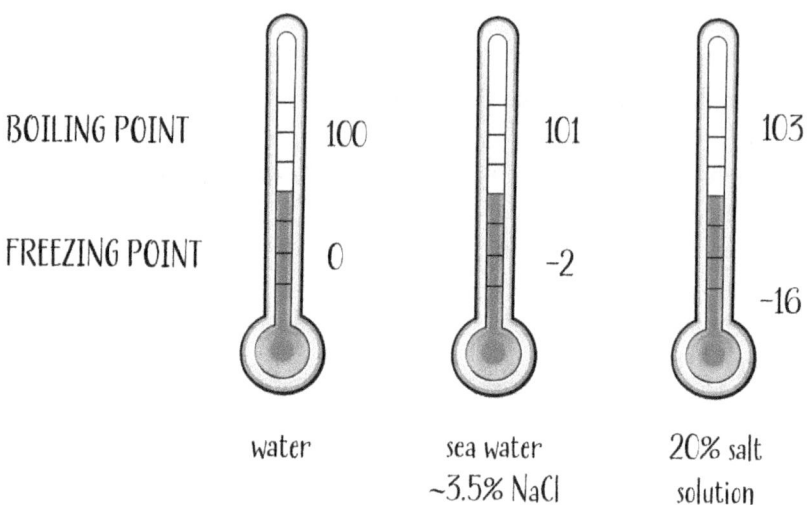

How does this work? The ice in the bag with the salt is much colder than normal ice. Temperature wants to equilibrate across the two items that are next to each other, so the milk gives its heat to the ice, and in doing so loses temperature—and starts to freeze.

Salt is a powerful ingredient. We add just a little bit to a big pot of boiling water when cooking and it increases the boiling point of the water. It makes the heat of the boiling water a little bit hotter, which cooks the pasta a bit faster. Salt has superpowers!

Art Museums with Children

Let it be said that I am an art history professor, so I had a vested interest in getting my daughters, ages five and seven, to like art. Going to museums is among my favorite things to do, and I love to share it with my kids. The trouble is, while kids tend to like science museums (full of interactive gadgetry) and natural history museums (dinosaurs!), the nature of fine art museums is certainly adult-oriented. There's a lot of staring quietly at things that do not move, that do not have buttons to push, and that do not have rows of six-inch-long teeth. Not exactly every child's dream outing.

The Lesson Game in Practice

But I've developed a system that has worked with my kids and can work for any parents interested in getting their kids excited about visiting art museums. It turns museum visits into Where's Waldo-style treasure hunts. What follows is the brief rundown, and some ideas that any parent can implement wherever museums are found, or even just while browsing art books.

Preview-Engage-Review as Applied to Museums

This is a system I use when teaching at university level, and also with my kids, and we cover it in its own chapter here. The idea is to whet appetites and preview something we'll be doing or seeing well before we get there. It's why we professors give out syllabi at the start of a course, and quickly summarize all that will be covered. It helps prepare our audience (whether a lecture hall of students or a car full of our children), lay the foundation and parameters of what we'll see, and spark initial curiosity. "Today, we're going to the National Gallery in London to see some of my favorite paintings," I might begin. "We're going to see a giant painting of a horse (George Stubbs's *Whistlejacket*), and a painting that was stolen by someone protesting against having to pay for their television channels (Goya's *Portrait of the Duke of Wellington*) and a painting of a boy being bitten on the finger by a lizard (Caravaggio's aptly-titled *Boy Bitten by a Lizard*)." This is helpful in that it gives my kids a sense of what to expect. Kids like that and find comfort in it.

Then, when we're in the museum, I let them loose to find the key things we mentioned in anticipation. It's step one of the treasure hunt trick I recommend for making art museums more engaging. So as soon as we get there, they can explore and search for some key objects. Particularly good are the first and third ones I mentioned. A giant horse and a boy bitten on the finger by a lizard are easily spotted by kids, without needing any a priori knowledge.

The "review" component of this approach is for the ride home, or dinner that night, or the next day (or all three). I ask them to summarize what we did and saw, what their favorite things were, what surprised them, and so on. This helps to cement the memory of what we did and even some of the names of the artworks or artists, through simple repetition.

Treasure Hunts in the Gallery

Simply wandering an art museum, particularly slowly and reading wall copy, is unlikely to hold the interest of younger kids. Fair enough, it doesn't always hold the interest of grownups, either. Therefore, it's best to give kids an active task. In addition to the opening gambit of asking them to wander around and find a few key artworks based on my basic description of them, I also have a similar approach when looking at individual artworks. Variant One is setting them loose and giving them a clue to identify which object I'm referring to. Variant Two is to look closely at a painting and, within it, find interesting details. This works best in group scenes, for instance the mysterious and intriguing paintings of Bosch or Bruegel. We've spent hours poring through my giant coffee table book of the complete works of Hieronymus Bosch, full of hybrid animals, monsters, devils and Alice-in-Wonderland-like details. Bosch's works are so weird that we play a game of "spot what's *not* weird," and they look for normal-looking animals, as opposed to, say, a fish with human legs. That's part of the "engage" component of the Preview-Engage-Review system. I do not let my kids passively half-glance at something, because I'm asking them questions about it. What do they see? What do they like? What don't they like about it? This also empowers them to feel good about having their own opinion (which an adult feels is worth inquiring about) and prompts them to look more deeply than the superficial glances that even many adults throw at most artworks they cruise by in a museum.

You can prepare a printed treasure hunt at home on paper that your kids can bring to the gallery. A checklist is good, especially if they are of reading age. Having paper and a pencil in hand also allows for them to draw things they see and like. This can be part of the treasure hunt (find a painting of a horse and draw it). Or the list can be of ten details they need to find and check off (or, if they can write, they should note the name of the artist in whose work the detail in question may be found).

These techniques turn the act of looking at art, which feels overly passive for children, into something more active and goal-oriented (a quest to find artworks or details within them), which is inherently interesting. To top it off, reward a successful treasure hunt with your children's choice of a treat—whatever they'd like to do. Repeatedly doing so will have a Pavlovian effect of associating the visit to a museum not only with the fun of the museum, but with the reward of the treat (ice cream, a movie, takeout Vietnamese, whatever they're into) afterward.

Cezanne and *Goodnight Moon*

Cezanne is credited with the invention of modern art. Or rather, he should be. My colleague at *The Guardian*, Jonathan Jones, recently published a column arguing as much. That while the textbooks tend to point to Picasso, and particularly his 1907 *Demoiselles d'Avignon*, as the first work of modernism, a shift in artistic style brought about by the interest of artists in the art and craft of non-European regions (Africa, Oceania, Asia), Cezanne was engaged in much of the same innovation without ever leaving his native Provence. Cezanne's leap forward was seen by traditionalists as a fold backwards: He flattened the three-dimensionality that, for centuries, artists had striven for—the goal of art was to achieve the naturalistic illusion that a flat canvas painting is actually a view into a three-dimensional reality. Cezanne took this three-dimensional reality and folded it, like undoing an intricate work of origami. He intentionally removed the illusion of depth and played with dimensionality, messed with our minds by toying with angles and foreshortening: One apple might be correctly painted to be seen from one angle, but the pear next to it is illustrated as if seen from a different angle entirely; thus the two should not exist in the same painting. He also, as Jones notes, broke down faces into masks, into blocks of color that resemble sculptures. This is most obvious with Picasso and Braque's Cubism, but they both cited Cezanne as their inspiration. Jones's article points out how odd it is that art history books disregard the admission by Picasso and Braque, who tried to credit Cezanne with this "invention" of modernism, while the historians like to credit Picasso and Braque.

Which brings me to what might be the greatest children's book ever written and illustrated, *Goodnight Moon*, by Margaret Wise Brown, with pictures by Clement Hurd. This slim picture book, for the youngest of children, is a super-minimalist text in which a bunny mother helps her bunny baby to sleep by saying "Goodnight" to a variety of objects around baby bunny's bedroom.

I'm writing this chapter on a transatlantic flight on my latest book tour, and I do not have a copy of *Goodnight Moon* with me. I don't need it. I've memorized it, each word and each picture. It's been a balm for both my daughters. If they are fussy, I begin reciting the words to this story, and they immediately calm. (For some reason, singing "The Star-Spangled Banner" used to also work for my elder daughter, but this story is guaranteed for both). I sometimes felt like the Monty Python sketch about the world's deadliest joke, in which a British soldier runs through the forest, surrounded by Nazi opponents, with no weapon but reading a German translation of the joke aloud, a joke so potent that it strikes down the enemy into fits of deadly laughter as he runs past them, reciting. I used a similar tactic on some occasions when my babies had trouble sleeping and cried. As I carried them in my arms, I began reciting the words to *Goodnight Moon*, and calm followed.

 The illustrations are deceptively simple looking. We see a room, angles askew, as if the artist isn't very good at depth (though of course this manipulation is intentional). We see objects in the room, simply drawn, the colors in bright blocks, with almost no shading. Ingeniously, as the bunny gets sleepier, the room gets darker. A fire in the hearth, beside the sitting bunny mommy, grows dimmer, the light outside fades, until the bunny is asleep and the room is completely night-dark. But before that darkness, there's this postmodern twist. The gem-colored bedroom scenes, which have alternated with black and white (rather, pen and ink) austere pages, now yield to a page with nothing at all on it. "Goodnight nobody." Then there is a false ending worthy of a Beethoven symphony. We expect the story to end with "Goodnight to the old lady whispering hush." But it does not. It's a false coda, and instead it goes on, floating us outside the window, beyond the warm, cozy bedroom, into the air and stars outside, flying heavenward.

 Curious about this super-powered text, I asked some child specialists. Dr. Carla Horwitz, who recently retired from running the award-winning progressive preschool Calvin Hill, in New Haven (of which I'm a grateful graduate), told me, "The book is so simple that you know there must have been an extraordinary amount of work to make it as elegant and simple as it is. The book has soothed many a child, and many an adult, as well."

 She continues: "I think there are many elements that make this literature that appeals on many, many levels. First of all, the rhymes and the rhythm. Then the fact that everything is a known element, close to the child, in fact in the child's room, so that everything named is an old friend. Going to bed

The Lesson Game in Practice

is a time fraught with much stress. Saying 'goodnight' is really a separation, and since children have so little experience, they don't know that it's brief, and that the daylight and the people they love will return. Surrendering to sleep is nearly the ultimate separation (other than death). And babies don't have a theory about reunion and the temporal understanding to realize the sleep time is brief. It might be forever! And it's in the dark, though this book actually gets dimmer and dimmer, but never pitch black. And you'll note that, when the bunny finally does fall asleep, the old lady's chair is finally empty. I never thought of her as the mother, more like a grandma or a nanny perhaps. But obviously she can be whatever and whomever you want."

Goodnight Moon was written in the year that Carla, and her husband Bob, a psychologist, were born. As Bob told me, "I wonder if it might have been read to us when we were little—we don't really recall. We remember it mostly as a favorite of our little girls, who are now thirty-somethings, and I imagine they'll read it to their kids, too, as you are doing with yours." He also notes some inside jokes hidden in the images, such as another book by the same author and illustrator, *Runaway Bunny*, which appears on a shelf in this baby bunny's bedroom. Bob continues, "What a loaded term that word 'goodnight' is. We say it to each other, as if we know that not all nights actually are good, and as if wishing would make it so. Kids are quite naturally afraid of the dark (so, too, are many adults), and not without reason: At the very least, it's hard to see where you're going, and easy to bump into things, but in some deeper way, it does bring up fears that the sun will never shine again, and that this night may be the beginning of the end. So how comforting it is to have someone saying 'goodnight,' over and over, acknowledging the presence of all that's in the room, still there tonight, as it was last night, still there tomorrow. And how comforting still to say goodnight to noise, as the book ends, and fall quietly asleep."

I asked for thoughts from my own father, Dr. James Charney, who read this to me and had it read to him and has now read it to his granddaughters. As a child psychiatrist, he is entirely aware of the power of soothing words and images, which actually give the slowly sleeping child a sense of control that bedtime otherwise lacks. "To me," he said, "what makes it so haunting is the incantatory quality of the 'goodnights.' The book is made to be read again and again to your child, and if you allow it to, it can put a spell on parents, too. You find yourself saying each 'goodnight' with a quiet and quieter sing-song rhythm, which just naturally leads to 'hush.' The Clement

Hurd drawings brilliantly mirror this: The objects in the room become more and more gray, the shading of each picture becomes faded, but never quite dark—nothing is scary but everything changes. Just like night should be. And the child enters that often difficult stage of sleepiness, not needing to fight it, because he is in control. He is saying 'goodnight,' in charge of the farewell for another day (or night), confident that all will be there for him to say 'hello' to in the morning."

The year that *Cezanne's Portraits*, an exhibit, opened at London's National Portrait Gallery also marked the seventieth anniversary of the publication of *Goodnight Moon*. Clement Hurd's illustrations feature the same collapsing of the illusion of depth that Cezanne initiated in his paintings of the late 1890s. The brilliance of these illustrations comes as less of a surprise when we learn that Hurd studied art with modernist legend, Fernand Leger. But modernist poetry is also an influence on this book, the stripping away of all that is not needed, even some punctuation, and the repetition of key words. This little book, which of course can be enjoyed without this sort of deconstructionist analysis, by those with tiny fingers and soft-closing eyelids, is a truly great work of modernist art, its text as powerful an incantation of modernist poetry as I know, and its illustrations richly in line with the tradition launched by Cezanne.

5 The Role of Screens in Learning

Conventional wisdom says that screens are bad for kids, especially little ones. I've heard it said that it's best not to let infants even see a screen (TV, iPad, smartphone) before they are two years old. That may be best, but it's not necessarily practical. It feels like the sort of advice that someone without a kid might give. It would also be best if kids never ate sweets, but in practice this is unlikely to manifest itself.

That said, it is evident that too much screen time has negative effects. Not that our kids' eyes will fall out (as some of us were once warned), but I saw how my kids got into a zone of screen-crazed focus that made them aggressive when told that it was time to stop, and promoted shorter attention spans and impatience. We grownups are guilty, too, of reaching for our phones whenever we have a minute of spare time—a minute! This issue is linked to the previous essay about the benefits of boredom. It's good to give your mind space to just space out.

The optimal option in a world in which screens are inevitable (and don't necessarily need to provide bad content) is for kids to recognize screen time as a privilege, not a right, and to have their screen time controlled and curated.

A friend developed a system of tokens. When his kids did something particularly nice, or helpful, or worked diligently, they would get a token. Tokens could be traded in for twenty minutes of screen time (a choice between screen options: TV or video games). But the trade-in could only take place at times when the parents offered it or by prior arrangement (as in "this Saturday you have the option of screentime after lunch if you want to use your tokens"). The only time screen time was available without tokens was when the parents invited the kids to a predetermined activity (a family round of Mario Cart or watching a movie on the couch together). This approach discourages mindless "vegging out" and channel surfing just to find some televisual entertainment and makes screen time (a) feel like an occasional treat rather than an expectation and (b) something to be planned, looked forward to, and curated, rather than "wastefully" random.

We didn't use the token system ourselves, though I see its merits, because we didn't want our kids doing things just for the tokens rather than out of a sense of responsibility. Our girls have always emptied the clean dishes from the dishwasher as their main "chore" (which is probably better to call "assist" or "help" since "chore" has negative connotations built into the word). We want them to feel like this is their contribution to the family, not "I'll empty the dishwasher and then I'll get a token." But I can see how balancing tokens for particular good deeds that aren't part of the family routine can work well.

Instead, we have screen time available only when we parents offer it (never when the kid wants it without an invitation). And we offer it only when all the responsibilities of the day have been fulfilled, or on a weekend, or when there is inclement weather. The kids never have access to screens whenever they want or without asking first.

When we do offer screen time it is (a) as a reward or a chance to unwind (for instance, to relax before a concert), (b) for a shared family experience (so they're not doing it alone), (c) when they have friends over (if they've also played together without screens), or (d) when the screen activity is curated. This last option is the subject of this chapter.

Use *Harry Potter* to Teach Your Kids: Turning Movies You'll Watch Anyway into a Fun Lesson Plan for Your Children

I first read, then watched, *Harry Potter and the Philosopher's Stone* (also known as *Harry Potter and the Sorcerer's Stone* in the United States) with my daughters when they were five and seven years old. It's a wonderful story, of course, and one you're likely to read and watch just for fun, because kids and parents both enjoy it. But for me, a professor interested in sparking a love of learning in my girls, it was just the latest in a planned series of activities we do together for entertainment, which I take as a carefully planned but easy-to-execute opportunity to teach.

A single movie night can turn into a bountiful learning experience for parents to share with their kids. It begins with discussing what we will see in the film and continues after the credits have rolled, in subsequent days, as we talk about what we've seen and some of the lessons that can be drawn from it. In this case, *Harry Potter* led to ten lessonlets, each of which took only a few minutes but which were easier to remember, and more engaging, because of their connection to the film. From how train stations work to castle architecture, from the real-life sets for Hogwarts to synonyms for "wizard," from basic Latin (used in spells) to an intro to chess (used to guard the Philosopher's Stone), an evening's entertainment can be used to develop a fun, organic lesson plan from the movies you'll watch anyway as a family.

I apply the same system with my young daughters that I do in the university classroom: Preview-Engage-Review. Before the movie starts, I "preview" the sort of things we'll see in it. That's not to give away plot, but to lay out some things to look out for and to look forward to. In this case, we've got a marvelous castle, Hogwarts, which is a boarding school for aspiring wizards and witches. We've got courses on magic, and a mystery to solve. During the film, I'm often pointing things out or asking the kids questions. This, I fully understand, could be annoying, depending on what you're used to. I find that engagement with my kids during the film helps them to be engaged *with* the film. When they were younger, even watching a movie they really liked, their attention would start to drift, and this helped keep them focused. As they get older my interjections are no longer necessary, but it does help if I point out some of the elements of the film that we'll later use for activities and lessonlets. Then, after the film, we "review" what we saw. I ask them what they liked best, what's the main thing they remember, which characters they liked, which spell they'd like to learn, and so on. This helps cement in the memory what we saw and empowers the kids to see that adults value their opinion.

In the days that followed, I pulled out activities and miniature lessons related to the content of the film, which were fresh in our memories. Here are ten lessonlets based on *Harry Potter*.

1. **Learn some (very) basic Latin.** There are uses of Latin in the film, particularly in the magic words through which spells are cast (*Alarte Ascendare*, which Gilderoy Lockhart uses to throw a snake into the air, links to the Latin *Ascendere* meaning "to go up"; *Amato Animo Animato Animagus* helps you become an "animagus," able to transform into an

animal, and the Latin *Amato* (linked to "love") and *Animo* (*anima* is spirit or soul), *Animato* is linked to the etymology of "animate." You get the picture). The kids wanted to have wizard's duels for fun, and so we learned some of the *Harry Potter* spells, with their pseudo-Latin which let us talk about some real Latin words from which the spells are derived.

2. **Castle architecture.** Hogwarts stirs the imagination, and it offers the opportunity to talk about castle architecture and do a virtual tour of some real castles that inspired Hogwarts. We designed our own castle based on the architectural components at Hogwarts: towers, ramparts, a great hall held up by buttresses, a draw bridge. You can get technical if you want to "level up" with your kids, and show them various column capitals and portcullises and mullions and that sort of thing, but for my young kids, basic shapes like towers and arrow slits were as technical as it got. Level up: we drew each component of a castle, labeled it with its name (because remembering the proper term for something is key), and then we each designed and drew our own castle based on those elements.

3. **Coats-of-arms.** The four houses at Hogwarts each have their own coat-of-arms (Slytherin's snake, Ravenclaw's raven). We talked about the origin of coats-of-arms (so knights, anonymous in suits of armor, could be identified) and looked at some famous examples from history (the noble Roman Barberini family has a heraldic sign comprised of bees, the Plantagenets had three lions on a blue ground). Then we designed a coat of arms for us, the Charney family. We leveled up by describing the difference between a coat-of-arms or armorial, and an *impresa*, an Italian term for a coat-of-arms for a single person as opposed to a family line. My daughters designed an *impresa* for themselves—an image and a slogan written on a scroll beneath it.

4. **Boarding school.** I attended a boarding school in the United States (Choate, which is old by American standards, founded in 1890) that felt magical, other-worldly and wonderful. Hogwarts minus the actual magic. I loved it. I also fulfilled the American fantasy of attending Cambridge University, which was even more Hogwartian. I took this as a chance to talk about my own boarding school experiences. It's a fascinating and slightly frightening lesson for tiny children to learn that older children can live away from home (and happily). Level up: We

took virtual tours of both Choate and my Cambridge College (Johns) and discussed what they would pack if they were to go away to study. This made the idea of leaving home to live elsewhere for a while and doing what you enjoy feel empowering, rather than intimidating.

5. **Parseltongue.** Snakes speak a language of their own that, somehow, Harry can understand. This led us to discuss how snakes in real life communicate. Under the guidance of wonderful Sir David Attenborough, we watched a documentary on snakes and used an animal encyclopedia to fill out our knowledge. Level up: draw their favorite snake from the encyclopedia and label some of its parts that we remembered (the forked tongue was a popular one).

6. **Synonyms for wizard.** Playing the synonym game is fun and expands vocabulary. You don't need to bring in complex synonyms that kids wouldn't have ever heard. There are plenty for "wizard." We tested how many we could name (and no worries if the meaning isn't precisely the same): magician, enchanter, warlock, witch, conjurer, illusionist, sorcerer, mage. . . .

7. **Scars.** Harry has a lightning bolt scar on his forehead from having been attacked by You-Know-Who. This is a chance to explain what a scar is, particularly if your kids have one. Skin's incredible regeneration works unless the cut is very deep, in which case a "ghost" of the cut remains, a scar.

8. **Arachnophobia.** In *Harry Potter and the Chamber of Secrets*, spiders feature—a lot of tiny ones and then one very large specimen. Harry's friend Ron is afraid of spiders, as are many people. This is a chance to learn the official term for a fear of spiders (arachnophobia) and the Greek *arachne* which means spider. This can be reinforced with double lesson power by also reading or telling the ancient Greek myth of Arachne. Level up: while we're at it, you can teach that the suffix, *phobia*, is also the Greek for "fear" and is attached to fears of any sort.

9. **Mythical beasts.** *Harry Potter* books include magical creatures invented by the author as well as traditional magical creatures with ancient origin stories. The J. K. Rowling-invented creatures can be fun, but are not particularly "useful" in lesson terms. But introducing kids to archetypal magical creatures that are referenced in countless stories and come from ancient myths is indeed useful and applicable in a wide variety of cultural and educational settings. So when Harry meets centaurs,

it's a good chance to define them (the torso, arms, and head of a man; the body and legs of a horse), and perhaps read an ancient myth that features them. The same might be said for hippogriffs, goblins, poltergeists and other traditional mythical beings which appear in these stories and many others. I like to reinforce understanding of such visually striking things by having my kids draw them. Level up: create your own compendium of creatures, and each daughter can then have a file of a drawing of each beast.
10. **History of magic.** The British Library ran an exhibit called "A History of Magic" that used *Harry Potter* as a vehicle to teach children about the real history of belief in magic and magical objects. We bought the catalogue, which is a wonderful book, combining images of real objects that were exhibited with illustrations from *Harry Potter* and the moments in the series that reference the objects on display. It's a constant source of fascination to browse and to read. Sometimes just reading an educational book together is lessonlet enough.

Of course, you can take this same concept and use just about any film or novel to put it into practice. Lessonlets can be drawn from anywhere, and a feature film or novel can be a rich source of them. I mentioned seven lessonlets based on the classic film, *Bedknobs and Broomsticks*, earlier in this book. I've drawn lessonlets from video games like *Tomb Raider* (which you'll read about shortly) or *Zelda* or, well, anything I can think of. Watching the Gilbert & Sullivan classic, *The Pirates of Penzance* (I grew up with the 1983 Kevin Kline version, and apparently knew all the esoteric lyrics by the age of four, at least according to Charney family legend), I pulled out lessonlets about swords (their different shapes and names), pirates, police, military rankings (Modern Major General, anyone?), Victorian prurience, the definition of "paradox" and more. Tailor the concept to whatever excites you and your children.

Introduce Your Favorite Childhood Video Games and Cartoons to Your Kids

Now that we have a world of entertainment at our fingertips, on demand, and computers in our pockets pretending to be phones we don't have to rush home for the start of *Scooby-Doo*. We can start it whenever we're ready. But with an infinite number of entertainment options available to my young children, I find myself wanting to introduce them to what I loved when I was their age. I recognize that my childhood favorites are not "better" in any objective sense (the world of Hanna-Barbera is arguably "worse" from technical, narrative and character development perspectives than any of the sophisticated children's fare on Netflix these days). But by showing them to my kids, and hoping they enjoy them, I feel like I'm opening up a part of myself to them, and bonding over something that I truly loved as a child.

The only problem is that I really want my kids to like what I liked. But what I liked is, from their perspective, a good deal less immediately gratifying, gripping and, well, entertaining than what is available now. How can we introduce our own enthusiasm for nostalgic classics when technology and attention spans are working against us? We want our kids to know, if not love, what we loved as kids, but their little brains are wired to prefer what's newer and more neurologically stimulating.

Today's cartoons and video games are more technologically advanced, and they've become more instantly gratifying. This is most obvious from the perspectives of pace, realism, and editing. Take, for instance, the classic Nintendo Entertainment System. The original 8-bit console I grew up with and couldn't wait to play (I was even an avid subscriber to *Nintendo Power* magazine) looks, by today's standards, very primitive. The controls are limited (two buttons, as opposed to today's controllers equipped with eight or more), the immersive experience of today's video games (which so often feel like you are playing through a live action film), and graphics seem quaint. Today, the NES appears to us the way the original Atari console, featuring classics like *Pong* (a "ball," actually a single green dot, very slowly bouncing between two "paddles," actually just green lines) did when we were little. Charming but nowhere near as immediately engaging as contemporary games. I bought the retro NES console, which comes preloaded with thirty games, and you just plug it into your TV. But initially, the games on offer did not excite my daughters as much as just about anything, no matter how simplistic, that can be played on a smartphone.

It's similar with cartoons. Those Hanna-Barbera cartoons have a place in my heart, but they are extremely simplistic, graphically and in terms of storyline and character development (or lack thereof—there isn't much character, beyond catchphrases like "zoinks" for Velma, "jinkies" for Daphne, and an odd orange cravat for Fred). Compare that to today's sterling cartoons, like *Trollhunters*, with cinematic action and true character depth, and the contemporary ones seem, objectively, better. They are also designed to engage the viewer more immediately, with none of the slower burn of past entertainments. Top this off with movies, and the black-and-white classics have a hard time competing for the attention of the young'uns when compared to today's slam-bang, color-rich pageants of action.

But the more modern is not objectively better, and can sometimes be less sophisticated, compensating with technology for lack of substance. It's not for me to say which era produced the "better" material. But what is important to me is that my kids should not dismiss older classics as inherently "boring." Yet, if offered either the 1986 *Legend of Zelda* on the NES or the 2017 "The Legend of Zelda: Breath of the Wild" on the Nintendo Switch, which would you pick as cooler?

Here are two tips that helped me introduce my daughters to the delights of my youth and allowed us to bond over them.

Start with the Classics and Work Your Way Newer

If you start your kids off with the idea that 64-bit (or far higher) graphic capabilities of video games are the norm, then it feels like a long step backward to switch to the old 8-bit console. It's like moving from Michelangelo's Sistine Chapel ceiling to the cave paintings. This doesn't mean one is objectively better than the other, but for younger minds less flexible and patient with subtleties, the more bells-and-whistles realistic option looks, well, better. The antidote to this is to start with the older and work your way newer. I learned this the hard way. We had a Nintendo Wii before I picked up a retro NES 8-bit console. The Wii is, by now, a bit old(er)-fashioned but it's far more immersive than the 8-bit. When we first played *Legend of Zelda: The*

Twilight Princess on Wii and then tried the original *The Legend of Zelda*, the Wii version was the one they went back for.

I had much better luck with cartoons and classic movies, because I had this idea of starting with the older and then working toward the newer, so that an appreciation for the older entertainments would solidify. I've been watching *Scooby-Doo* with my girls since the eldest was around three years old and they much prefer the original series, from the 1970s, to the version of the series made today.

Classics Begin Bite-Sized

The other technique I've found effective in introducing retro nostalgic classics is to begin with bite-sized bits, particularly YouTube clips of best-of, favorite moments. I use this when I think that my girls are probably too young for the material, but I'm curious to see if they go for it. For example, I'm a great Monty Python fan, but that's pretty sophisticated silliness. So, I "auditioned" various scenes. They loved the "fish slap dance," but they didn't understand the appeal of the "twit of the year competition" or the "dead parrot sketch." I'll circle back in the future, but they've since asked to watch the fish slap dance on multiple occasions, so I consider this an incremental victory.

There's a particular resonance and delight when our kids love something that we loved as children, and these tricks can help bring it to your home, wherever that may be.

How to Serve Your Kids a Slice of Nostalgia Through Film

The pull of nostalgia is a powerful one. We parents had favorites growing up: favorite TV shows, movies, books, and games. We've introduced how video games and cartoons can be presented to our kids. It's the same for old films, as we'll see here. Not every kid has a father who is a child psychiatrist with an expertise in film. (Dr. James Charney contributed to this story, and in chapter 7 both he and my mother, Diane Joy Charney, will write a few words, too.)

Start with the Older, Advance to the Newer

I borrowed a method from tasting menus for food and wine. You start out with the simpler, rawer, less complex, and work your way up. Now this doesn't mean "better," that, for example, a raw oyster is inherently less delicious than a breaded, roasted oyster covered in hot sauce and béarnaise. But to start with the bells-and-whistles version makes it harder to appreciate the purer rendition. The situation is similar with wine tastings, which are curated to introduce younger, fresher (less sophisticated) wines first, and then move on to those with more happening in them.

This is no direct analogy to film, because there is sometimes more happening in the older classics, in terms of complexity of ideas and character, than the newer ones. But attention spans have reduced over the decades and, to be perfectly blunt, the classics risk boring those brought up on contemporary fare.

I saw this firsthand with my daughters. When the eldest was around two years old, she loved a Slovenian classic from her home country called *Kekec*, a black-and-white film from 1951 about the adventures of a warm-hearted, plucky shepherd boy in the picturesque Alps. It was a big hit with her, despite the fact that it is old-fashioned by any standards, particularly so from the perspective of American film, which was far ahead thanks to the limited bankroll of what Yugoslavia was producing. Now that she's seven, she finds it a bit boring, because she's used to much faster-paced, colorful, quick-edited contemporary films. But the trick worked because she already has a nostalgia for it. She remembers having liked it, and so though she honestly considers it to be slow and less of a grabber, it has a place in her heart, and she does not dismiss black-and-white films as inherently uninteresting.

Now there's no need for you to set up your own kids with a Yugoslav classic. It's best to pick the oldest films that you remember enjoying and think your kids might like and go from there. The overall message is to introduce older films as early as possible to provide a foundation of positive experiences that will help your kids give older stuff the benefit of the doubt later.

Nibble the Classics

It can be tricky for young children to maintain focus for a ninety-minute black-and-white classic, even if it's one of the greats, like one starring Charlie Chaplin or the Marx Brothers. I inspired in my kids a real love for the Marx Brothers by showing them selected favorite scenes on YouTube. A three-minute YouTube clip is in no danger of feeling over-long, and today's kids associate the very platform of YouTube (rife with silly cats, videogame walkthroughs and "best of" compilations) with high entertainment. Take advantage of this and slip in some clips of classics. I got my girls into the famous "stateroom scene" from the Marx Brothers' *A Night at the Opera*. It's less than three minutes long. In it, several stowaways are hiding in a tiny stateroom on a cruise ship, and they haven't eaten for a while. Groucho Marx, who is the ticketed person staying in that room, calls room service to bring up a meal, ordering everything on the menu, plus dozens of hardboiled eggs. More and more staff and guests show up and want to do various things in the room—clean up, give a manicure, fix the pipes, until the tiny room is bursting with people. Then the punchline: The stewards show up with the room service order, open the door, and a flood of occupants tumbles out of the over-stuffed room. It is comedy brilliance concentrated, and my girls thought it was hysterically funny. They would've been unlikely to remain focused for the entire film (which is full of funny moments but does appear rather slow by today's standards). But this much was a gem that they repeatedly asked to be shown.

I had a parallel experience with the classic musical, *Singin' in the Rain*, my father's favorite movie. I was indoctrinated with a love for musicals through him, and this has the double nostalgia of being a film I like and being his favorite. But for very young children, it can be slow going. So I started with YouTube clips of three favorite song-and-dance numbers. "Moses Supposes," "Good Morning" (one of the happiest songs of all-time, and what I often sing when waking my girls), and the completely ingenious "Make 'em Laugh." These have slapstick elements, a lot of dancing, pure joy and catchy songs. Since they are the best part of any musical—the "storyline" is often filler between the songs—we went straight to the best bits and it worked. My girls loved it and regularly ask for Donald O'Connor, the supporting actor in the film who is an underrated dance and comic genius. Then, with various musical numbers to look forward to, it was easy for my kids to watch the whole ninety-minute film, because any of the bits that were slower for children were rewarded with the songs that they knew and loved.

Recall that I used the same tactic with a favorite film of my youth, *Bedknobs and Broomsticks*. The scene that fascinated me was where Angela Lansbury, an "apprentice witch," uses a spell called "Substitutiary Locomotion" to animate a museum of suits of armor to chase away an invading force of Nazis. It provided a great enticement into the story. I first showed them just this clip, and it had the same magical effect on them that it did on me. Then it was their idea to watch the entire film, not mine at all (wink wink).

I hope that these ideas might help you film lovers out there introduce an appreciation for older classics in even the youngest of children.

The Movie Menu

Everyone will have their own favorite films, and each parent will naturally find contemporary films themselves. But what about some of the past classics that might have slipped under your radar? There are no guarantees that these will delight your children as much as they have mine, but if you're looking for cinematic inspiration, these are fine choices to try out. We had far more on our list than these fifty, but they make for good places to start. One thing to add: There's sometimes inertia with kids wanting to watch movies they already know and love over and over again. There's comfort in this and nothing wrong with it, but it's good to keep adding new movies to the mix. Remind them that every film they love now was once a new one they hadn't seen before (and weren't sure if they would like). Consider a "new movie night" once a week (or once a month, whatever suits). It can be something that they look forward to.

1. Abbott and Costello Meet Frankenstein
2. Ace Ventura
3. A Christmas Story
4. Any Disney cartoon
5. Asterix the Gaul
6. Babe
7. Bedknobs and Broomsticks
8. Big
9. Black Stallion
10. Charlie and the Chocolate Factory
11. Dumbo
12. E.T.
13. Elf

14. Enchanted
15. Fantasia
16. Harry Potter movies
17. Home Alone
18. Hook
19. How the Grinch Stole Christmas
20. How to Train Your Dragon
21. Howl's Moving Castle
22. Hugo
23. The Absentminded Professor
24. The Court Jester
25. The Iron Giant
26. The Lego Movie
27. The Love Bug
28. The Marx Brothers' Horse Feathers
29. The Music Man
30. The Muppets Take Manhattan
31. The Never-Ending Story
32. The Parent Trap
33. The Pirates of Penzance
34. The Princess Bride
35. The Red Balloon
36. The Sound of Music
37. The Wizard of Oz
38. Laurel and Hardy's *The Music Box*
39. Lassie Come Home
40. March of the Penguins
41. Mamma Mia
42. Mary Poppins
43. National Velvet
44. Old Yeller
45. Paddington 1 and 2
46. Pee-Wee's Big Adventure
47. Singin' in the Rain
48. Star Wars
49. Toy Story
50. W. C. Fields's *Never Give a Sucker an Even Break*

Superpower Your *Tomb Raider*: Making Video Games Educational

My kids love video games. Your kids, I'm sure, love video games. Even I enjoy video games. I loved them as a child (growing up with the original Nintendo Entertainment System, with its 8-bit graphics that seem so charmingly dated now). I like them today, too. And that's okay. It is not morally reprehensible to let your kids play video games (within reason, of course), and it's even better if you play with them and they become a chance for bonding, a shared experience.

Video games can make for a real learning experience. It's not true for all types of games, and screen-time should still be regulated to a reasonable degree, but they can be instructive. Let's look at how this system can work in practice using a very popular game (in general and at my house these days): *Tomb Raider*.

First off, how can we regulate the playing of video games so they are a treat, a reward, not an expectation and not a zombie-fication of our children? In our family, video games are reserved only for the following occasions: inclement weather (which makes my girls delighted each time it rains), when someone is at home sick, or on days when they have to visit a doctor or dentist (as a reward). This works well for us, but it is certainly not an absolute golden rule, and each family should make their own system. The important thing is to stick with your system and hold fast to the rulebook you write. Kids love to wiggle their way around rules and they're good at it. But they also thrive on predictability and consistency. Whatever your household rules are, they should be strictly adhered to. Whatever you do, it's good to make screen-time not an expectation but a reward, a treat, and therefore valued.

Logic Games

The games that are most valuable, that offer more than pure entertainment and a dash of hand-eye coordination, are those that develop logic or have engaging storylines. The logic puzzle games like *Tetris* can, at first, look similar to games like Candy Crush or Dots or Bubble Witch. But those are much more passive. You have to connect a certain number of similar shapes,

The Role of Screens in Learning

so it's a bit like a word search, but they're not as neurologically stimulating. Logic games like actual puzzles, proper word searches (which teach reading and different ways of seeing), "What's wrong with this picture?" games, memory games (like *Memory*, *Mastermind*, or *Battleship*), word games (like Scrabble) and geometric puzzles like *Tetris* are far better. Classic games, like backgammon, checkers, and chess, are also very good for developing logic. When possible, endorse such options over, say, *Fruit Ninja*.

But these types of games are not particularly social. They're hard to do together, with interactions.

The *Tomb Raider* Tactic

The games that are best for a shared bonding experience are those that are more immersive, with complex puzzles or actions required, but with a minimum of killing. I'm not of the opinion that shooting games promote real-life violence, but they have a mindlessness and crass component that I'm not into and I don't think can be that good. If there is violence in a game, it should be cartoonish. That's why I like the very old-fashioned Nintendo games. Mario stomping on a turtle-turkey hybrid feels much more acceptable to me than, say, ripping your opponent's spine out of his body in *Mortal Kombat* (though, in all honesty, I was a fan of *Mortal Kombat* in my youth and don't feel any the worse for it).

Lately my family has been playing *Tomb Raider: Anniversary* on the Nintendo Wii. I like the Wii because most of the games require body movement, not just thumbs. This game isn't one of them, but it has a rich storyline and just a little fighting (the odd centaur statue that comes to life or T-Rex that happens to occupy a lost Peruvian valley) and a lot of problem solving and acrobatics. As my girls navigate heroine Lara Croft through obstacles and retrieve artifacts and relics, I not only play with them but talk through what we're doing and seeing.

Each encounter is a chance for learning. We fight a pair of animated centaur statues (as you do), who can turn Lara to stone with their eyes, and we have to show them their own reflection in a polished shield to defeat them. Here we have three lessonlets drawn from one boss battle—the fight with the big enemy at the climax of a level.

- We talk about what a centaur is, half man and half horse, and afterwards read a Greek myth involving a centaur
- We learn a new word, "petrification," to properly describe being turned into stone.
- We tell the myth of Medusa and how Perseus defeated her by showing her own reflection in a polished shield, which was clearly the inspiration for the centaur boss battle.

The enjoyment of video games, their immersive quality, helps kids retain lessons learned through them better than if the same lessons were taught—the same stories and vocabulary—without the reinforcement of the game. That was just the start. Here are seven more:

- When Lara puzzles her way through Peru, she finds settlements inspired by Machu Picchu. This seemed like an opportunity and my girls were intrigued to do a virtual tour of the real Machu Picchu and to see photographs of my wife's visit there.
- Lara does rubbings of relief sculptures as part of her adventures, so we took our girls on an outing to do real rubbings of reliefs at an outdoor museum near our home.
- Lara is quite the gymnast, and some of her moves intrigued our girls, so we watched some Olympic gymnastics competitions and debated on how Lara would do in such a setting.
- Lara swings on ropes, vines and her grappling hook, and so we added a new vocabulary word, "brachiation" (the act of swinging with your arms from one rope or vine to another, à la Tarzan). Not the most useful word, but once they knew it, you'd be surprised how often it is used in our household.
- This led to an intrigue in Tarzan, the original brachiator, so we saw the classic black-and-white movie and read the story.
- In one section, set in Lara's family mansion, there is a puzzle involving a sundial marked with Roman numerals. This led to a lesson on what a sundial is, including making one ourselves.
- Then we had a lesson on how to read Roman numerals.

The Role of Screens in Learning

All these lessonlets came from playing a single game, from an entertainment that we think of as passive and not really "good" for our kids. But, in fact, it can be made so.

The approach is designed to be adapted by parents to whatever interests them and their children (no need to stick to *Tomb Raider*).

6 Novelty and the Power of Slowness and Boredom

I used to never allow myself to get bored. Whether I was exercising, folding laundry, emptying the dishwasher, or even answering nature's call, I was entertained. This would normally involve playing with my phone; putting on a TV show in the background; or listening to music, a podcast, or an audio book. There was a time when one's mind was allowed to wander, but now, with a world of entertainment available to us at all times as easily as pulling out a phone, boredom is now exceptional, abnormal.

This chapter looks at some parenting tactics that may surprise: how allowing your kids to get bored now and then is a good thing, and how slowness both helps children and us parents to better savor and remember the beautiful moments with our kids.

The (Super)Power of Boredom: Why Letting Your Kids Get Bored Is a Gift

I thought this was a good thing—that time spent bored was time wasted. But then I started jogging. I found the act of jogging to be, well, boring and so I would pass the time by listening to music or podcasts or even dictating rough drafts of articles like this one into Voice Memo. Then a friend who is a running coach told me to try jogging without any additional entertainments. Ugh, I thought, that makes the prospect of my thirty-minute jog sound like work. She explained to me how beneficial mental downtime is to stimulate the mind. When your mind wanders, she said, it looks for ways to be engaged. The mind doesn't like to be bored, which is why we're always turning on external entertainments. But when it is bored, it clicks into a more active mode. You'll see, she said.

And so I tried it. And it was just as she said. I'd begin jogging and, for the first ten minutes or so, I would space out, my eyes rolling, thinking about all the other things I'd rather be doing. Then I'd suddenly notice that I had new ideas popping into my mind: a new article, a book concept. I'd up my pace to get home in time to write down all these new ideas that had come to me, magically, while jogging. And then I realized, doing this day after day, that it was the positive effect of allowing my mind to wander, undistracted. I was empowered through boredom.

Which brings me to my children. My liberal parenting conscience does not want to allow them to get bored. I feel, subconsciously, like I'm somehow failing them if I'm not either proactively engaged with them myself or setting them up in some way to be otherwise engaged, teeing up their drive, as it were. Just leaving them to their own devices feels unacceptable. You know what? Doing just that can be a great benefit, and a decent measure of allowing our own kids to get bored does them a favor. There's a danger to remaining too passive, in childhood and later in life, if everything is handed to you, even entertainment. My instinct tells me to either play with my kids whenever I can, or to suggest what they should play when I cannot. But this requires no imagination on their part. It is boredom that triggers the imagination. We idealize the imagination in children, but how can we stimulate it? One of the ways we can do so, and truly help our children, is by being occasionally more passive than our own conscience might first deem acceptable.

Perhaps you've seen the scene repeated as I have? It goes like this: "Dad, I don't know what to do." My daughter means this literally, not existentially. I can immediately think of a dozen things. I could imagine just reminding her that there are dozens of toys and puzzles and books in the playroom. I could set her up with a game or a movie. I could stop what I'm doing to play or to read to her. My liberal parenting instinct, like a legless creature within me, squirms around urging me to do something proactive. But I restrain myself and say, "I hear you, but it's good to sometimes have to figure out for yourself what you should do or play next. If someone else were to always give you suggestions, you would never try to invent games on your own." And then I exit the room and go back to whatever I was doing before.

The inevitable result is that my daughter whines for a minute, lies on the couch looking up at the ceiling, moans slightly, exhales deeply . . . and a minute later she's come up with her own solution and is off playing.

What she and her sister play in these moments is often more engrossing, for longer periods of time, than whatever I might've suggested. It's because the kids figured it out themselves. They dipped into their imaginations and solved a problem ("I'm bored") and are embracing their solution. They embrace it more energetically because it is theirs. They have ownership of it; it is their solution. This is a professor's trick—it's better to lead students to come to a conclusion themselves rather than tell them the conclusion and say, "memorize it." The act of concluding, of inventing reinforces the solution and empowers. My kids are also more likely to commit to the new game they invented out of boredom, because they took the effort to come up with it, and therefore value it more than something handed to them.

It's the old "Give a man a fish and he'll eat for a day, teach a man to fish and he'll eat for a lifetime." It's the same with a hunger to be entertained. Tell your kids what to play, and they'll play for an hour. Help your kids invent what to play themselves and they'll be entertained for a lifetime.

My discovery of boredom while jogging, and how it unlocked my own imagination and creativity, has led me to encourage my kids to do the same when it comes to play. Boredom can lead to the superpower of self-sufficiency and a strengthened imagination in children, too.

The Beauty of Silent Togetherness

When I was growing up, I had a nanny, Eleanor, who was like a second mother. She was a presence in my life from my first month until she passed away, when I was in college. Through my elementary school years, her husband, Anthony, would pick me up at 3 p.m. from school and I'd stay at their house until my parents were finished with work, around 6 p.m. Our main activities were passive: I would watch cartoons from 3 to 5 p.m. (in the following order on USA Network: *Scooby-Doo*, *G.I. Joe*, *Transformers*, and then *He-Man*, which was replaced in the lineup when I got a bit older with *Thundercats*). Anthony would sit in his easy chair in a little sunroom off the living room and read the paper. Eleanor would sit in an oversized chair in the living room, doing word searches or crossword puzzles, while I lay on the couch nearby, covered in a loosely knit brown, yellow and orange blanket, drinking chocolate milk made with Hershey's chocolate syrup and snacking on toasted, buttered bread that had been sliced into squares for me to eat easily. When the cartoon run was over, we would have dinner together, wonderful Italian-American classics (Eleanor and Anthony were children of Italian immigrants), like macaroni or "pasta fazul" (*pasta e fagioli* or pasta with beans in Amalfi dialect) or "pasta padan" (*pasta con patate* or pasta with potatoes). Anthony would slice Italian-style white bread and ask, "Want some bread, Fred?" And for dessert, Eleanor would peel an apple and slice it into quarters. She did all this with a simple knife, drawing the blade toward her thumb without ever slipping or cutting herself, which I always thought was an amazing trick. Then my parents would pick me up.

This was a remarkably consistent routine. I spent these wonderful hours with these wonderfully loving people who considered me family, but there was very little active interaction. We didn't talk much. We didn't have much to talk about. But that did not matter at all. They were a wholly loving presence, and their presence felt good, like a hug, soothing, warm, and safe.

Sometimes we feel that we are interacting in a meaningful way only when we are talking or doing something. This book is mostly about *doing* things in order to connect better and more with our children. It's useful to understand that you can have that connection without doing anything to speak of. Your very presence in the same room as your children can be gift enough. You don't have to interact. You can each do your own thing. But the vibe, the aura, whatever you want to call it, of a loving family in the same space is, in itself, a powerful potion, a great gift.

This passive time together will not stand out in memory, or rather it will appear to be a single memory, when you think back on it, all those hours, days, weeks of just quietly cohabiting the same space merging into one memorial moment, as if it were all one continuous happening. But don't sweat it. Being realistic, most of your time with your children will be along those lines. The lessonlets and Lesson Games that are the focus of this book are the outliers. They are the one-to-fifteen-minute blips in your otherwise routine days. They will stand out most, and make you feel most like you are being a proactive, well-meaning parent. But don't discount the long, quiet, passive periods. Kids can feel the love and the ability to share space without interacting, and to feel entirely at ease in silence is the mark of true comfort.

On Consistency and Novelty

Remember mix tapes? I guess it depends on how old you are, but I grew up making mix tapes of favorite songs back when it took a good deal of effort to do so. I would wait for songs to appear on the radio, leap into action to record them onto a cassette, and pause it when the radio would, annoyingly, play commercials before a song had ended. Then I'd move songs from one tape onto another, carefully arranging the songs in an order that seemed right (and sometimes that would convey hidden messages of affection to recipients of the tape as a gift, girls I had a crush on). I would decorate the mix tape with sketches of stars in blue pen. I guess this was a thing, because one of the punk bands I like, The Ataris, has a great song called "Song for a Mix Tape" that starts "Tonight I made you a mix tape and I decorated it with lots of stars."

Along came CDs and Minidisc players (a brief but ingenious technology) and things changed, but what really changed how we listen to music was Napster and YouTube, the idea that music should be free and on-demand, which has recently been replaced by subscription all-you-can-eat music services like Spotify and Google Play Music. Now my daughters have learned to say "Okay Google" and they can get any song they want to play whenever they want. Mix tapes are no longer needed. But my girls do need to remember the names of the songs they like—the whole names and the names of the artists who perform them—otherwise Google gets confused.

Today's ability for children who cannot yet read to tell a computer what they'd like, and the computer serves it up for them, is a great step forward. But it requires that the kids know the correct names of whatever they might be after.

On Consistency and Repetition

The best parents are as consistent as possible in whatever rules they lay out for their kids to follow. Deviate, let it slide, fail to follow through and the consistency is lost, the kids have "won," and the parents have ruined their authority. When you pick your family rules, whatever they may be, the mark of a parent who is doing what's best for their kid is consistency—even if that consistency means not giving the kid what they want, when they want it.

What kids find scariest is not knowing what is expected of them, having to constantly guess and walk around on eggshells. One day they can eat in front of the TV, the next Mom shouts at them for doing so—this feels unfair to them (they need to know the rules in order to stick with them) and is disconcerting, like a house with furniture and floorboards that move on their own, so you never know where to step and when your next step might send you tumbling. We parents can update or alter rules, but this should always be laid out clearly and with an absolute consistency from the moment the new rule is explained forward.

For us, examples of rules that suit our family include that video games are only an option if it's raining, or that the girls always have to empty the dishwasher, or that there can never be a bedtime without the brushing of teeth. I'm not here to recommend rules for your family, that's your business and you'll know far better than I which works best for you. But it is objectively true that it is better to be consistent for parents to maintain their position of authority and not let the kids "play" them. It's bad for kids to get what they want, whenever they want it. It leads to the expectation that this will continue throughout life, and that is thoroughly unrealistic. So whatever rules you set, be consistent.

Trying New Things

This can be seen in the world of foods, where kids are not usually adventurous. I always tell them "there was a time when you'd never had Nutella and it looks suspicious and gross to you" and that usually wins a discussion about whether they should try something new. We have a food policy that accepts that kids genuinely don't like a lot of sophisticated or different flavors that we adults enjoy—but they must taste everything once. If they've had a proper taste (licking something and fleeing doesn't count), which means a real bite or spoonful, and if they don't like it, no problem. But not trying is strictly forbidden, and we're not shy about sending someone from the table without their meal if they refuse to at least try something. In truth, I think we've actually had to resort to this draconian measure only once or twice. Set the standard and remain consistent and you needn't lay down the law often. Show your kids that they can play you, and your authority is undermined. It will be very difficult to win it back.

This comfort in repeating what is known includes food, film choice, music, and games. I feel this, too. I love bacon cheeseburgers and would happily eat them daily. I love *Airplane!* and I'm happy every time I watch it. "Roots Radicals" by Rancid is my favorite song and delights me every time I listen to it. But variety is the spice of life and the foundation of an interested young mind. So how do we introduce variety while still letting kids enjoy the comfort of repeating what they know they like?

There are a few ways we approach this. One is to designate a New Movie Night. For a while, we used Mondays. That night we would watch something the kids had never seen before. That was the only option, or no screen at all. If my wife and I had "cracked" even once and bent to the kids' desire for the umpteenth screening of *Ice Age 3: Dawn of the Dinosaurs* (which is a classic), then it would've never ended. The kids would have demonstrated that they were psychologically stronger than us parents and our attempts at broadening their horizons would have slipped down a steep slope. Instead, we have their pick of movies on other movie nights, but Monday is for something new.

When it comes to foods, we don't want to prepare entirely separate meals, one for the kids and one for the grownups, but we also do not want to force kids to eat something that they actually don't care for—and my wife and I love super spicy things, which wouldn't be for young kids anyway. So, we might prepare a separate meal on some occasions, but we reserve a single spoonful of whatever we're eating for them to try. If they don't like it, no problem. If they like it, super, they can have more. But if they don't try it—they miss a meal. (As I mentioned, I think they've only actually missed a meal once or twice, ever—we established our authority by following through with the punishment for not trying something new and it was not subsequently challenged, as we showed we are not to be messed with).

In the realm of music, I try the same thing. I want to gradually expand my kids' horizons, even if they generally prefer the core of songs they know and love. For every ten new songs I play them, maybe they'll like one and add it to the household virtual mixtape. Part of this is linked to my nostalgia and the desire to share the things I loved in my youth with my kids, in hopes that they might enjoy it, too. I never want to be pushy. I don't want to pressure them into liking something (or saying that they like something) that they don't. But I want to give them a rich selection of things that they can choose from and decide what they take to heart themselves. So I'll ask them to "taste" a new song.

Here's our music approach. I play them a single new song each day. We usually do this when we otherwise have "lost" time. Time that is not taken away from other activities but we use "in between time," while we're doing something else or working toward something else. We might also play the new song when we're cooking or bathing or emptying the dishwasher (which is their primary household chore). The car is ideal—you drive from point A to point B, and the duration of the drive is perfect for trying out something new. A new movie is a commitment, ninety minutes or so. A new song is only about three minutes. A *soupcon*, like a single bite of a new food.

I usually don't tell them "This is the new song of the day," but just play something and see if they like it. If they do, I tell them something about it, and try to help them remember the title and artist. If they don't, no problem, it was still experienced, even if in a passive, osmosis sort of way. And if they do like it, then it will refresh the perpetual playlist of the moment, which I will continue to refer to as a mixtape. Expanding their potential "playlists," literal ones consisting of songs, but also movie lists, books, art and foods is all good and will raise them up well-rounded, experienced little humans.

How to Travel with Your Children: Tips for Car Rides, Holidays, and Virtual Travel

"Are we there yet?"

No, we're not there yet. We just started. And you can only sing "99 Bottles of Beer on the Wall" so many times or listen to the same CD on repeat, before madness sets in. Fortunately, there are all sorts of tricks for managing longer trips with young children—or indeed any sort of activity that requires sitting for a long time and waiting.

The first trick is to divide your time into roughly fifteen-minute intervals. Fifteen minutes is a chunk of time that a child can grasp. It's about half of an episode of *Scooby-Doo*, for instance. It's digestible. It doesn't feel like forever. So take your drive or your wait and think of it as a big cake that you'll look at in terms of fifteen-minute slices. That drive to Aunt Gertrude's house takes ninety minutes, so that's six fifteen-minute slices. Your kids, if they're anything like mine, may fall asleep for half of that, so you've got three "slices" to cover in terms of entertainment. A favorite album might be forty-five minutes of music, and that's three slices handled (provided you can survive listening to that album *again*). I'm leaving aside screen-related solutions, like letting the kids watch a DVD or play videogames during the drive. My kids would get nauseated anyway, and I want to feel like I'm spending quality time with them, even if we're "stuck" in the car together, so I don't just want them to be set up with something passive.

What are the activities that we play in fifteen-minute bursts? We've covered many and we'll turn to others in a moment, but one thing to keep in mind is to quit while you're ahead. I'd rather stop playing a game after fifteen minutes or so even if the kids are still into it, rather than get to the point when their enthusiasm wanes and they shift to considering the game no longer interesting. Think of it like eating ice cream. Would your kids be more likely to want to come back for more ice cream in the future if they have a single scoop and would happily eat a second one, or if you order them four scoops and they get through 2.3 and leave the rest? You can maintain the excitement of activities and games by stopping before they are categorized as no longer fun.

I Spy

The classic game requires each player to pick something they can see and say, "I spy with my little eye . . ." and then they say what it is and others have to look around to see what they've seen. "I spy with my little eye . . . a hairless dog!" (That's not at all weird; our dog, Hubert van Eyck, is a Peruvian Hairless.) This works best when you are not driving (things that you can "spy" go by too quickly in the car).

Name That Tune

Kids rarely have lyrics memorized but sing tunes with "dummy lyrics" that sort of half sound like what the lyrics actually are. (I do that, too, with Slovenian songs by my favorite musician, Vlado Kreslin, and in theory, I speak Slovene). So you take turns singing a song (or humming it) and the others have to guess which song it is.

Twenty Questions

We play limitless variations of this game. We take turns picking a category of thing (animal, dinosaur, country, food, movie) and the players ask questions about it. For an animal, we might ask "Is it carnivorous?" "Does it walk on four legs?" "Can it fly?" "Is it a decapod?" (My girls love *Moana*). We have twenty questions or guesses—if we can't figure out what it is after twenty, then the picker wins that round. Whoever guesses is the next picker.

Name Ten

We pick a category (food, carnivorous animals, big cats, cities in Europe—whatever seems appropriate to the interests of your kids), and players take turns naming ten of them, keeping track on their fingers. For trickier topics you can play Name Five.

The Translation Game

This works best for bilingual families (my family speaks Slovenian and English) or families learning a new language. Offer up a word in one language and try to stump the other players with the translation. You can "level up" and make it trickier by going from the secondary language into the primary language (either the first language or, in our case, the language spoken by the mother), which is normally more difficult. You can "level up" further by translating phrases (like idioms for which there is no direct translation but more a thematic one).

The Theory Behind the Games

These sorts of games promote some key abilities that will benefit your kids when they become students. They are encouraged to remember the proper names for things. Learning doesn't help much if you can't recall exactly what something is called. The ability to be precise and to memorize proper names are useful skills. Thinking by category is also important. That's why it's useful to think of foods in groups (vegetables, fish, meat, grains) because once you categorize them you can think of them in terms of shared characteristics and they can be sorted and stored in our memory more easily and with more useful detail. All of these games are a type of test that is fun, and it's good for kids to get used to being tested. Testing will happen all the time in school (and in life) and to think of tests as a "fun" challenge, not something scary or overly judgmental, will be beneficial later on. Repetition and articulation help memorization, so each time they name ten carnivorous animals, for instance, the list is reinforced and the memory is held more tightly. And kids love to show off their knowledge. It's empowering, and this is an ideal way to make kids proud of themselves.

A Way to Virtually "Travel" from Home

Developed during isolation time, I came up with a version of "traveling" on gently educational virtual trips as a way to engage, teach, and expand the feeling of the limited floorspace that we can navigate.

There is a world of virtual tours available, some newly so, a nod to the current situation in which places that once relied on paid tickets have made virtual tours available for free. Others are regularly free, but we tend not to notice outside of this time of isolation. Every day my girls and I take a virtual tour of a different museum or landmark. The Georgia Aquarium, the Natural History Museum (in DC, New York, and London—my girls are into dinosaurs), the British Museum, the Musée d'Orsay, the Vatican Museums, to name a few. And Machu Picchu, the Pyramids, the Great Wall of China. Below you'll find a list of tours that I've already done and recommend, including links. Some are official websites or tours, others are simply walkthroughs made and uploaded by tourists. The key is to make the experience deeper and more engaged and educational by talking about what you will see ahead of time, to whet the appetite—we'll find the location on a globe and maybe zoom into it via Google Earth. Then we talk during it, asking lots of questions. (What do you see? What looks beautiful to you? What's the most interesting thing? Would you do this yourself?) Then talking about it afterward, which helps them remember and internalize what we saw and learned.

By way of example, our "tour" of the world's largest aquarium (in Atlanta, Georgia) was courtesy of a random, amateur teenager with a good camera. We talked about what we had seen at an aquarium in person when we went in Vienna last October, what we were hoping we'd see in this video tour. We spiced up the tour with questions and encouraged dialogue: Which fish is the most beautiful? Can you find a yellow-tailed fish? Do you see any fish that was in *Finding Dory*? Which is cuter, a penguin or a seal? And so on. I don't worry about the weight or actual educational value of the questions and there are no wrong answers, really. It's about together-time, focusing on something cultural and/or new, engaging with full attention (no parents playing with phones), and feeling a sense of access to a world broader than the current isolating climate.

To keep my girls entertained we chat throughout the virtual tours, mostly asking them about what they see, what they find interesting. If they're up for fifteen minutes, that's great. If longer, also great. To keep it a positive experience, I always try to stop before they get bored, Their attention span is narrow, but if something is interesting, it is interesting.

This sort of activity will go a long way not only to feeling immersed in art and culture, and feeling productive instead of entirely passive, but also to feeling like you are expanding. You can "travel" beyond the walls of your home, which suits any situation and budget.

7 Empowering Grandparents

My family and I are very lucky to have proactive, enthusiastic, tireless grandparents who love engaging with their granddaughters. My parents are both former Yale professors and writers themselves, and they offered to bring in the grandparents' perspective to this book. They go by Nonna (Italian for grandma) and Greppen (which sounds like a Gruffalo-ish cartoon creature, but it's how Eleonora pronounced Grandpa before she could pronounce Grandpa, and so Greppen he remained). They wrote their contributions in two periods, once when Eleonora and Izabella were five and seven, and once when they were ten and twelve. These two phases require different approaches, and in both cases they are writing from the perspective of grandparents who do not live nearby (in fact, they live in a different country).

Virtual Grandparenting 101

Though the pandemic may have heightened the need to figure out ways to be present in the lives of loved ones from a distance, grandparents often live far from their grandchildren, and the number of visits is, understandably, limited. While nothing beats an in-person visit, there are ways to maintain a more regular, close bond even when apart. This is one of the blessings of technology. Not long ago, a letter by post, or a phone call, was the best we could do. Now sending video messages instantly and speaking live via video calls allow grandparents (or other remote relatives and friends) to be virtually present, even on a daily basis. You get everything but hugs.

My parents split time between New Haven, Connecticut, and Orvieto, Italy. One is a seven-hour flight from us in Slovenia, the other a seven-hour drive. But we didn't really study approaches to virtual grandparenting, and put them into practice, until isolation time. Suddenly there was no impending physical visit. Even as I write this, we're not sure when we'll next see each other in person. But we've developed an approach that has worked beautifully for them to spend time with Izabella and Eleonora, do their own version of lessonlets, and do so regularly.

If we were to break down our approach into some general tips, it might look like this.

1. Sending videos to each other is quick, easy and nonintrusive. You look at the videos when you want to and film them when you can. Quick selfie videos, or videos showing something you've done or made or eaten, no longer than two minutes, are a perfect way to feel a sense of immediacy. Parents can encourage kids to send photos of videos of things they've made or done (a Lego house, a drawing of a donut dancing with a milk carton, whatever they're into). If they've learned a new talent, dance, song, then making their own video of it and sending it to loved ones is a great way to increase their sense of pride. It's especially fun if they shoot the video and narrate, presenting their achievement from their own perspective.

2. Schedule live video chats but with a specific activity already planned. We found that just setting up a video chat without any structure was a bit awkward. The kids didn't necessarily want to "chat" the way grownups might, and there wasn't much focus after they initially said hello to Nonna and Greppen. But if there is an activity planned it works much better. Nonna and Greppen found some great projects to do together.

3. Reading stories over live video works particularly well. Greppen has taken to reading short stories or chapters in a book to our girls. Each session, which we schedule almost daily and the girls really look forward to, is relatively short—fifteen minutes or until the chapter or story ends (the precise time isn't important). The best for our age group are stories with illustrations. If it's a physical book, then Greppen will hold up the pictures for the girls to see. But we've also gotten fancy and if it's an eBook, then we have a copy of it open on our iPad at home, and Greppen and Nonna appear on a smartphone next to it. (In our tradition, Greppen reads and Nonna laughs enthusiastically, and sometimes very giggly, along in the background, which is particularly delightful as an accompaniment.)

These virtual grandparent visits are a highlight and also give us parents a break, as the kids are being "babysat." Once they're into a story, they can't wait for the next session. It becomes a reward for them, so you can schedule it as such. After they take a bath, for instance. For activities that are not ongoing, it works best to preview what they'll do together. "Okay, today Nonna and Greppen want to make plasticine dinosaurs with you. They'll make them in the United States and you'll make some here, and then you'll compare what kind of dinosaurs you made"—that sort of thing. So they know what to expect and there's a targeted core activity that becomes a medium for general chatting and spending time with each other.

I'll pass the mic to my mother to explain the approach, and then my father will jump in with his insights.

Virtual Learning with Dr. Diane Joy "Nonna" Charney

Since few grandparents are lucky enough to live in the same region as their children, "virtual grandparenting" has gone from an occasional option to a necessity if we want to maintain regular contact and feel like a presence in our family's lives. So what is the best way to do this?

Long-Distance Lessons

This can be a good time for grandparents to share their passions and talents. In the case of my husband and myself who began our own relationship fifty years ago over four-hand piano duets, long-distance music lessons for our granddaughters via Facetime have been rewarding. We gave them a brief start at playing piano in the way we learned it. Now they're progressing on their own via computer. Having planted the seed, we are delighted to watch their progress. And maybe the distance protects everyone from being too pushy about approaching the instrument "our way."

Living so far away has been an extra incentive for us grandparents to be on the lookout for possible activities to do together virtually, and to get more comfortable with the technology that will bring us together safely. For example, despite being computer challenged, I discovered a special button on YouTubes that allowed me to pause or slow down a fantastic drawing video to a speed where my old-timer self could follow along with it and match the kids' superior dexterity.

Using YouTube as a Medium

A particular activity that was a hit with all of us—a five-year-old, a seven-year-old, and two seventy-three-year-olds is "How to draw animals with your hand."

Of course, we had to do them all, and here's how we went about it. My husband, who understands technology more than I, volunteered to control the YouTube video while we three "girls" were the wannabe-artists who, following the brilliant artist on the screen, traced our own hand and miraculously turned it into an animal. Among the many features that made this so engaging was that the three of us were doing it together in "real time," after which we could compare and comment on each other's "masterpieces."

This activity lent itself to many variations. It occurred to me that we could do it as a version of charades, which appealed more to younger granddaughter "B," for whom the quick drawing was difficult.

My idea was to stop the video *before* the animal being drawn was revealed. Everyone could try to guess what it was going to be, and we were usually surprised, which was part of the excitement. Another variation:

Imagine what other things could be drawn from a particular hand position. If we liked the idea of an alternative animal that might emerge from the same hand position, then we could try on our own to draw it.

After completing each animal drawing, we enjoyed praising each other's work, but we especially liked the idea of taking photos of all of our efforts of the day—usually four or five different drawings. With the fifteen-minute maximum in mind, trying to keep activities short and fun, we agreed that each of us would photograph our animal drawings and email them to each other to form our own picture gallery—a chance to document and compare our work. I'm keeping these as a record of the good times we had creating our own menagerie.

Adjusting for Various Ages and Interests

That one of our granddaughters is five and the other seven brings me to the topic of sibling issues and how this time with our grandchildren can offer a chance to deal creatively with sibling differences in age, style, talents, interests, and personality via individual activities as well as those aimed at a mixed group.

Here, I'm thinking of how when we are all together it's a bit like the multilevel learning in the old one-room schoolhouse. When that works well, there can be a sense of leadership and mastery for some and learning opportunities for others. But if there are enough adults to go around, there can be different paired combinations of a grandparent and grandchild that allow an interaction to be tailored to the moment and interest of each child.

Coloring Together as a Point of Departure for More

The free templates offered by museums of paintings from their collection to color can offer other rich opportunities. For example, an 1818 Turner painting of a sailing vessel can be a source of stimulating questions such as, "If you were on a ship like that, where would you like to travel to?" or, "What would it feel like to be on that ship? Do you think you would like it?"

There's the history of different types of boats that could be brought up: clipper ships, schooners, packet boats, man-of-war ships, and more.

And, of course, the history of artist J. M. W. Turner and what else was going on in the art world then.

As another example, a George Stubbs 1763 painting of a zebra could not only be colored, but also turned into a cutout paper sculpture that could move. The instructions were accompanied by a short history of how zebras got to England from South Africa, and explained that most people then thought zebras were just horses with stripes!

Exploring the Natural World from Home

Among the surprises that have come our way as unwittingly sexist grandparents has been finding out that our girls are even more excited about dinosaurs than their father was. Our online visits have offered a chance to broaden their interests and ours—to branch out from dinosaurs to bird calls via brilliant apps that let them click on a bird to hear its song. We found three sites that we all liked. The first was a homey-looking YouTube, clearly a labor of love, that featured mini-videos of eighteen different birds. Another had drawings of fifty birds presented in squares that little fingers could not resist clicking on.

But perhaps best of all was the interactive site, "Discover River Birds" from Barcelona's Museu del Ter. It features beautifully colored drawings of thirty birds in their natural habitat. No need to even click on anything. As the cursor passes over each bird, it bursts into song. I decided which were my favorites, and we liked comparing our choices.

Give a Tour of Whatever Is Happening Near You

In addition to the activities designed by professionals you can also make the most of what may be happening at the moment at grandma and grandpa's. For example, we made use of a dramatic home repair event occurring just outside our window. While Grandpa Jim was reading to the kids, workers happened to be shoring up our fire escape stairs for the building. I grabbed my phone to make a video because I thought it might be intriguing for our granddaughters to see the smoke and sparks flying and then try to figure out what might be going on out there. It was a real-life version of the charades that our younger granddaughter adores. They were fascinated and enjoyed figuring out what those sparks were all about.

Similarly, we love seeing what's going on outside their window. Everyone's experience is different and not everyone has Slovene grandkids whose other grandma and great-grandparents live on farmland that feels exotic to us city slickers. We watched fascinated as they picked cherries, yellow raspberries, and ate red currants over ice cream. Last week we saw them watching rented baby goats being unloaded onto the property to serve as living lawnmowers. Then there were the baby chicks and newborn kittens. Each change of scene stimulates questions and conversation.

Let the Kids Be the Stars That They Are

A key takeaway from our Grandparent Time has been a reminder that kids enjoy being a star. I was reminded of how important it is to be a good audience and to encourage them to photograph their own creations. If we watch an activity in progress, we say how eager we are to see the final or next step. If they're cooking, I say I wish I were there to lick the bowl (and I'm not kidding!). When I saw five-year-old "B" having a bit of trouble getting her thick, yummy batter that looked like chocolate pudding into the cupcake cups, I asked if the MasterChef junior knew the trick of using a second, separate spoon or spatula to help get stuff off the first spoon. I loved watching her sing along as she worked. Our own singing baker! And a pretty neat one at that!

Cooking Long-Distance

And while we're on the topic of food, I must confess to our being pretty obsessed "foodies." An idea was floated that we grandparents could make an archive of short videos of family recipes with the grandkids. This struck me as a great way to cover more than one agenda. I'm thinking that an activity like this would appeal to grandparents in general who are looking for a way to remain part of their grandkids' lives. Our first attempt, however, now affectionately known as the "Messy Macaroon Massacre," was far from a success. Even though we had never had problems with this recipe before, major and very (different!) things went wrong on both sides of the Atlantic. But we all had a great time anyway, comparing fiascos and our respective fixes for them.

Fortunately, there's more than one recipe in our repertoire, and many family traditions and keepsakes that we'd like to transmit as part of our legacy. Of course, to be a grandparent brings many joys along with increased awareness of the life cycle. But we love the idea of superpowering our grandkids and especially the motto that accompanies the book: "Don't count the days, make the days count."

Virtual Reading with James "Greppen" Charney, MD

Much of the year my wife and I live about a seven-hour drive from our granddaughters. So, though we visit them as often as we can, Facetime and WhatsApp have become vital connections. With the pandemic, and with us caught a full ocean away, they became an even more vital link. We tried to have a live video visit every day, and failing that, an exchange of photos and comments on our day and theirs. Their parents have been very good at keeping us in the loop.

Knowing we weren't likely to be able to actually be there with them any time soon, these video visits took on a new importance. We wanted to really try to engage the girls in a different way. To get as close as we could to feeling "with" them. That meant, for us, looking for things we could do together—even though we were some six thousand miles apart. Not just chatting (though the girls are good at that), but finding activities that encouraged a back and forth sharing.

Sharing a Love of Reading

What I've been doing lately and enjoying very much, is reading to the girls. The author and independent bookstore owner, Ann Patchett, had written an article about her belatedly discovering the children's author Kate DiCamillo. Friends had been recommending DiCamillo's books for several years, but she had never given them a try. Once she did, she found herself reading everything that DiCamillo had written. She says that her young adult novel *The Miraculous Journey of Edward Tulane* is one of the best and most touching she has ever read, period.

DiCamillo is unusual in that she writes for children at every stage—picture books for the very young, short, illustrated chapter books for new readers, and books for older children and young teens. Her writing is clever and funny, taking a delight in language that children really enjoy. And she can turn on a dime and make an observation about music or friendship, or find joy in the ordinary, that makes you want to stop and share it with whoever is near.

I went in search of her picture books as a place to start. There are three *Bink and Olly* books, two girl friends who are very close and very different. Bink is small, impulsive, and is always thinking about her next meal—usually pancakes. Olly loves to imagine she is a grand princess, or climbing a high mountain, and brings Bink along for the adventure. Olly also makes really good pancakes.

There is an especially funny and sweet story about their visit to an actual state fair. But I'll let you discover it for yourself—and with your kids. What was a delightful coincidence for us is that the size and personalities of the two friends in the book matched the ages and personalities of our granddaughters, so they really could identify. But even without that extra dimension, these stories were keepers. Our girls asked me to read them over and over.

Then we discovered the next level of DeCamillo, a series of short chapter books about the denizens of Duckawoo Drive in a small, mid-America town: the Watsons, who had adopted a pig they named Mercy, who slept in her own bed and loved buttered toast; the elderly Lincoln sisters, grumpy practical Eugenia and sweet daydreaming Baby; Frank and Stella, the children next door; Francine Poulet, the animal control officer; and assorted other characters.

If one book focused on Baby Lincoln, you could be sure that Mercy the pig would show up, too. If it was a story of how Mercy saved the day, the Lincoln sisters or another local would be there. These books created a little world that enthralled the girls.

Buttered toast became their new snack-of-choice thanks to Mercy.

We would stop reading often to look more closely at the witty illustrations (DiCamillo doesn't illustrate them herself, but her drawing partners have been very well chosen), or to guess how this character or another was feeling about the offbeat thing that was happening, or to guess what would happen next. When there is an unusual word, I check with them to be sure they know what it means—asking them first what they think it might mean. That often pulls us away from the story to talk about the peculiarities of language. Kids like words (especially our granddaughters, who are bilingual; English is not their first language). Talking about the book while you are reading it, as well as after you have finished, is very much part of being together.

For the chapter books, which we would read over several days, I would ask the girls to remind me what had happened earlier—both to check on how much they understood the story and whether they were still interested in continuing. If they weren't (it hasn't happened yet) I would have switched to something else.

We haven't moved on yet to the more grown-up novels like *Edward Tulane*. I'll keep that one and the others she has written for older children, for another year.

Of course, DiCamillo is not the only author with whom you could entrance children. What was fun for me, however, was discovering in DiCamillo an author I had never heard of—and finding her so good.

The girls and I have enjoyed my reading books to them from my childhood and from the childhood of my son, their dad. Books like anything by Dr. Seuss, *Where the Wild Things Are*, *My Father's Dragon*, *Charlotte's Web*, *Winnie-the-Poo*, or *The Phantom Tollbooth* have all become favorites, often read more than once.

Their dad has been reading them the *Harry Potter* books, which are much more complicated than anything I've read them so far. They are really enjoying them too, which surprised me because I thought they were written for much older children (say age ten and up). I wonder if these more sophisticated books may need the bedtime routine and physical closeness that their parents can provide, and that Facetime just can't match.

I love it each day when I get a WhatsApp message asking me when I am free to read to the girls. Those thirty to forty-five minutes are precious, and fun. I am glad I can offer that time to free up their mom and dad from childcare for a few moments, but I get so much out of it, too.

The Superpower Reading Menu

My parents and I have put together this subjective selection of books that are great for parents (or grandparents) to read to their children. They are from various eras and have been arranged roughly in order of complexity, starting with the books that have a higher picture-to-text ratio or shorter, simpler stories and working up toward more text-heavy, picture-light books. So as not to repeat the same authors too often (for instance, every Dr. Seuss book is worth reading), some entries cover an author or series in one go. These stories are complex enough that there is no simple one-line moral or lessonlet emerging from each. For this reason, the list does not include a paragraph per book on what to glean from it. Parents reading should pause often, ask questions of the listeners to be sure they are following (and if there's an exotic word, to be sure they understand it), and then ask some questions after reading, even the following day, to review what was read. Often a simple question like "which part did you like best?" or "which was your favorite character" is enough. You might also encourage children to draw a scene from the story themselves or invent a story with the same characters. Of course, slightly older children can read some of these books by themselves, but *Empower Your Kids* focuses on interactions between parents and kids, so the aim is to read aloud (preferably while snuggling). Audiobooks are a legitimate option, especially for car rides, but these should not be used instead of reading directly to your kids. We encourage the menu/candy shop browsing approach to choosing our evening read, by having all the children's books on the lowest shelves in our study. The girls can each pick one book, any they like, from the shelves. It's delightful to see them choosing carefully, sometimes a new one, sometimes a favorite old one, but they are empowered by choosing what we'll read.

Some of the books are particularly useful later on. A grounding in early childhood of key, iconic stories that recur in references throughout school will be invaluable. These include biblical stories and apocrypha, mythology, Aesop's fables, *Arabian Nights*, and fairytales from the Grimm Brothers, LaFontaine, and Hans Christian Andersen. These canonical stories will inevitably be referenced in classes far in the future, and if your children are familiar with them from childhood, their memory of them will be an advantage. Such stories allow parents to upload some information now, in a fun format, that will be "useful" much later, but it is still a proactive and long view thing to do. While there's no need to only read stories that will be useful as points of reference in the future, on the other hand, if they happen to be good stories your children enjoy *and* they are useful points of reference for later, then that's double value.

The Western Canon Junior list we've prepared (my parents and I) is a lite version of what our Yale University colleague, Harold Bloom, presented in his famous book, *The Western Canon*—iconic, resonant books. But there are great versions of Bible stories and ancient myths for kids. And there are kid-friendly core stories in the fairytale vein that are just as influential. So many Disney movies are based on the fairytales of Charles Perrault, and the Brothers Grimm, for example.

The practicality of reading such stories to your kids must be, first and foremost, because they're fun, magical stories that both you and your kids will enjoy. The added bonus will be that the stories, situations, and characters will subconsciously nestle in your children's minds and one day, when they're sitting in a literature seminar at college, they might recognize that the postmodern novel about which the teacher is lecturing has borrowed themes from the Prometheus myth—and wow, will the teacher be impressed!

1. *Pat the Bunny* by Dorothy Kunhardt
2. *Goodnight Moon* and *The Big Red Barn* by Margaret Wise Brown
3. Dr. Seuss's complete oeuvre
4. *Curious George* stories by H. A. Rey
5. *The Giving Tree* and others by Shel Silverstein
6. *It Could Be Worse*, *We Can't Sleep*, and others by James Stevenson
7. *Madeline* stories by Ludwig Bemelmans
8. *Ferdinand the Bull* by Munro Leaf
9. *Where the Wild Things Are*, *Eloise*, and *Chicken Soup with Rice* by Maurice Sendak
10. Aesop's Fables
11. Biblical stories
12. Greek and Roman myths (I grew up with D'Aulaires—if you want to be fancy, try Nathaniel Hawthorne's 1893 *The Wonder-Book for Girls and Boys*)
13. *Boris and Amos* and others by William Steig
14. *The Polar Express*, *Jumanji*, and others by Chris van Allsberg
15. *Snowflake* and others by Cerrie Burnell
16. *The Phantom Tollbooth* by Norton Juster
17. *Berenstain Bears* books by Stan and Jan Berenstain
18. *Mercy the Pig* stories by Kate DiCamillo

19. *My Father's Dragon* by Ruth Stiles Gannett
20. *Charlotte's Web* by E. B. White (which was actually the name of my cat)
21. Classic Disney comics like *Mickey Mouse, Donald Duck*, and *Uncle Scrooge*
22. *Mrs. Piggle-Wiggle* series by Betty MacDonald
23. *The Very Hungry Caterpillar* by Eric Carle
24. *Harold and the Purple Crayon* by Crockett Johnson
25. *The Borrowers* by Mary Norton
26. Charles Perrault's fairytales (he established the fairytale as a literary genre and wrote the definitive versions of "Little Red Riding Hood," "Cinderella," "Puss in Boots," "Sleeping Beauty," and many more)
27. Grimm's fairytales (they wrote their own darker retellings of classic fairytales, like "Hansel and Gretel," "The Frog Prince," "Rapunzel," "Beauty and the Beast," "Little Red Riding Hood," "Rumpelstiltskin," "Sleeping Beauty," and "Snow White")
28. Hans Christian Andersen's fairytales (completing the trifecta of core fairytale authors—and Disney inspirations—he wrote "The Emperor's New Clothes," "The Little Mermaid," "The Ugly Duckling," "Thumbelina," and "The Snow Queen"—which *very* loosely inspired *Frozen*)
29. *Arabian Nights*
30. *Watership Down* by Richard Adams
31. *The Velveteen Rabbit* by Margery Williams
32. *From the Mixed-Up Files of Mrs. Basil E. Frankweiler* by E. L. Konigsburg
33. *Winnie the Pooh* by A. A. Milne
34. *Asterix and Obelix* comics by Goscinny and Uderzo
35. *Just So Stories* by Rudyard Kipling
36. *Spirit: Stallion of the Cimarron* by Kathleen Duey
37. *The Wizard of Oz* by Frank L. Baum
38. *Are You There God? It's Me, Margaret* by Judy Blume
39. *Little House on the Prairie* series by Laura Ingalls Wilder
40. *The Wind in the Willows* by Kenneth Grahame
41. *Johnny Tremain* by Esther Forbes
42. *Diary of a Wimpy Kid* by Jeff Kinney
43. *Tintin* comics by Hergé
44. *Black Beauty* by Anna Sewall
45. *20,000 Leagues Under the Sea* and others by Jules Verne
46. *Alice in Wonderland* by Lewis Carroll

47. The dark, imaginative novels of Roald Dahl (*The BFG, Charlie and the Chocolate Factory, James and the Giant Peach, George's Marvelous Medicine, The Fantastic Mr. Fox*)
48. The gothic spooky novels of John Bellairs (illustrated by Edward Gorey)
49. *Anne of Green Gables* by Lucy Maud Montgomery
50. The *Harry Potter* series by J. K. Rowling

Nonna's Perspective on Empowering Your (Grand)Kids

In thinking about what grandparents can do with younger children and older, because many of the activities we liked previously were related to or based on art, which has been an ongoing passion for our granddaughters, I'm noting that with some variations those ideas have evolved to have staying power.

A case in point—I have turned my bathroom into an art gallery that features our granddaughters' creations over the years. These have increased in sophistication as they acquired the ability to write and make their own books with great flair and imagination. Special occasions are marked by complexly illustrated stories with titles like "NONNA THE QUEEN OF SALADS" that feature animated vegetables running amok as they vie for a place of honor in the salad bowl. Every birthday party invitation becomes an opportunity to make a special card tailored to the lucky recipient.

Although the girls lack the hoarding tendencies of their Nonna, I think it amuses and pleases them to see their art over the years on proud display. I like to remind them of how much I value whatever they make, and particularly what they have made for me. A recent addition is a highly original vase of a bouquet of paper flowers made two years ago by my younger granddaughter, Izabella. The vase is made of the innards of a paper towel roll, and each of the "flowers" sports its own stamen. Now how could anyone, especially a fanatic gardener like me, even think of throwing away such a masterpiece?

It has been an extra treat to watch the musical seeds we planted when we began teaching the girls to play piano in the way we learned it. We put our original piano books from more than seven decades ago to good use. They are now up to playing from my forever favorite *Oxford Piano Course Book Two*, currently a collector's item originally from 1929. I love seeing that its wonderful tunes and illustrations have stood the test of time. It has the added nostalgia value of including my own undistinguished early compositions that our girls are eager to surpass, and do. They think it's usual for kids their age to compose their own tunes.

In talking about our particular family music adventures, however, I don't mean to suggest that all grandparents are necessarily likely to have a piano background complete with favorite instruction books from 1929. I only mention this to encourage fellow grandparents to bring in things you recall fondly from your own youth and present them with enthusiasm. I'm reminded that not everything needs to be new, shiny, and wrinkle free. Older stuff (like us, ourselves!) can still be relevant and cool.

But now that our granddaughters have become serious musicians themselves, they are teaching us more about their distinctly individual personalities and talents. It's been a thrill to encourage them as they practice their respective instruments and to applaud their frequent performances. They have inspired us to try to improve as well. I have been a mediocre flutist since the fifth grade, but I went back to taking lessons to try to keep up with my number one granddaughter who took no time at all to be able to play circles around me. I leave it to her to win the gold medals, but we have fun playing duets together.

Among the unexpected thrills of growing older with grandkids came when ours reached the age of when I was enthralled with the Betsy-Tacy books. We read the first chapter of the 1940s series to each other, and Eleonora liked them, too! She loves mysteries, and I'm not sure what she would make of the Nancy Drew series that I could never get enough of when I was her age. Maybe we'll give it a try. With respect to the question "Are You the Same Person You Used to Be?" although I'm a lifelong teacher of diverse students from preschool age through college, I feel newly born as the lucky Nonna of two extraordinary Slovenia-born granddaughters who are always teaching me new things.

As the oldest of four accustomed to winning the favorite games of our childhood (Clue, Monopoly, the card-based Spit and Concentration), to have the tables turned when I play with my skilled granddaughters is an unexpected treat. It can be humbling in a good way to learn and model how to lose gracefully.

The German boardgame we've all most enjoyed recently called Activity combines Balderdash, Pictionary, and Charades. The beauty of this game is the way it can be adapted to any age (in our case, nine and seventy-eight) and the varied skills of the players. If the questions are too hard, we like to add our own to the ones that come with the box. This was necessary because we were using the Slovenian version of the boardgame, but that added to the fun. In this team game one player has to act out in pantomime, illustrate, or use other words to define the phrase written on the card they have picked. The object of the game is to get your team to guess the target phrase so you can advance around the board. To accomplish this requires quick, creative thinking on everyone's part, and the nine-year-old got a lot of satisfaction from being able to hold her own against the rest of us. We grandparents who were newcomers to this game were delighted to discover how much we liked it.

We have also found it fun to compare old favorite building toys with new ones. Despite the seductive power of today's Magna-Tiles, during every visit to our house the forever appeal of the wooden blocks that will outlive us all is obvious. Our girls rush to them and never seem to tire of erecting freeform constructions of increasing complexity. These can accommodate stuffed animals, Lego creations, figurines and other small objects, all of which inspire imaginative story making that can go on for hours. This is another example of how old favorites from your own youth that might include what you did with your own parents or grandparents, whether physically or in your mind's eye, can find new life.

When it comes to food, I'm glad that Grandpa a.k.a. Greppen James, who is the better chef, has written about the cooking adventures that are a big hit with both girls. Since we are a family of foodies, we like to share the taste memories of favorite candies, cakes, and foods like egg-in-a-peg. These can spark memories of "childhood" from all of us—it's just that ours go back further!

Living most of the year in a climate-friendly corner of Umbria, Italy, I devote many hours a day to working in the garden, and it's easy to find chores for Izabella and Eleonora to help. It makes them feel grownup to have their own gardening gloves. and who doesn't like to pick and eat strawberries, peaches, pears, apples, or grapes along the way?

Of all the activities we do, one stands out for its irresistibility. It has many facets that can be adapted to ever-growing kids. Ours never seem to tire of setting up a "store" where they sell my scarves and hats and more. Laundry baskets become counters to display their wares; fake money and price lists are composed. We often incorporate talent shows that feature our music and tap shoes. The girls decide the roles each will play in our extravaganzas that require a fashion model to show off the garments, a master of ceremonies (usually me) to keep things rolling, and a cashier/saleswoman to answer questions and take money.

The setting-up itself can be the best part—especially if there happens to be an empty freezer box or other odd materials for props and alluring signs that call out to be decorated.

Once the rest of the family is invited to participate in the event, the excitement builds. A climax comes when each "customer" models his or her own purchases, and "prizes" are awarded for the best combinations. The photos and videos we take along the way make the fun last, and who knows? These may become a legacy for the next generation!

Could it be that the comfort of family rituals and legacies is the key element of all these activities? As challenging as it can be to keep up with our granddaughters, I just found a lovely quote from Lori Stratton in Crow's Feet on *Medium* about that:

"What I hadn't understood about grandchildren is you get to see all the best parts of life again, only this time you know how fleeting and precious those days are. I would go through all the difficult events in my life over and over again if I knew that it would always end with me being surrounded by a brood of grandchildren."

I understand just what she means.

Greppen's Perspective on Empowering Kids

WhatsApp was a vital connection with our granddaughters during Covid. I can't imagine how things would have been without their daily videos, and the chance to chat with them live in the app.

WhatsApp remains in regular use (and of course you can use whichever messaging, video, and call app you like). What is new is that each granddaughter has her own chat with me and Nonna, and we have two group chats for the whole family together. Both girls are very good at keeping in touch.

They know I am interested in everything they do, and they are eager to share. I get to see their latest drawings, videos of them dancing to music videos, and the medal or certificate they get for doing well in recitals or music contests (they have a lot of them in Slovenia, part of the rigorous music training they get at the conservatory, giving them confidence in performance and an ease in front of an audience).

But as wonderful as it is to connect with my granddaughters virtually, nothing beats spending time with them in person. Here are some of my favorite ways to empower my grandkids when we are together.

Books and Bonding

With Eleonora, now twelve, I often ask her about the latest book she is reading. She is a serious reader like I was as a kid, enjoying burying herself in a book. She has worked her way through most of *Harry Potter*, stopping short of the last two books as she realized how dark the story was getting (and how long those last books are). I encourage her to tell me what she likes about the book and what she doesn't, not just telling me the plot but exploring with me about how it is told. Though the books are available in Slovene now, she reads them in English, which still amazes me.

Both girls are bilingual and have an enormous vocabulary, but Eleonora is the one who passionately loves to read. She taught herself to read in English when she was eight years old, in order to begin the *Harry Potter* books. Her latest enthusiasm is the *Jurassic Park* books of Michael Crichton, and she is beginning to work her way through the *Lord of the Rings*. I think she enjoys talking to me about these books, and I sure enjoy hearing about them.

I have recommended lots of my old favorite books to her and she seems eager to try many of them.

Izabella, now ten, is developing her own approach to reading. I discovered that she likes to read comics when her parents and I introduced her to the Carl Barks graphic novel adventures of the Disney characters Scrooge McDuck, Donald Duck, and the duck family. These long, illustrated comic book tales from the 1950s and 1960s are considered classics. They are clever and funny with an Indiana Jones vibe (lost treasure, pirates, the evil Beagle Boys). Top quality comic books like these are terrific choices for a child who prefers images to words.

I read several of these wonderful stories to the girls when we are visiting, and Izabella is now reading them on her own. I love it when I discover one of the girls' new favorite passions; it makes it so much easier to choose presents for birthdays and holidays.

Noah grew up with the Asterix and Obelix longform comic books, first with me reading to him and then with him enthusiastically reading them on his own. Asterix is a tiny, clever fellow who gains super strength when he drinks a magic potion. He defends his village in ancient Gaul (modern France) when Rome ruled the world. Obelix is a big lug who always has super strength, having fallen into a cauldron of magic potion when he was a baby, but he's not very bright. They are the best of friends and have some forty adventures fighting Romans in Gaul, Egypt, Ancient England, Germany, and much of ancient Europe. The stories are translated from the French and are witty and silly in turn, with character names such as the magical Druid Getafix, the chef Clovogarlix, the architect Edifis, and the Roman centurion Nefarius Purpus. The stories are fun for kids and adults and are great books to read together.

But you never know. It turns out that these books were not yet hits with our granddaughters, nor was the Tintin series, another I would have guessed they'd have liked. I mention the Asterix books because they are really good and worth considering, but what you loved may not always be loved by the next generation. For every success I have had introducing the girls to a book or movie that I loved, there will always be a few that simply don't work for them.

Our batting average has been pretty good. But no one bats a thousand! The key is to offer suggestions with enthusiasm, then leave them to breathe and decide on their own whether or not they'll take them up. More often than not it's a question of "when" rather than "if." Eleonora has read every John Bellairs novel now, but when we first introduced her to them, their gothic spookiness was a bit too spooky. She picked one up later and then binged on them all.

Sharing Family Traditions

We have several family traditions that mean a lot to us. Every Christmas Eve, I used to read two favorite books to young Noah: *The Night Before Christmas* by Clement Moore, with illustrations that have always defined the holiday, and *The Polar Express* by Chris Van Allsburg, a more modern book with wonderfully evocative illustrations and a gentle story. I read these books to Noah every Christmas Eve of his childhood life and now I read it to his girls. During Covid, I read to them online using WhatsApp or Facetime. They had their own copies of the books, so we would turn the pages together—me in Italy, they in Slovenia. This year we were together again for Christmas. How very special to resume reading to them while we snuggle together looking at the pictures! Noah is right there too, *kvelling* (a wonderful Yiddish word which means overwhelmed with pleasure at the happiness of a loved one). These life-long traditions can mean so much, not just to a child but to the adult she becomes.

We have enjoyed introducing the girls to American traditions that are unknown in Slovenia. American culture does have a tendency to leak into other cultures. Halloween in Italy did not exist as a holiday until fairly recently. They did observe the Day of the Dead on November 1, a day to go to the cemetery and honor loved ones who had passed away. But the idea of children dressing in costumes, knocking on neighbors' doors and declaring "trick or treat" for candy was only known through the movies. Suddenly, now, it is a thing in Italy. And to a lesser extent, in Slovenia, too. Because it was essentially unknown in Slovenia when the girls were born, we came up with a contained version that did not depend on the neighbors.

We grownups would hide in separate rooms of the house and the girls, dressed up as Maleficent from *Sleeping Beauty* or Anna from *Frozen*, would knock on each door, announcing "trick or treat." We would feign surprise and give them a treat. Then they would retreat to the living room floor to count their "loot" and choose the one or two pieces of candy they were allowed to eat that night. We would watch Disney's *The Legend of Sleepy Hollow* (with the Headless Horseman, which did not scare the girls at all---but you do need to be sensitive to the possibility of upset, and judge according to their age and sensitivity to such things). They also liked Tim Burton's *The Nightmare Before Christmas*, which frankly, I find spooky but does not seem to faze them at all (go figure!).

We do an American Thanksgiving whenever we can manage a visit that is close to the holiday. It doesn't matter if it's not on the traditional day. After all, no one in Slovenia (or in Italy) has a holiday on the day of American Thanksgiving. You can make any day you choose a holiday of your choice. As with most families, the fun is in the cooking, the feast, and the gathering of family. That is universal and fairly easy to make happen anywhere.

However, it is almost impossible to get an American-sized turkey in Europe. One time Noah ordered one from his local butcher, and when he went to pick it up, instead of the eighteen-pounder we were expecting, it was the size of a slightly obese chicken. He had to scurry and ask his mother-in-law to bring her famous stuffed pork ribs dish to complete the meal, otherwise we would all have starved! We have learned to order two if there will be many coming to dinner. The girls like to cook with us or just keep us company while we bounce around the kitchen. It is a day-long party, starting with the cooking, and then the feast, and then recovering from all that food with a movie or a board game.

These cultural differences are forever interesting to the girls (and to us grown-ups new to our adopted country, Italy). They love to hear us talk about when we were kids (or when their father or mother was a child) and how we remembered these holidays and family traditions.

It goes both ways. We find Slovene traditions fascinating and exotic. For instance, in Slovenia whenever you enter a house, you put on slippers. There is always a basket of slippers for guests by the front door. Children learn to put on slippers in kindergarten and they wear them every day at school. Teenagers too! It is just their normal. We got used to the tradition and we now follow it in our house in Italy. As I write this, I am wearing slippers.

Board Games Are Family Fun

In the midst of Covid, I bought Eleonora a very nice wooden chess set, and a book teaching her the rules. She read it right away. Because Covid kept us apart then, we started playing together online. There are several good apps that allow you to play chess in real time with anyone in the world. *Chess 3D* is the one we used. I was in Italy, she was in Slovenia. We would make a date for a game and look forward to it. She is a fast learner and pretty soon she was playing to a draw and now she regularly beats me (I am a terrible chess player and had not played in years when we started together).

Now that we can visit again, she has resumed her interest in the game. And, I have to admit, she has gotten even better. My definition of success is now no more than managing to prolong the game so it is fun, before losing gracefully. I am not losing on purpose. She is simply a better player than

I am now. And I am proud of that. She is pretty proud of herself too and loves that she can beat Greppen in a game I taught her.

Note to myself: I need to study the chess book I got her to have any chance of winning a game.

Speaking of games, both girls and their parents love board games and when we are with them, game night is almost any night that school homework doesn't get in the way. Favorite games now are Clue (or Cluedo in Europe), Monopoly, Ticket to Ride (a clever game where you compete to be the first to complete complicated train routes in nineteenth-century Europe), Dixit (creative storytelling based on exotic illustrated cards) and Activity, which Nonna described above. Any one of these games can bring the family together (a significant improvement on each person staring at their smartphone screen, as though in a private bubble) since anyone from age six and up can enjoy playing.

Cooking and Eating Together

I love to cook, and the girls do too. Both parents are very good cooks and often include the girls baking cakes, making cookies or preparing dinner. We have a family tradition for breakfast of what we call "egg-in-a-peg" (egg-in-a-hole is another name for it). Inspired by the classic English breakfast, it is basically an egg fried in butter sitting in a hole cut in a slice of bread. The bread becomes lusciously buttery and the egg is delicious. Though they have learned to make it themselves, and they do a very good job of it, they always ask me to make it for them. I love that. My wife comments that this is like they're still enjoying being read to, even though they both can read to themselves. Or that even though they are old enough to walk home from school on their own, they like us to walk with them when we are visiting. Some of our best conversations happen on those walks.

Or it might simply be that I make a killer egg-in-a-peg that magically just tastes better.

When they were younger, the girls were reluctant to get their hands gooey touching dough or other foods. But now that they are older the hands-on aspect of cooking has become a fun feature that we can share.

During visits they have begun to ask me to teach them some favorite dishes: Spaghetti Bolognese, twice-baked potatoes, bagels from scratch (I made those with their Dad, too), brownies, Thanksgiving stuffing. I hope we will begin to do some more adventurous dishes in the future, but having these in our pocket is a great start.

What favorite dishes from your family might your children enjoy cooking with you? Even better, what are their favorite dishes that you have made for them over the years? It can be a precious gift to teach them to make it with you.

There are so many mini lessons that you can include in a cooking session: following directions, reading and understanding measurements, especially when one recipe might be using grams and another cup measures. Figuring out how to convert one to the other, so the recipe can work, recognizes that different cultures count things differently, as well as introducing the importance of knowing when in cooking, like so many other projects, you need to be precise, and when it's okay to improvise.

Slovenia has wonderful food. So does Italy. So eating out is part of the regular rotation of activities during our visits. I have favorite restaurants I ask for us to go to, places the girls seem to love too. There is a wonderful Chinese restaurant in the capital, Ljubljana, called Chang. No visit is complete without at least one outing there. The girls know just what to order, starting with their favorite dishes, which surprisingly includes cauliflower—it's a sign of a good restaurant if they make cauliflower so good that young kids can't wait to eat it as a main.

But many children don't like cauliflower, broccoli, or spinach. Ordering together in a restaurant needn't be a challenge, a landmine of foods to be avoided to protect your child's preferences. Though we encourage our granddaughters to tell us what they like (and don't like) and respect that, we also will insist they try something new. Their parents are good about this, and we try to follow their lead. In fact, this can be a game the grown-ups can play as well, because most of us have established foods we think we don't like, simply because we decided we didn't like them long ago. I had too-chewy calamari (squid) as a child and for years convinced myself it was not something I would ever order in the restaurant. But at a seafood restaurant recently on the Connecticut shore, someone ordered the calamari and exclaimed at how delicious it was, offering me a taste. Reluctantly, I tried it. And it was delicious—it was nothing like the rubbery dish I had as a child—and suddenly it was something I really liked. You may have a story like that to tell your grandchild as you encourage her to try something they think they don't like. You might order something that is new to you and her and take your first tentative bite at exactly the same time—and then compare notes.

Traveling Together Is a Special Treat

We have been lucky enough to share several outings with the family. We met for five days in Vienna to celebrate Noah's fortieth birthday—a surprise coordinated by our daughter-in-law Urška, which Noah knew nothing about until we arrived at the same restaurant there! A whirlwind of museums, parks, cafes with amazing pastries, Wiener Schnitzel, Goulash, wursts of every kind (with horseradish and hot mustard) and, the girl's favorite: hot chocolate *"mit schlag"* (whipped cream).

The girls are naturally curious and it's always a surprise what they find interesting in a museum. There is almost always something. If not, we can make a game of "Where's Waldo" for instance, inviting them to find hidden details in a painting. Noticing how one artist always has animals in the background, and (something our art historian son taught us) that the sixteenth-century painter, Carlo Crivelli, always hid a green pickle in every painting. In Vienna we also went to the zoo, and to a music museum with displays of ancient instruments, and a staircase with steps that sounded different notes when you stepped on them—you could tap out a melody going up and down. Since Izabella plays the violin and Eleonora plays the flute, this place pressed the right buttons.

A trip across the border to the town of Graz in Austria, just over an hour away, was another treat. The girls love museums, playgrounds, exploring the open-air markets, and seeing the exotic buildings (Graz has a historic tower clock with dancing figures), discovering the different foods and manners of the country. Each specific difference can be a learning moment, a chance to try to understand why they do things that way, and how much variety there can be in the way people live.

The Movie Connection

I write books about movies and have loved them all my life. Our visits are another chance for us to watch favorite movies together and for me to introduce them to new ones—and, frankly, for them to introduce me to new ones that they have discovered. Disney's *Moana* is a perennial favorite, and a wonderful example of a feisty, competent, and confident young girl. I remembered enjoying *School of Rock* when it came out, with the comic actor Jack Black boisterously breaking the rules at a staid private school, but what seems to me best about the film as one to watch with your grandkids is how he discovers what is special about each child in the class, and finds a way for them to make a real contribution to the illicit rock band he is making of the class. It may be Hollywood hokum that he also discovers that he loves to teach and is good at it, but it's an optimism we could all use a dose of now and then.

Our granddaughters have been introduced to the great old Hollywood musicals, usually at first by just watching YouTube clips of individual numbers, like "Good Morning" or "Moses Supposes" from *Singin' in the Rain*. These are catchy tunes with happy energetic dancing that inspires them to get up and dance too, even when the movie isn't playing. This is something we can do with them, though I think they are often happy to be in their own world while dancing—as long as a parent or grandparent is watching appreciatively.

Whatever films inspire them to imitate and elaborate on the stories or the songs and dances, are worth watching with them. If it's an old film and you have a memory of how it affected you when you first saw it, share that experience. It puts another story in their memory bank, letting them get to know you better, not just as a grandparent but as a person. Some of the most meaningful conversations start with such a simple tale.

Time flies, and it is so precious, measured by how quickly Eleonora and Izabella are growing up. We need to be flexible and attentive as their interests change and their personalities develop, knowing that what worked last year may become ancient history. We feel so lucky to be part of their world, watching them discover it and themselves, and being grateful that they remain enthusiastic about sharing it all with us.

Vive la Résistance

So, let's say you suggest a project for today and your child doesn't want to do it? What do you do?

Well, there is a magic in the idea of the Lesson Game and its lessonlets. That magic is flexibility. This isn't meant to be school. There is no set agenda—or there shouldn't be. The goal is to engage your kids, to be involved with them in a way that you both enjoy. So, if one suggestion doesn't fly, with the many ideas here, you can just move to another, until one puts a sparkle in your child's eyes. If she isn't in the mood for reading, perhaps a walk in the nearby woods will excite? Or going for a bike ride, or practicing rollerblades? If that doesn't do it, maybe it's time for her to help you cook dinner or bake something for dessert? So, what does she want to bake? Have a couple of delicious-sounding cupcakes or brownies ready to suggest. Or, even better, pull out the cookbooks and make a project of studying them together and choosing just the right recipe for the moment.

What can make this easier is having backup ideas at the ready. If you feel like you have to invent something else to do when confronted with your child just not getting excited about, say, coloring, it can increase your anxiety, your frustration, or otherwise leave you feeling off balance. We are not all so good at coming up with a new idea on the spot. Especially if you think it's a pretty good idea, to have your child reject it can lead to annoyance that little Charlie doesn't recognize how clever you are, or hurt feelings that he doesn't appreciate how hard you are trying. But it's not about that. Charlie just doesn't want to sit still now; he needs to burn off some energy or do something that requires less concentration (or maybe more).

In other words, at that moment you are out of sync.

So how do you stay in sync? Asking is a good start—include your child in the decisions, let her know what you are thinking about and ask her if she likes the idea. And if not, how would she make it better? "Let's not color dinosaurs today, let's make up our own monsters and color them." The other day our granddaughters were shown one of Vincent van Gogh's landscape pictures, with his strong bright colors. Their mom suggested they try to copy it, making their own picture inspired by his. She did it too. They had a wonderful time drawing and coloring together and then sharing their masterpieces with each other.

If the girls hadn't wanted to do that, their mom could have suggested they browse through the book of paintings and make another choice. Or choose another book for inspiration. Here, you are staying in the realm of coloring and drawing, a quiet activity maybe after a more active day, but you are encouraging the children to help decide just what the drawing project will be. When they can feel ownership of the activity, whether it's entirely their idea, or just a tweak of something you presented to them, enthusiasm follows.

Another option is to offer them a short list of things to choose from. For example, you pick three activity options (your own or from the Superpower Menu), and let your child choose which of those to do today. This lets you, as a parent, lay out what you are up for doing, but gives your kids a sense of power by allowing them to choose from the short list.

It's important for you as the grownup to try to be more easily flexible, to feel okay shifting gears and not taking it personally if a suggestion falls flat. Your kids are pretty creative and they often (but not always) know what they want. Or maybe it's better to say they know (again, not always) what they *don't* want. So, it is good to start with your idea for the day, unless your child comes to you with a request. That request is always the best place to start, and if it fits with the time you have that day and is something that can be turned into a lessonlet, go for it. If it is something that you would have to put off for another day (because it takes too much time, or requires advance preparation, or costs too much), your explanation becomes a learning moment. Planning to make that request work, or to find a version of it that will satisfy, is another exercise worth doing, and increases the odds that your child (and you) will be happy with it.

Routines Soothe

There are so many things in life that are confusing, especially for children (but for grownups too). Sometimes the best we can say is "we don't know." That's hard for grownups as well as kids to wrap their heads around. One way to help, and to give a sense of control when things are out-of-control, is to set up routines.

Predictability, as Noah mentioned in the previous chapter, routine can powerfully calm anxiety. Again, we are not talking some sort of rigid schedule. But having a shape to your day can really make a difference. If your child knows that there is one activity expected each morning, and another at a set time in the afternoon, for example, the hours pass more easily. This can be different on different days, or at least in part, the same every day. If your child's school has been giving him work to do, it would be good to designate a set time each day for him to sit down and do it. The reward for that would be something he gets to choose to happen after.

Whatever you do, as long as it's together then it's time well spent. The pleasure felt and the attention paid creates memories and opens up the world for you and your kids. And that's a wonderful thing.

8 Cultures of Education

Parenting systems from countries other than our own can offer useful tips, alternative perspectives, and ideas. Sometimes experiences can reassure us that we're already doing the right thing, but often a new concept can be added to our menu of parenting tactics—this has been the case for me, as an enthusiastic American expat who has lived in many different European countries.

This chapter provides insight into how teaching styles differ, particularly between where I have lived for a decade—Slovenia—and where I grew up, in the United States, and studied, in England. It sheds light on how countries educate in different ways, via varying traditions, some of which I find more effective than others. Read on if you're curious about some of the distinctions, and the principles upon which I build my own lessons, whether I'm teaching post-graduate students or a five-year-old.

Positive Parenting in Early Childhood Education

Through no merit of my own, I feel that I've had the best possible education, throughout my life. I had to get good enough grades to make it into the institutions I aimed for, though I was never a top student. But I really have both good fortune, and my parents' decisions, to thank for what is quite possibly the world's best education. However, while I studied at elite institutions like the University of Cambridge, that is not where I received the most important lessons. The most important step to any child's education comes in the first ten years of life.

Before we begin, let us consider a brief chronology of my schooling. We will then consider what I got out of each institution, and what lessons we can draw from the experience. I began, around age three, at a multi-award-winning preschool (which, in the US system, comes before kindergarten, and is more of a day-care center than a proper school). Calvin Hill (founded by the father of the former NBA basketball star Grant Hill) is a tiny, highly regarded preschool run by a family friend, Dr. Carla Horwitz. Just what is so unusual, avant-garde, and powerful about the Calvin Hill experience is something we will return to. Any teacher or professor can employ these methods, but relatively few do, outside of the North American system, where it is expected and required.

From kindergarten (age four to five) until high school, I attended a private day school called The Foote School. For high school (age fourteen to eighteen) I went to a boarding school called Choate Rosemary Hall. I attended a small liberal arts college for university called Colby College, in rural Maine. It is tiny by US standards, only twelve hundred students, and is an excellent school, but I went for two reasons: (1) I was recruited to play on their squash team, and (2) I didn't get into any of the more internationally famous universities, like Yale and Brown, because my grades were good but not great.

Both in high school and at college, I studied abroad. I lived in Paris, on an academic high school program, when I was sixteen, studying in French. And during college I lived in London, when I was twenty, studying acting. After college, I moved to Europe, studying first for a master's at the Courtauld Institute (a part of University of London specializing in art history), then a Master of Philosophy (MPhil) at University of Cambridge (also studying art history). I began a PhD at Cambridge but transferred to the University of Ljubljana when I met my Slovenian future wife, and finished my doctorate there (in architectural history). I've taught students of various ages for many years, from advanced high school students through postgraduates, and taught for institutions like Yale and Brown (the two universities I didn't get into as a prospective student).

I included this list from my CV simply to demonstrate the diversity of my education, in a variety of countries and subjects. But while there have been many differences, there are a few important consistent points that are worth highlighting, and which tend to be lacking from Slovenian, and indeed continental European, education. Yet these points could be introduced, for they cost nothing—they would simply require a shift in attitude and approach.

One of my earliest memories of school took place at the Calvin Hill Pre-School, and I must have been four years old. During the day, I would build structures out of wooden blocks—sometimes elaborate fortresses, in which

I would conceal small spaces where I would place toys, hiding them within "secret" compartments. When the end of the school day came, we would have to dismantle our carefully made constructions and put the blocks away, to be used the next day. This could be mildly traumatic for a young child who had spent an hour or more carefully building his creation. Recognizing this, at the end of each day, a teacher would make a quick drawing of the structure I had built, write my name on it, and tape it to the wall for public display. This may seem like a very small thing, of no particular importance, perhaps even silly—but it was not. This is just one component of the hugely valuable, critical lesson that I was taught, passively, every day at Calvin Hill: that anything I do is of value and is something to be proud of. This lesson, in miniature, expanded within me to teach me the most important lesson that a child can have, the embodiment of the "American dream" that has now become a requisite dream and belief for every successful person in a capitalist, democratic environment: that you *can* do anything you want to do, provided you work hard and are smart to achieve it.

I remember little else of my time at Calvin Hill, but I recognize that this self-confidence was the most important lesson I have ever learned. We learn self-confidence from three sources: teachers, parents, and experience. Experience is what we have the least control over, and it comes with time. But parents and teachers can teach the value of whatever you do as a child, by showing proactive interest in whatever a child produces and shows interest in. It doesn't matter if a child's drawing or construction is objectively good or not—what is important is instilling the sense that there is a value in anything the child sets his or her mind to. American parents tend to be over-the-top with praise of even mediocre output. This is certainly better than too little or no praise. Children should not be taught, from the earliest age, that being lazy or doing a halfway job is praiseworthy. And as Dr. Horwitz says, "If a child doesn't really think that something is that good and is praised anyway, they may get the idea that the praise isn't honest, so it backfires. Honest and not over-the-top praise for the work (or the effort or determination or persistence) is what we look for." But whenever there is genuine interest and determination, a level of passion and attention to detail, the product or action should be praised.

This early childhood lesson in self-confidence is a microcosm—much more than just what must happen for a four-year-old to grow into a confident, alpha-personality adult. But it is a detail like this that we remember. I cannot thank enough the system at Calvin Hill, and the staff who implemented it, for teaching me to believe in myself. Students eventually learn to read, write, and do their multiplication tables. But it is a rare and hugely powerful gift, to teach a child self-confidence.

In the first ten years of their lives, we have the opportunity to teach our children self-confidence—this is the most important outcome of all those lessonlets. That is the single greatest gift you could give them, to help them through the rest of their lives. Teach them that all they do, all they work hard at, is of value. If they learn this, then the world will be theirs.

I spoke to Dr. Carla Horwitz, an expert in early childhood education and the principal of Calvin Hill, about what to look for when choosing daycare, preschool, or kindergarten for your children. Of course, in Slovenia parents have far less choice—their children tend to go somewhere local, when space is available. In the United States, there can be an abundance of choice, and parents are occasionally known to over-complicate. But there are certain things to look for, and that one should ideally expect, in the best preschools.

Here are some suggestions from Dr. Horwitz:

- My recommendations come down to looking at what kind of relationships there are between the children and the staff, as well as with the family. Relationships are central. A good physical plant is always nice, but wonderful care can happen in church basements and in places that are not state of the art if the caregivers and teachers understand, respect, and appreciate children; know the developmental stages and the behaviors associated with them so as to provide a stimulating (not over-stimulating) comfortable, safe and loving environment; respond quickly to children's needs and allow for children's own initiative and interests—even babies have these qualities! Not having a rigid schedule, being flexible yet organized (there should always be structure underpinning any program, but it should take the needs of the children, the teachers, and importantly the families into account) is also necessary.
- Also crucial are group size and child to teacher/caregiver ratios. A too-large group, more than eight infants—actually too many for my taste—or toddlers is too many children in one space and it would be very hard

for them to get the attention they need. And the ratio should be 1:4, though for infants 1:3 is better.
- I think group care for infants under twelve months is problematic. I'm wary of institutional care for babies, for many reasons, including that they get sicker more often.
- Trust your own gut intuition. Can you envision leaving your precious child in the care of these people? Do they make you feel welcome? Are they warm? How long have they been there? What is their training (courses do matter, and an intellectual understanding of theory as well as a good sense of practice is important, but so are the caring instincts and ability to read a child as well as communicate with the parents).
- How do the staff talk to each other? Are they collaborative and respectful? You can tell a lot by how the adults treat each other, though that doesn't appear on too many lists.
- Are the children in the program generally comfortable, relaxed, and happy, and involved in play and other activities?
- Are there sufficient numbers of adults with specialized training in early childhood development and education?
- Are all areas of a child's development stressed equally, with time and attention being devoted to cognitive development, social and emotional development, physical development?
- Do the staff meet regularly to plan and evaluate the program?
- Are parents welcome to observe, discuss policies, make suggestions, and participate in the work of the program?
- Are staff alert to the health and safety of young children and of themselves?
- Is there a balance of active and quiet activities with room for individual as well as group times, and do the children get to play outside and explore the natural world? This is really important to me, and too many American programs really have no opportunity for kids to play outdoors with appropriate space, materials and supervision. I hope Slovenia is different.
- Lastly, use your nose. If it's smelly it's not well cared for, and then neither are the children!

These recommendations from Dr. Horwitz are, of course, assuming an ideal situation in which parents can choose between multiple preschools, to find the one they feel most comfortable with. This is not possible in much of Slovenia, although there are good Montessori or Waldorf schools that offer slight variations that may be preferable for some parents. But the tips are useful all the same.

Six Things an American Father Has Learned from Raising Kids in Slovenia

There have been a series of top-selling books on just the concept of national styles of parenting from which we could learn a thing or two, from Pamela Druckerman's *Bringing Up Bebe*, about raising children the French way (which is primarily about parents doing whatever they would like to do and the children happily conforming and following the lead), to Amy Chua's *Battle Hymn of a Tiger Mother*, about Chinese parenting (where an authoritarian insistence on practice and achievement is thought to be beneficial in the long run, even if difficult for children from moment to moment), to Rina Mae Acosta's *The Happiest Kids in the World* (about Dutch parenting habits, "how parents help their kids by doing less"). With a demonstrable audience of parents curious to know how it's done abroad, and what tips they might implement at home, the Slovenian approach is worth considering.

My family and I live in what I consider just about the best place to raise children, in Kamnik, Slovenia, a small town capped by three castles (and six microbreweries!) that is clean and safe and charming—imagine a Slavic version of a gee-whiz Norman Rockwell sort of town. I have become friendly with a number of specialists in schooling and child development and parent-child dynamics here on, as the locals like to say, "the sunny side of the Alps." Feeling in a reasonably good position to weigh in on the Slovenian approach to parenting, I examined my own experiences and also polled a handful of local experts. Here are six things that I learned.

1. **Shift responsibility and consequence for decisions onto the children.** My first port of call was the book, *Connect to Your Teenager: A Guide to Everyday Parenting* by Leonida and Albert Mrgole. The Mrgoles are

a hugely popular Slovenian therapist couple specializing in helping parents have a better dynamic with their teens. Their primary lesson is shifting responsibility and consequence for decisions away from the parents and onto the children, so that children recognize that they are responsible for their own destinies. This is both empowering for the children and it relieves the pressure of being authoritarian from the parents. It helps children recognize that the choices they make result in consequences that they will either be happy with, or not. The key phrase is to offer your child a choice: "You can choose to do your homework and go to the concert this weekend, or you can choose not to do your homework and therefore you will not be able to go to the concert. It's up to you." This is a powerful potion that works regularly, but it seems to me just like generally good advice. Is it particularly Slovenian?

2. **Universal rules no longer exist . . . but once they did.** This more enlightened and liberal approach to parenting is in stark contrast to the more traditional, patriarchal, and authoritarian method that was generally prevalent in Yugoslavia. Ivana Gradišnik, the head of Slovenia's branch of *Familylab*, says "No more is there a one-and-only outside authority to go by. Parents have to decide—decide for themselves—and then take responsibility for their decisions and the consequences of those decisions. And that is difficult."

3. **Don't overdo it with the praise.** One of the first things that Slovenians notice about Americans, whether they know Americans in person or gather data from popular culture, television, and film, is a tendency on the part of American parents to overpraise. Past generations of Slovenian parents, particularly during the time of Yugoslavia, tended to under-praise. There was an accepted level that children were expected to attain and sustain, which involves good behavior and also doing reasonably well in school. Achieving this expected level was not normally deemed praiseworthy. It was an expectation, so praise was doled out in moderation if at all, and many Slovenes look back in retrospect and say they received far too little of it. This meant that they felt rather under-supported. On the other hand, Slovenians often mistrust the enthusiasm and praise lavished by Americans, whether rating a local pizza place or talking about the achievements of their children. They see Americans as praising too much, with too enthusiastic a hand, and as a result they are not sure what is genuine. The current generation

of Slovenian parents try to strike a nice balance, it seems, recognizing that children thrive on positive reinforcement, but still thinking that American parents tend to overdo it.

4. **Aim for a Buddhist level of contentment.** In Tito's Yugoslavia, most of the country was part of a single comfortable but working-class social order, as might be expected in a socialist country. Just about everyone had the same clothes, bags, shoes, toys, and so there was little room for kids, or their parents (as is often the case), to showboat their distinctive social status. Materialism has infiltrated Slovenia as one of America's primary exports, but only in the last two decades. Here it is present but not ubiquitous. Since there is far less of the discrepancy between the haves and have-nots than there is in the United States, just about everyone in the country lives reasonably comfortably and would self-describe as content. There is something to be said for contentment, and it is a more modest approach than Americans tend to have. Americans tend to feel that they are either on top of the world or miserable, and if they are miserable then someone else is likely to blame. Slovenians have a more modest expectation of what life should bring, and this is reflected in an upbringing in which you don't see the American insistence on their children achieving superlatives, but where being content and cared for are the priorities.

5. **Curb the competitiveness.** Parenting in the United States can involve nervousness about universities and the job market that result in pressure on children at a very early age—the cliché about parents worried about their kids getting into the "right kindergarten" that will start a chain reaction leading, the thinking must go, to inevitable success thirty years later. This is almost entirely absent in Slovenia. There are also only a couple of universities in this country, and the state of the economy and job market is such that having a university or even postgraduate degree is no guarantee that a Slovenian will find interesting, ready, and gainful employment. So, the argument that to have a good future you must do well in school is much harder to reinforce here, because it simply is not as universally accepted as in the United States. There are also almost no private high schools and the universities are state institutions. This means that there is nothing really to compete for, in terms of doing well in school. This alleviates the pressure to do well in school that American

parents tend to force on their children, but the negative is that it is hard for parents to explain to children why they must study hard.

6. **Encourage independence.** It is unusual, from an American perspective, that Slovenian children expect to live at home until they marry. There is a danger to this, that Slovenian children become overly reliant on family taking care of them (in terms of cooking and laundry and household chores). To counteract this, self-aware parents take action. Tina Deu is a mother of three who writes an enormously popular parenting blog in Slovenia. She describes putting her fifteen-year-old to work in the summer and sending him to the bank to open his own account. "There is no shortage of 30-somethings who still live in their childhood room," she says, "or who move only as far as the top floor of the family house, so Mama can still wash their undies and iron their shirts." In order to help her children become more independent in a context in which it is likely that they will remain at home until adulthood, or possibly beyond, Tina insists that her kids do for themselves whenever possible. They are on their own to take the bus to sports practice, for instance, instead of the parents acting as a taxi service. Sounds good to me.

I'm delighted to learn a thing or two from my adopted homeland and think my children will be the better for this more international approach.

Tips for Multilingual Families or Learning New Languages

Our family is multilingual. I'm American, my wife, Urška, is Slovenian, and we live in Slovenia. We also have a family house in Italy, so we thought of adding Italian, but we don't speak it perfectly and it didn't feel organic to speak it to our kids, so we set that aside for now. Our girls attend German class, since we're right next to the Austrian border. My wife lived in China and used to speak good Chinese. I lived in France and used to speak good French. Foreign languages are fun and a constant point of interest for us.

With this in mind, there are some lesson games that we like to play that focus on the multilingual side of our life. We both apply them to our two fluent languages, English and Slovenian, but also for languages we want our girls to learn (German and Italian). Some of the ideas presented here are best applied to multilingual families, but others can be for any family in which the kids are learning a new language, at whatever level that might be.

Whatever Your Activity, Pick One Language at a Time

Whatever we're doing, we're likely to be speaking in two and a half languages. By that I mean that we'll jump between English and Slovenian from sentence to sentence, but also sometimes from word to word. For their first few years of speaking, the girls didn't really distinguish between their languages, at least not consciously. They always did know to speak only English with my parents and only Slovenian with Urška's. When they grew more cognizant of the languages, we started doing activities exclusively in one language. For instance, we might have a lunch only in Slovenian. This helped them to distinguish the languages and consider them as two separate routes, as opposed to one, braided trail. That's because speaking two languages in the course of a conversation or even a sentence isn't useful and can amount to not conveying anything at all to your interlocutor. When we play games that involve speaking, like Name Ten or What Animal Am I Thinking of—and especially What Begins with This Letter—we'll designate which language we're playing in for that round.

Play Translation Games

We've already mentioned the Translation Game as a pastime on car rides. It really is both fun and empowering, as it highlights to children that they know two languages well, allowing them to show off their abilities. It works just as well with monolingual families who are learning a new language. The words can be basic (colors, numbers) for beginners. I know approximately no German so my daughters are already ahead of me. We can still play the Translation Game in German for some super basic things, like colors or foods or numbers (as long as we don't go higher than nine; after that I'm stumped). You can level up by shifting from a single word "How do you say 'lizard' in Slovenian?" to a phrase "How do you say 'Happy Birthday to You' in Slovenian?" Level up even further when there's an idiomatic phrase that doesn't really translate, at least not directly. See which direction is easier for your kids, from English or into English.

Alternate Language Consumption

Kids tend to have a mother language and a second language that may be fluent but isn't quite as integrated into the psyche and being as the mother language (which, naturally enough, is normally that spoken by the mother). Our family is pretty equal between English and Slovenian, and it's good to cultivate a balance (and to work on whichever seems weaker or less developed). A way to do this is to alternate which language is "consumed" in cultural activities, and prioritize whichever language seems like it could use more work. This means reading more books in the weaker language, watching more films or TV in it, speaking it more. If the languages feel equal, then just alternate—if we read one novel in English, then the next one should be in Slovene.

Try Your Best to Stick to Your Native Language

I speak Slovene fluidly but not fluently. I have extensive conversations in Slovene, I teach in Slovene, I have business meetings in Slovene, I have friendships exclusively in Slovene, but I never actually studied it. I learned mostly from speaking with my mother-in-law (*hvala Babi!*). I never memorized declension endings so I'm always guessing (Slovenian has declensions like Latin—it also has a dual verb form, for two people, which is rather romantic). Almost every sentence I utter has a grammatical error in it (or multiples). I'm intelligible, and I get away with sounding "cute" (I'm told), but it certainly ain't correct. I try to speak only English with my girls, so as not to accidentally teach them my incorrect grammar. It's not always possible, but as close as can be to each parent speaking their native language is preferable.

To Learn a New Language, Assign All Cartoons to It

We have controlled cartoon doses at our house. There are a lot of cartoons, don't get me wrong, but not all the time. We do have a few screen-related things that the girls can pretty much have as much as they like. One is documentaries (particularly nature documentaries—David Attenborough is our homeboy). The other is cartoons and movies in German. Since German is the language they are studying (I use the term loosely), anything in that new language counts as "educational." Kids will watch cartoons. A lot of them. They seem to be just as happy regardless of the language. I've found our girls intently watching a cartoon in Indonesian—they seemed perfectly content. So if they can, by osmosis, absorb a new language, and a single language that they are consistently exposed to, that is a very good thing and will help them advance (likely far more quickly and well than the weekly lesson they have now, which is more of a playtime, anyway).

Start Languages as Early as Possible

Studies have shown that the human brain absorbs languages far more quickly in the first five years or so. At that early age, kids are like sponges and don't even have to try—simple, extensive, consistent exposure to a language is enough for them to internalize it. As they get older, it becomes more difficult and requires much more effort, study, memorization to learn languages and more regular practice to retain them. The earlier you can introduce a new language, the better and easier it will be.

However Many Languages You Speak (or Need), Learn More

Learning foreign languages is wonderful for the brain. Foreign language study stretches it, keeps it active, elastic, young. It's recommended that for adults to learn and practice a foreign language can stave off mental deterioration. For kids, foreign languages expand their knowledge, and the ability to speak other languages is, quite simply, one of the best advantages they can have later in life. It provides professional and lifestyle opportunities, or just enhances holiday making. Pile on foreign languages, the more the merrier. Whether or not you really need to speak other languages, or your kids do, it's a good skill to cultivate.

Meditation and Mindfulness for Kids

Slovenia was the first place where I considered meditation and mindfulness. The concepts have their adherents around the world, of course, but they strike me as more universally applied, whether through a spiritual practice like Buddhism or secularly, outside of the United States, where I grew up.

In Japan "forest bathing" is prescribed by doctors to help with stress and anxiety. In Slovenia, while they don't call it that, long walks in wild woods are a go-to recommendation whenever life feels overwhelming. The slower, more deliberate pace of life, even in Slovenia's capital, has encouraged my appreciation and mindful approach to life.

If parenting preteens sometimes feels like trying to capture mist in your hands—one moment they are focused, the next lost in a world of screens and distractions—you are not alone. In our digital age, where attention spans are ever shortening and the pressure to achieve mounts early, teaching children mindfulness techniques is not just beneficial, it is essential. Parents can guide their children toward a more mindful existence by helping them develop patience, observation, and appreciation for the present moment. These are ideas borrowed from other cultures (hence the placement in this chapter on lessons from abroad) and practices—meditation and mindfulness—but they can help any and all of us, at any time of life.

Embracing Stillness

Mindfulness is about teaching our children to be present: to taste food instead of gulping it down, to hear music rather than simply letting it play in the background, to truly listen to a friend instead of thinking about what they will say next. It is about learning to appreciate the moments in between the milestones rather than rushing ahead to the next thing.

Mindful Appreciation: Savoring the Present

Many parents lament that their children seem to be in a perpetual state of restlessness, always seeking the next source of entertainment. Video games, social media, YouTube—the dopamine rush of digital engagement keeps their minds leaping forward, rarely stopping to savor a moment of stillness. One simple way to counter this is to introduce the practice of mindful appreciation.

For example, during family dinners or walks, you might pause and ask your child to take a moment to notice something beautiful or enjoyable—the way sunlight filters through the trees, the scent of fresh bread, the warmth of a hug. Encouraging children to "behold" their surroundings trains their minds to slow down, fostering gratitude and awareness.

Managing Stress with Controlled Breathing

Children can learn to control their own physiological responses through breath. Preteens often struggle with performance anxiety—whether it's a big test, a music recital, or speaking in front of the class. In these moments, their thoughts race, their hearts pound, and panic sets in.

One of the simplest yet most effective mindfulness techniques is controlled breathing. Teaching a child to inhale slowly through the nose for four counts, hold for four, then exhale for four can be transformative. This "box breathing" technique, used by musicians and even Navy SEALs, not only calms the nervous system but also restores focus. Before a test, a child can take a few deep breaths at their desk, grounding themselves in the present rather than spiraling into worry about the future.

Taking a Moment: Creating a Pause Between Stimulus and Response

When a child feels overwhelmed—perhaps after an argument with a friend or when frustration mounts over a difficult homework assignment—encouraging them to "take a moment" before responding can be invaluable. This moment can be as simple as closing their eyes, taking a slow breath, or stepping away to reset. The ability to regulate emotions, rather than be ruled by them, is a skill that will serve them well into adulthood.

Integrating Mindfulness into Daily Life

Mindfulness does not have to be a rigid practice. It can be seamlessly integrated into everyday activities:

- **Mindful Mornings**: Start the day with a minute of deep breathing before school.
- **Mindful Eating**: Encourage your child to take a few moments to really taste their food.
- **Mindful Listening**: Teach them to truly listen to a friend or sibling without interrupting.

- **Mindful Creativity**: Encourage drawing, writing, or playing music as forms of mindfulness.
- **Mindful Bedtime**: End the day with gratitude—one thing they appreciated that day.
- **Mindful Journaling**: Encourage kids to keep a journal or diary without any expectations or requirements for how often they write in it or what they write about. Be sure that they know it is a private place for them—they can share it with you if they like, but you will respect their privacy and not read it. It should be a place where they can "dialogue" with themselves; writing things out helps you process a feeling or experience and consider it in a new way.

By teaching our children to slow down, breathe, and appreciate the present, we equip them with lifelong tools for resilience and joy. In a world that constantly pulls them toward the next distraction, mindfulness offers them the gift of presence—a valuable skill they can cultivate anew each day.

Applause for You, the Reader

Congratulations for being such a wonderful parent. As I mentioned at the outset, it goes without saying that, if you picked up this book, you are in the top percentage of caring, proactive, intelligent, and extra-mindful parents. Your children are in great hands, and I hope that some of my ideas will make your parenting a bit easier, perhaps with some added fun, added closeness and added memories with your kids.

A big thanks to my parents for coauthoring some sections, to my wife for the illustrations and design, and of course to my girls, Eleonora and Izabella. *Rad vas imam.*

Thank you once again, and now onto the final section. The Superpower Menu!

9 The Superpower Menu

This section of the book is designed to be a source of inspiration for what you might choose for lessonlets for your kids. They are my ideas collected during years of Lesson Gaming, all of which I've used with good results at home. This is not meant to be a to-do list. Use any you like, skip any you don't. My list is skewed toward my own interests and those of my children, and yours will inevitably differ. I've divided them into themes because it encourages learning and recollection to group together lessonlets on a certain theme—dinosaurs or the Middle Ages or outer space—rather than bounce around various, unconnected themes. It also feels satisfying, in retrospect, to look back and feel that you and your kids have done a lesson block on this theme or that. "We did a lesson block on Ice Age mammals and watched all the movies in the *Ice Age* series" feels better than dancing between mammoths, then the planets, then suits of armor, then back to sabretooth tigers. But, again, don't push your kids or yourself too much. Them wanting to learn is the most important thing, structure is secondary.

There are 365 lessonlets in this book, and you've already seen at least 53 of them. They were listed in the main text, so for the sake of space, we're not going to repeat them here. Here we have the remaining 313 or so (but who's counting, right?). What you'll find are initial ideas, a few sentences on how to execute them and what your kids can glean from them, and a few ideas for leveling up. What we're not including are step-by-step instructions for each. This is to keep the book length manageable (it would be well over five hundred pages if we were to include detailed instructions for each) and also because I'm not here to micromanage how to teach your own kids—you'll know how to teach them and what they'll respond to better than anyone. I'm here to give you some points of inspiration for the overall approach to inspiring a love of learning in children and 365 points of departure. I don't know *how* to best teach most of these lessonlets myself. I look things up (online or on YouTube most often) for anything I'm unsure of, which is most things outside of my particular specializations. So, I'd recommend that you do the same. There are multiple ways to do any of these activities so find what works best for you and your family. These lessonlets are primarily for younger children (under age ten) but some of the "level-ups" are good for older preteens, so select what best suits your kids and their interests, abilities, and age.

Once you've done a Lesson Game (and extracted one or more lessonlets from it), it's good to review what you learned the next day. This can be done just by asking questions, or you can gamify it by making a treasure hunt, the answers of which require remembering what was learned, or a trivia game with prizes (like gummi bears or blueberries) or, if you have more than one child, they can quiz each other. This will reinforce what they've learned and is fun in and of itself.

Enjoy and happy learning!

***

1. **Bake Cookies**
First bake the world's simplest cookies, or even get things started with store-bought frozen cookie dough that you just slice, lay out, and bake. The easiest cookies ever are: 1 cup peanut butter, ½ cup brown sugar, 1 egg. Mix, spoon onto a baking tray, bake at 170°C/340°F for twelve minutes. Voila!
Level up: Shape the dough, decorate with toppings, then graduate to more complicated recipes (like oatmeal raisin or black and white cookies).

2. **Make Syrup out of Spruce Tips**
Pick spruce tips in the spring. Place them in alternating layers with sugar in a large glass jar with a top. When filled, leave out in the sun for at least a month, pressing the mixture down every few days. Pour out the resulting syrup through a filter. Use the syrup for sore throats and coughs (and parents, mix it with schnapps for a healthful tipple).

3. **Meet a Kitten**
Introduce your kids to a baby animal (kittens are recommended). Let them gently hold it. Talk about why kittens have their eyes closed, why all baby animals seem to be gifted with cuteness to make them endearing to parents.
Level up: Explain how baby mammals feed.

4. **Make a Sourdough Starter**

You can use raw potato, sugar, water, and flour. Give it a place to "live" (a Mason jar, for instance). Have your kids name it and write its name on the jar. Ours is Herbert.

Level up: Feed it every three weeks with equal portions water and flour. Then use it to make bread. Level up further by making trickier baked goods, like brioche or croissants. Then get a sourdough cookbook (we like *Sourdoughmania* by Anita Šumer) and work your way through it.

5. **Do Rubbings of Various Surfaces**

See how the surfaces come through on the paper.

Level up: Find carved stones and rub them to reveal what's written; ask how old your kids think the carvings are and what they represent.

6. **Go on an Adventure in Your Backyard**

Choose a goal (for instance, finding five acorns, climbing a hill, whatever you like). Tell them about some historical adventures (Marco Polo, Scott of the Antarctic, Vasco de Gama, etc.).

Level up: Make the adventure a treasure hunt with a checklist of what to find. Add a compass and teach about the cardinal points and how (and why) the north is magnetic. Have your kids photograph or make a video recording of the adventure.

7. **Bake Something Beyond Cookies**

Try simple cinnamon sugar poppers made from premade puff pastry. Cut the pastry into strips. Roll each strip into a ball. Drop the ball into a bath of melted butter, milk, sugar, and cinnamon. Roll it around then place it on baking paper on a tray and bake for twelve minutes at 160°C. Let them cool and start popping!

Level up: Make a frosting dip for them. Make more elaborate cinnamon rolls. Make your own puff pastry.

8. **Get in Touch with Nature**

Let your kids touch nature. We're often too distanced from it. We watch documentaries or take walks and observe, but there's nothing like tactility. Start with a lady bug (unobjectionable, not gooey, no teeth).

Level up: Pill bug, earthworm, snail, slug

9. Microwave Sweets

This is easy, delicious and can be done anywhere with a microwave, even if you don't have access to an oven. Talk about what key ingredients go into cakes and brownies (eggs, flour, butter or oil, sugar, a rising agent, chocolate). A microwave works by heating the water that is in foods at a cellular level so it steams the sweet from within. We started with cake in a mug.

Level up: brownies, three-layer cake (with Nutella between layers and freestyle decorations on top)

10. Videogame Lessons

Look, kids love video games. In moderation, they can be great and even learning experiences. Don't just see video games as a distraction that gives parents some downtime. Take fifteen minutes to play with your kids, proactively, asking them about what's going on, the backstory, and so on. They're great for learning to read, for understanding English, and the best games aren't mindless but involve strategy and problem-solving.

Level up: We played *Zelda* on the Wii, and when the hero turned into a wolf, we discussed the term "lupine," meaning wolf-like. Then we added other animal terms, like bovine, canine, feline, leonine, aquiline, porcine, etcetera. Then we fought some bad guys. It was awesome.

11. Make Tiny Books

The British Library has a collection of tiny books made in the Victorian era for girls to read aloud to their dolls. They have a website with some didactic info and various children's authors making their own tiny books, plus instructions to make yours at home. We folded an A4 paper into eight rectangles and cut them into four sections to bind like a book with a brightly colored cover and an elastic for the spine.

Level up: Then we each wrote a story and illustrated it. Then we read them to each other.

12. Let David Attenborough Be Your Guide

Attenborough is the benevolent god of nature documentaries. He can do no wrong. He is calming, informative, engaging. Set up any of his documentaries and let him guide you. But be a proactive participant. Ask

your kids questions throughout and after, repeat key facts and be sure they are understanding what is happening in the documentary.
Level up: Work backward as Attenborough's older documentaries will require more focus from your kids than the newer ones.

13. **Track Animals**

Look for animal tracks in the wilderness, whatever is native to your area. We followed deer tracks and talked about distinguishing different types of tracks (paws vs. hooves vs. cloven hooves).
Level up: Try tracking insects. There's another Noah Charney who is a biologist specializing in insect tracking. With a name like that, he's got to be good!

14. **Tree-Spotting 101**

Walk in the woods and have your kids gather different leaves. Identify which tree they match. Talk about some of the characteristics of the trees. Then send them on treasure hunts with a checklist to bring back a leaf each, without using the original leaves gathered as a reference. Can you name the trees these leaves go with?
Level up: Go with more exotic trees, bushes, or grasses.

15. **Spot the Weird in a Hieronymus Bosch Painting**

You don't have to be an art historian like me to play this lesson game. Bosch is famous for his fantastic, weird, hybrid creatures, but his paintings also contain "normal" animals. Introduce kids to great art by having them spot the normal animals and the invented or hybrid ones. Start with *The Garden of Earthly Delights*.
Level up: Try other Bosch paintings; paintings by other artists; or go to a museum if you can and play the game live, in front of the original art.

16. **Learn About Shadows**

My daughter asked me why shadows are sometimes long and sometimes short. Super question. We set up a demo with a toy and a light to show the location of a light source, like the sun or a flashlight, and how it casts shadows of various lengths depending on where it is in relation to the object.

Level up: Go outside in the sunshine and reproduce shadows; have your kids estimate shadow length and location based on where light sources are; look at a painting with strong chiaroscuro (the play of light emerging from shadow) and ask them where the light source in the painting must be.

17 & 18. Learn Roman Numerals/Read Sundials

These can be done while playing *Tomb Raider: Anniversary*, as we did it. We were playing *Tomb Raider* and encountered a puzzle involving a sundial with Roman numerals. It was a great chance to teach them. We learned the basics of Roman numerals. Then we learned the basics of sundials. We put the two together and made a sundial out of paper, marked it with Roman numerals, and made a dial out of a piece of cardboard. We put it out in the sun and tried to make it work.

Level up: Write out 1 to 10 (or I to X) in Roman numerals; do some basic math using Roman numerals.

19. Gather Elderflowers

Elderflowers are wonderfully tasty and easy to transform into a drink and dessert. Gather them as far from a road as possible (so they won't be dusty). Take the fullest flower clusters and fry them in simmering oil. Let them drain on a paper towel, dust with confectioner's sugar and eat! Dry the other flowers to make tea or soak them in water with sugar and lemons to make a cordial.

Level up: Make an elderflower syrup by heating the cordial and thickening it with sugar and a bit of gelatin.

20. Adopt a Critter for a Sleepover Party

A lucky snail was picked up in the blazing sun and might've been an ex-snail had we not intervened. Instead of just bringing him to the shady woods, we adopted him for a single night before releasing him. We looked up what habitat would be ideal for an overnight and made a terrarium out of an empty jam container. We talked about the environment, plants, and food it might need. We handled it gently. It was a great chance to see nature up close. We left it in the jam jar but with the top off so it could leave whenever it liked.

Level up: Make an overnight terrarium for another creature who is somewhat more complex, like a frog.

21. Make Your Own Coat of Arms

We got into coats of arms from *Harry Potter*. We talked about their use (identifying armored knights in battle and at tournaments by painting the family armorial on a shield). We copied the Hogwarts armorial.
Level up: We then invented a Charney family armorial.

22. Fruit Picking

Take the kids to pick a fruit of your choice, outdoors or at a nursery. It's both a lovely time outdoors and a chance to teach about how fruit grows, the role of pits/stones to propagate trees, how birds eat and—yup—poo the pits to help create new trees (kids think this is hilarious). Then make one or more dishes starring that fruit.
Level up: Make a list of fruit to pick and make a point of going on an outing to pick each; make baked goods, juices, and jams out of the fruit.

23. Shop at a Superhero Store

The girls set up a shop with toys "for sale," but each had a special power, so they seemed like useful tools for battling evildoers. They set prices for each, depending on the extent of the powers, and gave out "money" in the form of blocks. It combined basic math with the concept of value, inventing powers, and even some basic haggling.
Level up: Buy increments or shares in superhero tools to practice fractions.

24. Learn the Value of Coins

Play "store" with real coins to start learning their value and recognizing them. Introduce divisibility (why should the coin with 2 on it be worth more than the one with 50?). And why should a larger coin be worth less than a smaller one?
Level up: Introduce paper money; introduce different currencies.

25. Make Your Own Van Gogh

Van Gogh paintings are actually pretty easy to copy, since they don't require realistic drawing skills and are really blocks of color that can be replicated with crayons or pastels. We browsed a book of his paintings and the girls picked one for us all to copy. We each made our own version of it. Meanwhile, we learned the artist's name, the technique of gloopy paint called *impasto*, and fun facts (like how he cut off his own ear—not sure if that counts as a "fun" fact, but it was certainly memorable).

Level up: Choose trickier paintings from his oeuvre; choose other artists who are more realistic in style; learn the names of the paintings you're copying.

26. Play with Anagrams

Anagrams are great fun and good practice for spelling and toying with the alphabet, as well as seeing things in a new way. The same collection of letters can have various meanings. We got into this through the second *Harry Potter* book, where the bad guy's name turns out to be an anagram for You-Know-Who. You can play with letters in lots of ways, but we have a tactile, analog board with stick-on letters, which I like. You can use Scrabble or Bananagrams tiles or make your own out of paper. See what can be spelled out with your kids' names.

Level up: Give kids a jumble of letters and ask them to spell multiple words using some of them; or make it harder and they have to use all of them; get really tricky and introduce palindromes.

27. Learn About and Draw an Exotic Animal

For a month one summer, we babysat a friend's axolotl. Yeah, I didn't know what they were either. So we made a lessonlet out of learning about them. You can do this with any exotic creature. Read an entry on them in an animal encyclopedia. Watch a YouTube documentary about them. Then draw one. While drawing, ask some questions about the animal that will review what you just learned/read/watched about them, to reinforce the facts.

Level up: Draw attributes learned along the way, for instance draw what the animal eats, draw a background suitable for their preferred environment, etc.

28. Turn Lemons into a Lemonade Lesson

Making homemade lemonade is fun, but it's also a chance to educate. Test and taste the balance of sweet (sugar, honey, or agave syrup) to sour lemon. Talk about why fruit like lemon has pits (to make lemon trees).

Level up: Try various additional flavorings (Melissa, mint, ginger, orange); talk about taste buds and test by rolling the lemonade over different parts of the tongue.

The Superpower Menu

29. Work on a Farm
Depending on where you live, this may be a daily occurrence or feel a lifetime away. But a day on a farm, working as much as possible, offers a great series of lessons both of how to do things (milk a cow) and where our food comes from (milk from a cow).
Level up: Take the basic farmed product, like milk, and process it into something else, like butter, cream, or cheese.

30. Military History Through Drawings
The girls wondered about differently shaped swords that they'd seen in various cartoons and video games. So I drew some of the most iconic and varied ones and we learned their names and basic shapes (broadsword, rapier, saber, scimitar, claymore). Then the girls drew them and wrote out the name, to create a weapon gallery.
Level up: Talk about how each was wielded and do some slow-motion play fighting to choreograph and help memorize basic distinctions (like piercing vs. slashing); watch HEMA (Historical European Martial Arts) tournaments online to see historians fighting with them for sport in traditional styles.

31 & 32. Egyptian Gods/Hieroglyphs
We took a virtual tour of the real tomb of Pharaoh Ramses VI (available online in a video-game-style navigable format). We saw real hieroglyphics and some gods with animal heads on the tomb walls. Then we opened *Picturepedia* to the ancient Egypt page and reinforced what we saw, learning some basics about mummies (whom we'd seen in *Hotel Transylvania* and *Scooby-Doo* episodes), some of the gods on Egypt (like Horus, with his falcon head) and some basic hieroglyphs.
Level up: Spell out some words transliterated with hieroglyphs (like your kids' names).

33. Show Photos from Your Past
A trip down memory lane is great for bonding and deepening your child's understanding of you and your background. Begin with the sort of photos that would be most interesting for kids, regardless of who is in them. This may not be a photo of you with Aunt Gertrude sitting on a rock, but a photo of a pet or your first time bungee jumping.

Level up: Show a complete series of photos from a particular time and place, quiz your kids about who is in photos they've seen before.

34. Care for Plants at Home or in the Garden

Give your kids responsibility for taking care of plants by watering them, first with your supervision, later on their own. It's a good early step toward responsibility for a pet. If a plant dries out because they forgot to water, then it can help drive home the point that responsibilities have consequences. Plants require delicacy (no overwatering) so this can bring out a new side to your child. Seeing the plant grow is a reward in patience.

Level up: Take your kids to a nursery and have them pick their own plant to take care of entirely on their own.

35. Learn to Make Cheese

There are rich, complex cheese traditions of the sort Food Network documentaries cover. Watch one of those. But then make cheese at home the easy way. You just need milk, vinegar and salt. Full fat, unpasteurized "raw" milk works best—easy to get in Europe, illegal in many parts of the United States, but even normal milk will work. Boil a gallon of milk and stir constantly. Then lower to a simmer and add ½ cup of vinegar, while you stir. The milk will curdle. Pour the curds into a strainer and rinse with cold water. Press them to get rid of extra liquid. This is your cheese. Flavor it with salt, but you can also add chives, pepper, garlic, whatever feels right. Now it has to dry, so wrap it in the aptly named cheesecloth, let it cool, then put it in the fridge. Voila!

Level up: Make more complex cheeses, like mozzarella.

36. Visit a Petting Zoo

Petting zoos are fun and also a great impetus to learn about the animals you'll see there. Use the Preview–Engage–Review system to first study up on the animals you will see before you go. Then have the kids name fun facts about the animals when you're there. When you're home, have them draw the animals and have a quiz about those fun facts, to see what they remembered.

Level up: Make a model of the petting zoo at home out of plasticine or just draw or paint one with all the animals present, and list the fun facts around the edges.

37. Needlepoint
Needlepoint is great for dexterity and respect for tools (the needle point isn't a toy). Draw a cute design on a piece of fabric and, with or without a stretcher, let your kid trace the lines with thread.
Level up: Opt for a more complex design; fill in sections with colored thread rather than just tracing the outlines.

38. Make Pancakes
Pancakes are easy—a cake in a pan. They've got the most basic ingredients (flour, egg, milk, sometimes a rising agent) but you can up your game with various add-ins. And there are several types of pancakes: Crepes, American, Dutch. This is likely the first thing your kids can cook by themselves, and it's universally loved. It can teach them about proportions of ingredients, either mathematically or just in terms of the proportions that have to be right for the end product to taste good.
Level up: Dutch pancakes are the trickiest, as they puff up in the oven if made properly, while crepes are so thin that they can also be hard to get right, so start with American-style puffy pancakes and work your way up; try making savory pancakes (blini) to top with sour cream and caramelized onions (or caviar, if you're into that sort of thing).

39. Knife Skills
Learning to use a knife safely and well is an important life skill. Start early and easy with a butter knife (or plastic picnic knife), one that cannot possibly injure anyone. Kick it off by slicing boiled carrots, which offer no resistance. Encourage equal-sized slices holding the knife with the tip on the cutting boarding then cleaving down with a repeated motion (the way chefs do, just in slo-mo). Move on to boiled hot dogs (which add a little more resistance and sometimes need a sawing motion).
Level up: Add different textured items to cut; teach how to safely cut rounded things (tomatoes, peaches) by first cutting one side to make a flat stand on which to balance the food in order to cut the rest without it dancing around.

40. Work with Chopsticks
Chopsticks can be tricky. I got nowhere until Travis Marshall (wonder what he's up to now) somehow taught me in second grade of elementary school.

Start by just letting kids play with them, and move on to trying to pick up large foods with good grip potential (like a slice of grilled chicken).
Level up: Grab slippery veggies or fruit pieces; pick up individual rice grains; if you're into *Karate Kid* then try to catch a fly.

41. Counting to Ten in Any Foreign Language

Learning foreign languages is an endless geyser of lessonlets and great exercise for the mind, whether or not you really need that new language. We've got a chapter on this, but in terms of lessonlets not related to picking up a new language entirely, a great way to play is to learn to count to ten. Depending on where you're from, pick easier languages first (in the United States, Spanish is the second language, while I grew up with French as the second language in school—in Slovenia, where I live now, the easiest to learn is Serbo-Croatian).
Level up: Tackle more exotic languages; turn to those with exotic alphabets, like Serbian or Chinese.

42. Playing "Store" to Learn About Coins

Every now and then on the landing in our house a store is set up. That's the aforementioned "Superhero Store," but that's more about the superhero tools than a lesson in shopping. This lessonlet focuses on prices and budgets. Distribute something that acts like coins (pieces of paper with numbers on them or, if you like, actual coins). Lay out household objects and assign them prices. Take turns buying. It's good for considering relative value of objects for sale, basic math and keeping track of your coins in order to buy what you need.
Level up: Have prices in decimals, not just round numbers.

43. Play the Translation Game

Mentioned in our chapter on foreign languages and on long trips, this game is ideal for multilingual families or those learning a new language at an advanced enough level to already have some basic vocabulary words. Try to stump the other players by asking for the translation of one word into your native language. Whoever gets the answer right asks the next question.
Level up: Go from your mother tongue into the foreign language (this is usually a bit harder); translate whole phrases (including idioms); translate whole sentences.

44. Play Name Ten

Start with a category (dinosaurs, vegetables, cities, etc.) and the player has to name ten of them. I might say "name ten fruits" and off the kids go, either as a team or solo. It's great for passing the time on trips and helps to organize concepts, objects, and words into categories, not just remembering the stand-alone word. Knowing that peaches, apples, mangos, and bananas are all fruits is helpful and a step up conceptually from just seeing an apple and saying, "That's an apple."

Level up: Make the categories more complicated, for instance "name ten carnivorous dinosaurs" or "name ten cities in Europe;" you can make this easier by playing Name Five or harder by playing Name Twenty.

45. Clean Around the House

Sound too good to be true for a lessonlet? Cleaning is only a chore if we make it feel like one. For kids, the younger the better, it can be a fun game. It's the opposite of a treasure hunt. Find objects where they shouldn't be, lying around the floor or the table, and return them to their proper place. You can sweeten the deal by giving a prize for helpers who help most (put away the most mess) and do so without complaining. You can make it more of a game by timing it (who can put away the most toys in five minutes), or a competition (whether this is a good idea depends on your kids and their dynamic).

Level up: Cleaning more properly (not just putting things away), like wiping the dining table or using a handheld vacuum cleaner.

46. Dance Routines

Kids love to dance, but you can make it a learning experience that promotes motor skills, concentration, and memorization by teaching them set dance moves. My girls started with "Macarena" and then we went with the 1980s Bar Mitzvah party favorite, "Electric Slide," both of which have a simple set of choreographed moves.

Level up: Have them emulate a favorite music video's dance moves (my girls love young dancer Maddie Ziegler, who appears in many Sia videos); get fancy with an actual dance style (like foxtrot or tango).

47. Yoga for Kids

Yoga is demonstrably good for everyone and everything. Whether you're into it is another story (I never could get into the groove, my wife loves it). Yoga for kids is beautiful for promoting patience, flexibility, the ability to follow instructions, body awareness and, in the meditative component, mindfulness. Find a yoga for kids video or a class and start with very basic moves (downward dog is always popular, as is tree pose and warrior pose). It can be even more of a game by suggesting that your kid practices enough until they can make their own yoga for kids video which they will lead.

Level up: With yoga you can level up indefinitely, over a lifetime, in both length of routines and complexity; see if your kids can memorize some of the names for poses—even the original Sanskrit names.

48. Make Your Own Volcano

Learn about volcanos through a documentary, then make one at home. You just need baking soda, soap and vinegar, although you can get fancier. Take a disposable glass jar and place it on a tray lined with foil (for easy cleanup). Fill the container 2/3 of the way with water. Add 4 tablespoons of baking soda, 1 teaspoon of dish soap and, if you like, 4 drops of food coloring. Stir. Drum roll. Then add 8 ounces of vinegar and watch the eruption.

Level up: Have your kids make a plasticine sculpture of a volcano with lava flow and use it to teach you parents about how volcanos work.

49. Bake Bread

We've covered baking cookies, but bread is its own thing. And it is surely a great life skill to be able to bake your own. Start with the very easiest—a bread flour mix to which you just add water, let rise, roll onto a baking surface and bake. You can do no-knead breads, but kids enjoy rolling and kneading the dough so don't be shy about it. It'll be a bit messy, but that's part of the fun (for them, at least). It's also a basic food chemistry lesson, particularly how the leavening agent works.

Level up: Move on to recipes for bread that doesn't come from a mix, to which you need to add your own yeast; take it up a notch with sourdough breads or gluten-free breads, which are trickier to make come out well; you can include braided loaves, marbled loaves (in two colors), or sweeter breads like challah or brioche.

50. Assemble a Sandwich

This might sound quotidian, but there's an art to making sandwiches that offers useful lessons. You can tell the (likely apocryphal) story of how the Earl of Sandwich wanted to eat with one hand while still playing cards and asked for meat pinched between two loaves of bread, inventing his namesake meal. Let your kids choose the bread (and perhaps slice it) and the stuffing (anything goes, from peanut butter and jelly to sour cream and honey to ham and mustard to whatever seems tasty). Let your kids make you lunch from various ingredients. It's empowering and inspires creativity and thinking about complementary flavors.

Level up: Make a toasted sandwich; go big with a club sandwich (three levels of bread).

51. Enliven Your Lexicon

Kids with elaborate vocabularies are extra cute. In a variation of the Synonym Game, or rather in preparation for it, introduce various words for the same thing. We did this by watching the classic Danny Kaye comedy, *The Court Jester*. There's a fall-off-your-seat-funny sequence that involves a vessel, a chalice, and a flagon. This was a chance to explain that each was a varied term for a cup, with slight differences. We drew each and then the girls memorized the whole comedic sequence. I like a five-year-old who can differentiate a chalice from a flagon.

Level up: Stump the family—we thought it was fun to try to get the girls to use, in casual conversation, words that their grandparents didn't know—we got them with "brachiation."

52. Identify Musical Instruments and Their Sounds

This is like a blind tasting for the ears. First show pictures of various instruments and play their sounds (there are websites that do just this, or you can use a synthesizer with various instrument options). Then play them again and have your kids guess which goes with which instrument.

Level up: Play a piece of classical music and have the kids list all the instruments they hear.

53. Send Them on a Treasure Hunt

This is a lessonlet that encourages problem-solving and puzzling and being observant. But it's also a good addition to *any* lessonlet. Treasure hunts can be thematic and linked to whatever your kids just learned the last week. You can make clues that are coupled with lessons. For example, "the next treasure is where we made lunch yesterday" or "the next treasure is where Mommy and Daddy dream." We use treasure hunts instead of tests to consolidate knowledge of the week. They are always a hit.

Level up: Require your kids to read a new clue at each location discovered, rather than having a single treasure (a candy, a toy, a coin) at each location; have your kids make treasure hunts for each other or for you.

54. Decorate Easter Eggs the Old-Fashioned Way (stockings and onions)

Ideal for Easter, decorating eggs the store-bought food coloring way is fine, but there's an old school approach that is more resonant. Collect onion skin for a few weeks leading up to Easter (or whenever you do this activity) and then boil as much of it as you have in water. Gather some wildflowers or blades of grass and tie them to the eggs with old pieces of stocking. Then drop the eggs inside. The onion skin provides a natural dye, coloring all the egg aside from where the flowers or grass stuck to the shell.

Level up: Add more complex designs and lay out blades of grass in specific patterns (like crisscrossed) rather than random.

55. Geography Quiz

Learning about countries offers lots of opportunities. You can find them on a map or globe, learn capital cities, national anthems, tourist sites, even gross national products (if that's your thing). We use an interactive globe that comes with a wand—you touch it to a country, and it tells you the country's name and there are built-in quizzes or facts. You can use this, or a normal world map or atlas or even Google Earth. Start with just naming continents, then move up to countries.

Level up: Step it up with capital cities, tourist sites, languages, and more.

56. Explore the World via Google Earth and Walkthroughs

This was touched upon in its own chapter, but Google Earth and YouTube "walkthroughs" offer an infinite well of goodness. "Travel" without leaving home to places that come up in conversation, or where you or relatives are from, or places you learn about through TV, film, or documentaries.

Level up: We try to be more organized and work our way through major sites by theme, for instance ancient Egypt, and we'll "visit" several sites in a row to solidify and deepen the lessons linked to this era.

57. Still-Life Drawing

This is a foundation of any drawing class. Let your kids assemble a still-life (a bowl of fruit, objects, or toys from around the house). Then ask them to draw it from whatever angle they like, with whatever medium they like. Drawing something forces you to look more deeply, in a more nuanced, patient, detailed way.
Level up: Use colors instead of just black and white.

58. Interior Design

How would you decorate various rooms in our house? With your kids, draw the bird's-eye-view of a room in the house and then make proportional cutouts of various furniture items (that you already have or invented ones). You can find cutouts to print online or make your own. Ask your kids how they would arrange furniture and let them choose wallpaper or rugs from online vendors with visual catalogues or paint walls.
Level up: Design a whole apartment or house with multiple rooms.

59. Design Your Dream House

What would your kids' dream house look like? Ask them to draw a view of it from various angles. Be sure they consider the rooms that need to be included, like bathrooms and a kitchen and bedrooms.
Level up: Make a blueprint (bird's-eye-view) as well as a frontal view; design a dream tree house.

60. Castle Architecture

I loved designing castles with defenses when I was very little. I spent some holidays in France visiting castles with my parents, and they really stimulated my imagination. So with the girls, we looked at a book on castles and talked about the different architectural elements and what they were for (arrow slits, drawbridge, portcullis, moat, towers, ramparts). This concept could be applied to any building type (churches, stadiums, airports, etc.).

Level up: Now it's time to design your own. We drew each component part and then the girls drew these assembled into their own imaginary castle.

61-71. Play Chess/Play Backgammon/Play Dominoes/Play Mahjong/Play Checkers/Play Chinese Checkers/Play Mancala/Play Reversi/Play Snakes and Ladders/Play Yahtzee

These are ten lessonlets in one, all to do with traditional board games. These games have their own rich cultural history and they promote logic, thinking ahead, and sportsmanship. They also naturally allow for leveling up simply through experience, becoming a better player. Chess, for example, is really the richest of them all. We began with Battle Chess, with animating fighting when one piece takes another, which adds a visual stimulation bonus for children. We also used some apps that teach kids how to play by only allowing correct moves for each piece, so kids can gradually learn. These are also good for promoting sportsmanship. Fun is the key, whining if you lose is uncool. Being cool when you win and when you lose is a sign of maturity.

Level up: Simply play at a more advanced level, either the computer or opponents; add in favorite games from your own childhood.

72. Play Croquet

Combining strategy with physical execution, croquet is beneficial for mapping out the playing area (and inserting the hoops) as well as playing. Learning that swinging as hard as possible is not the best way to win is useful for little kids. And as they grow stronger, you can sprawl out the field of play.

Level up: Let your kids set up the field of play; add in the option of smacking your opponent's ball away if you bump it (this can get nasty, so judge whether your kids will benefit from this rule).

73. Learn the Rules of a Sport

The world of sport is a layer cake of goodness. You can play the sport yourself, enjoy watching matches, engage with stats (which can be a fun rabbit hole down which to tumble for older kids) and understand rules. Pick your sport. I tried to teach my girls baseball, and it's very tricky if you don't grow up with it organically. That qualifies as a level up. Something

more straightforward like basketball is good, or darts, billiards, track and field, you name it.
Level up: Complex sports like baseball or cricket.

74. **Pick a Sport and a Team to Cheer for and Learn Their Players and Stories**
Watching sport is much more fun when you have a team and follow its stories, melodramas, statistics, and successes. I grew up a Red Sox fan for baseball. When I moved to England, I wanted to watch football (a.k.a. soccer) but opted to choose a team to follow in order to make it more fun. It was arbitrary that I picked Manchester City. They had just been bought by wealthy owners but were being teased and looked down upon, so they had an underdog story to them despite their enormous new riches. So I became a Man City fan by reading the always ingenious and hilarious *Guardian* football section. When I lived in Rome, I added Roma to my list. If you already follow a team sport and a team, then teach your kids all about it. Get them the kit to wear and cheer while watching games. If you don't have one yet, choose one. It's a great family bonding opportunity and there are many lessons to find within them, particularly if you like statistics.
Level up: Let your kids choose an entirely new team and sport and join their enthusiasm for it.

75. **Make Coffee or Tea for the Grownups Just the Way They Like It**
We parents are always making things for our kids, so how about we turn a little switcheroo into a lessonlet? Teach kids to make you coffee or tea just the way you like it. It empowers the kids to be able to make something grownup for a grownup and they'll be delighted to do something nice for you. Start with just adding a teabag, milk, and sugar to a cup and you handle the boiling water for tea. When they get older, they can do it all, including boil water in the kettle.
Level up: Make more complicated drinks, like espresso shots or cocktails (no tasting allowed for juniors).

76. **Shadow Animals with Your Hands**
The game of making animal shapes with your hands in front of a light source, and casting shadows on the wall, is likely one you've done already.

But make it into a lesson about shadow and also imitation of the shapes of animals and their heads. See how many you and your kids can do, then make a game of guessing what it is you are making. You could also put on a shadow play together, with a light making a shadow for each and have the shadows interact.

Level up: Make more complex animal shapes; act out some of Aesop's Fables or other animal tales your kids might know.

77. Learn to Whistle

This is one of those activities that I couldn't for the life of me figure out how to explain to my kids with verbal instructions (and I'm a professor, so I'm supposed to know this sort of stuff). But it's a useful thing to learn and kids feel like it's a proper superpower. Sometimes imitation is the best way to learn, rather than a complicated explanation. Inhaling and whistling first seems easier than proper whistling through expelling air.

Level up: Perform some whole songs by whistling, then play the game of "Name That Tune" with whistling.

78. Learn Your National Anthem

Turn patriotic and teach your kids your national anthem. You can practice singing it together. At first they'll probably just sing what sounds sort of like the lyrics but aren't really, and that's fine. Getting the tune right is step one. Talk about what a national anthem is and when it's normally played (at medal ceremonies, before sporting events, etc.). Some national anthems, like America's beautiful "Star-Spangled Banner," have interesting origin stories.

Level up: Help your kids memorize the proper lyrics; learn the national anthem of another country.

79. Identify Flags

At some point early on in school, kids are likely to do an exercise in which they color in their national flag. This is good to do at home but expand your horizons and learn the flags of other countries, too.

Level up: You can make or print flashcards and quiz your kids on which flag is associated with which country; learn all the flags of a continent; let kids invent a flag of their own imaginary country.

80. **Identify Geometric Shapes**
Learning the proper names of things—whatever they may be—is useful early on and critical during student years. So try out geometric shapes next. Have your kids draw them (using a ruler preferably) and write out their names. Then you can make or print out flashcards to quiz, first on simpler shapes (triangles, circles, squares) and graduating to more complex (rhomboids, pentagons, ovals).
Level up: Use the shapes to make abstract patterns by assignment, for instance "make a pattern using four triangles, two circles and three squares."

81. **Learn Single Vanishing Point Perspective**
This is a popular one with art historians. The discovery of how to mathematically calculate and create accurate perspectival depth so that a two-dimensional object like a painting looks three-dimensional to the eye was the biggest advance of Renaissance painting. The easiest way to reproduce it is to draw a horizon line. Then draw a dot somewhere along it. That's our single vanishing point. I like to add a sun setting over the horizon with that dot as its center. Then draw two lines emerging from that dot and running to the bottom edge of your paper. This might look like train tracks that disappear over the horizon. Now add lots more lines, all emerging from that dot on the horizon and running to the bottom edge of the page. These are called orthogonal lines and they'll look like rays shooting out of the vanishing point. Finally, on the half of the paper below the horizon line draw horizontal, parallel lines, many of them, but with a trick: those nearer the bottom of the page should be spaced more widely apart and those nearer the horizon line closer and closer together. This results in a three-dimensional plane. We imagine that each resulting square would be the same size if we looked at them from above, but from the perspective we've established, those nearer to us, the viewers, appear larger and those we imagine are farther from our eyes appear smaller. Remember the movie *Tron*?
Level up: Add figures to this plane, making those standing closer to the bottom of the page (which we imagine as closer to us, the viewer) larger and those nearer the horizon line (farther from the viewer) proportionally smaller.

82. Identify Artistic Styles

Call me an art historian, but I think this is a great game. Learning artistic movements, even the most basic distinctions between them, is great and ups the level of museum visits significantly. Show your kids multiple examples of each style. Try styles that are very different at first: Abstract Expressionism vs. Realism, Sienese Gothic vs. Surrealism, Fauvism vs. Cubism. Work your way up to those with subtler differences (High Renaissance vs. Mannerism). Then have a quiz, showing a painting and asking them to name the style.
Level up: Raise the bar by having kids memorize the names of some painters or even individual paintings in each style; have your kids draw or paint the same subject (a bowl of fruit, a horse?) in a variety of artistic styles.

83. Learn to Juggle

Juggling is great for concentration and hand-eye coordination. Start with a single ball throwing it up gently and catching it with the same hand. Then throw with one hand and catch with the other. Then a ball in each hand, tossing the ball to the other hand in an X pattern. When you feel confident, add that third ball. Beanbag balls are good, but the easiest to learn with are things that have a lot of hang time, like tissues or air-filled balloons. Heavier, more compact things are hardest.
Level up: Work your way to juggling heavier objects; add a fourth item to juggle; try to do something else while juggling (walking, dancing, blindfolded).

84. Drill Sports

Drills for sports are fun on their own and develop coordination, whether or not your kids play the sports in question. Juggle a soccer ball (a.k.a. a football) to keep it off the ground and see how many touches you can make without it dropping. Play tennis against a wall and see how long your rally with the wall can last. Dribble a basketball and see how long you can keep it up, including dribbles between your legs.
Level up: Drill with a partner, juggling a ball between you, keeping up a tennis rally, trying to steal a basketball from one another.

85. Play Mirror My Movements

Make like a mime, or that great scene in *Duck Soup* where Harpo Marx plays a mirror game (copied in a famous *I Love Lucy* skit). Two players stand facing each other just a foot or so apart. One leads and moves any way they like while remaining in place. The other player has to copy their movements as precisely as possible, so they appear to a bystander to be a person and their mirror reflection. This encourages concentration and allows you to teach about mirrors.

Level up: Have the player intentionally do the opposite of what the lead player does.

86. Blind Taste Fruit or Vegetables

This stimulates the sense of taste and encourages memorization of names and flavors. Slice up a selection of fruit and/or veg. You can show your kids which you choose and let them taste in advance, or make it trickier and keep it a surprise. A plate of apple, pear, peach, grape, banana—whatever you and your kids like.

Level up: You can sneak in something they've not tried before and see what they think, as tasting should be blindfolded; you can integrate several varietals of the same thing (Granny Smith, Braeburn, Pink Lady, and Golden Delicious apples have very subtle differences).

87. Memorize and Recite a Poem

Really? Well, yes, we all had to do this in school and there is a reason for it. It's not just a parlor trick, but memorizing and interpreting a poem, *feeling* the words, is good for reading deeply, and also performing is empowering. So have your kids pick a poem, memorize it and recite it in front of the family. Tell them the story of the poem and the poet, help them understand it thoroughly, not superficially.

Level up: Recite more complex, longer poems; recite a poem in a foreign language; write a poem and recite it.

88. Put on a Puppet Show

Maybe you have puppets at home, or you can make some hand puppets from socks? You can watch a puppet show and repeat it, but it's much cooler if you either write one with your kids or improv—decide on your characters and a situation and what should happen by the end of the scene, and then let her rip. Talk about the history and tradition of puppets in various cultures and the psychology of why talking through something else

can often be a vehicle for children to express more complex internal issues that are hard to bring up directly.
Level up: Make your own puppets and write your own puppet show; make a video of the puppet show, like a short film.

89. Learn about Magnets

Magnets are magical and a chance for a lesson on attraction and repulsion. They are also fun to play with. I grew up with a set of metal geometric shapes that you could balance on a magnetic board and stack into three-dimensional structures.
Level up: Play with magnet strengths and see how heavy a load each one can lift or attract.

90. Navigate with a Compass

Carrying on from the magnet theme, teach your kids to find their way with a compass. Step one is to learn the cardinal points, and this is best done with a map. Have your kids draw their own compass and label north, south, east, and west. Once they get the hang of the main four, add the incremental steps (north northwest, etc.). Explain why a compass will always point to the north (there's a magnet in the compass that can spin freely—it always ends up pointing toward the Earth's magnetic field, which is about a thousand miles south of the North Pole, in Canada. Knowing roughly where you are and knowing which way is north allows you to figure out how to get elsewhere.
Level up: Set out in the woods with a compass and a map and ask your kid to guide you.

91. Plan What to Pack

Pick an expedition (real, like a holiday to the beach, or invented, like a holiday to the beach) and ask your kid what they think they should pack to go there. Decide how many days you'll be away, help them know what the climate will be like that time of year, and ask them to make their packing list. If you like they can actually pack, and you can teach them some basics of packing (rolling shirts to avoid wrinkles and maximize space, for instance). They should pack only what they can reasonably carry themselves. This helps them think ahead.

Level up: Ask them what the whole family should pack, which might include things like medicines, toiletries, chargers, and other items that kids usually don't think twice about.

92. Longitude and Latitude Treasure Hunt

Explain the basics of longitude and latitude. Find your own location this way and a few others (maybe a grandparents' house).
Level up: When your kids get the hang of it, send them on a virtual treasure hunt. Give them ten coordinates and ask them to find what cities or famous sites are found at each set of coordinates (without using the internet).

93. Fire Safety

This is a lessonlet that can save a life. Teach your kids about what fire is, how it is made, why it appears in nature. Emphasize the severity of messing with it (if you feel it is appropriate, show them video of uncontrolled forest fires, the devastation of their aftermath, or even selected pictures of people with mild burn injuries—nothing too scary, but enough for them to understand how dangerous fire can be). Then teach them fire safety. The fact that heat rises, for instance, and most deaths due to fire are from suffocation, so if there's ever a fire, they should get as low to the ground as possible, and so on.
Level up: Introduce fire-extinguishing methods (various fire extinguishers, using water, smothering a flame) and even basics of burn first aid.

94. Stretch Like an Athlete

Stretching is overlooked in sport and life, but it's hugely beneficial. For kids it's also fun. So introduce a basic stretching routine, do it regularly with your kids, then let them lead you in a routine of their choice using the stretches you taught them.
Level up: Have your kids design a stretching routine and let them lead you through it.

95. Practice Coin Tricks

A coin can be a font of fun. There are whole books of coin tricks, but you can start with flipping a coin, guessing "heads or tails" and talking about percentages and chance. You can talk about the history of coins and learn their value. You can roll the coin around your knuckles.

Level up: Learn a disappearing coin magic trick or four-card-monte style sleights of hand.

96. Write in Different Fonts
Kids often learn to write and read in caps and move on to lowercase. But once they've got that covered, you can show them various fonts and encourage them to write out the alphabet or their name in that font. Then they can pick their favorite or even invent their own font.
Level up: Try to write while looking in a mirror; or if you want to get crazy, make like Leonardo da Vinci and practice writing so that the words are only legible when you look at them using a mirror.

97. Grains
Kids might think "bread is bread," but there's a world of grains out there to try, wheat being just one of them. Barley, rye, buckwheat, millet, Kamut, and alternatives like rice and corn can all be introduced. First, go over the process of growing, harvesting and processing each grain. Then try baking bread made with each grain. You can do a taste test, baked or store-bought, to introduce your kids to the flavors and textures.
Level up: Make it a blind tasting; taste the grains when prepared in different ways (polenta, pearl barley, risotto).

98. Memorize Birthdays
I used to know lots of birthdays (and phone numbers and addresses). Memorizing things, unsurprisingly, helps improve memory and the speed of recall in general, and it's a necessary skill for school. A good way to start is to help kids memorize their own birthdays, then those of family members.
Level up: Add other important dates, like holidays; add historical dates of important events.

99. Origami
This art form is simple for kids to practice, just folding paper and often making fun animals, but it's also sophisticated and can be tricky to do. It moves from simple to hugely complex, so there's room for expansion and it shows how a single, basic thing—a piece of paper—can transform into anything. Learn about its rich history and tour some impressive

examples of it online. Particularly videos of experts creating work quickly are fascinating.
Level up: Move on to more complex design; try to design your own origami project.

100. Target Practice
Whatever your missile of choice (we like water guns or those Velcro balls that are like proto-darts), help your kids hone their aim by practicing hitting a target from various angles and at various distances. They'll feel good about visible improvement.
Level up: Introduce some basic physics, like the force of gravity pulling projectiles down so aim a bit higher than you'd think to.

101. Beauty Salon
Makeup is a grownup thing, and there's no rush for kids to wear it regularly or outside of the house. But it can be fun to put it on, it can be fun to style your hair, to paint nails. There's also an artistry to it, applying it with subtlety, that you can teach. You can find looks online and try to match them. You can describe what cosmetics are made of and the history of them (ancient Egyptians used lead—bad idea).
Level up: Let your kids do their own styling to mimic a photo they found; let your kids style you.

102. Make Your Own Soap
With the raw material of glycerin soap (you can use lye, but it can be more problematic) you can design and make your own soap. Pick a mold, add natural coloring and your choice of fragrance oil. Explain how soap works—dirt attaches to it and falls away when your rinse it off with soap. Kids like the fun fact that, just a few generations ago, a bath was a rare event, monthly in many cases. With homemade soap, bath time is extra fun and feels more like a personal accomplishment.
Level up: Make various soaps to give as gifts; make shampoo.

103. Face Painting
Halloween face painting can be done any time. Face paint is easy to come by and you can paint your kids' faces like animals or characters. What makes this educational is the way it promotes looking more deeply. Let your kid

paint your face in imitation of an animal and they start to notice details of the animal—the prominence of whiskers on a cat, for instance—that they otherwise would have glossed over. It's a similar depth to having to draw something from a model but includes the fun of dressing up.
Level up: Shift to more complicated designs that are more realistic.

104. Animal Sound Charades
Moving like animals is fun but so is making their sounds. Teach your kids about the sounds animals make and then play charades by having to name the animal imitated.
Level up: Add more exotic animals (everyone can moo, but how about mimicking a giraffe?)

105. Role-Playing
I loved role-playing games as a kid. Dungeons & Dragons, *Final Fantasy*. Introduce role-playing first with your kid as him or herself. Describe a situation involving them and ask what they would do next. It provides imaginative hypotheticals that let you explore how your child would react and allows you to suggest possibly preferable reactions.
Level up: Play role-playing games like Dungeons & Dragons or video games, so your kid designs and leads a character.

106. Is It Moral?
A role-playing game in which you lay out scenarios and what a character does, then ask your kid if what they did is moral. Your definition of morality is your own, so tailor it to suit. It tests your kids to do the right thing and lets you guide them and suggest more moral ways forward.
Level up: Have your kids explain to you (or write out) the family's rules on moral behavior.

107. Solubility
A simple chemistry lesson can come when mixing your kid's favorite powdered drink into water. They see this a lot but now you can put a name to it. That's what so much learning is all about. Explain how various liquids can dissolve various solids at various speeds. Take a variety of forms of sugar: cube, normal, confectioners. Use a stopwatch and add the same weight of each to the same amount of water and see how long they take to dissolve,

once while stirring once without. You can try it with salt (finely ground and chunky) and then reverse the process and boil the water to evaporate it and see if you can end up with salt at the bottom of the pan.
Level up: Introduce saturation—when a liquid cannot absorb any more dissolved matter; step deeper into the chemistry.

108. Dance Moves to Match Video
It will likely happen naturally that your kids will mimic a video of people dancing. Doing so can be developed into a lessonlet that helps them learn focus, memorization, balance, and coordination. Tell them about the video and song they're dancing along to. Let them choose which to try out. It can be a game in which the closer they mimic the moves they see, the better.
Level up: Introduce formal dances (tango, fox trot) and the terms that go with them; make a video of them dancing along and then run the video of them alongside the original to see how accurate they are.

109. Basics and History of Martial Arts
Like so many nineties' kids, I watched *Karate Kid* and was hooked. Martial arts are brilliant for kids, teaching them discipline, training, toughness and the always useful skill of being able to defend oneself. Introduce a variety of martial arts through videos, discuss the history of the martial art and the philosophy (the bigger you are doesn't mean the better a fighter you'll be).
Level up: Learn some basic moves; enroll them in classes.

110. Wrestling Greco-Roman vs. Sumo
It's not only boys who find fighting fascinating (you should see my girls as unicorns doing battle with dragons and/or dinosaurs), so introducing kids to the rich cultural traditions of combat is a winning lessonlet. If *Street Fighter II* has taught us anything (and what hasn't it taught us, really) it's that styles of fighting are of particular interest. So introduce your kids to two wrestling traditions, Greco-Roman and Sumo. Show them clips of competitions and introduce some moves. Ask what differences they notice in the rules and techniques. Asking what kids notice is always a good thing—it tells them that their opinion and view is important and encourages them to look deeper.

Level up: Learn some basic moves to try out (in slow motion); pick a "favorite" competitor and follow their career for a while—sport is more fun when you have someone to cheer for; enroll in classes for either.

111. Vive la Différence
As we've said more than once, simply asking your kids for their opinion empowers them in many ways. It also encourages analytical, deconstructionist thinking, scanning for differences like the Spot the Difference kids' game of two nearly identical drawings with a few hidden differences to seek and circle. This lessonlet recommendation is really an approach to which you can apply any concept you like. It can be images (two photographs or perhaps two *Annunciation* paintings, one by Crivelli one by Leonardo), two songs ("500 Miles" by the Proclaimers and the punk cover of the same song by Down By Law), two roughly parallel sports (the aforementioned Greco-Roman vs. Sumo wrestling, or baseball vs. cricket).
Level up: Ask your kids to be the quiz masters and ask you what the differences are; print out two images (like two *Annunciation* paintings) and have them label the differences and also the similarities.

112. Name That Tune
The old game show is fun to play at home. We began inadvertently. My girls would be singing something, using dummy lyrics and barely managing the tune, and my wife and I would try to figure out what the heck they were singing. But it becomes an organized game when you've built up a library of songs and can try to stump each other by singing, humming, or whistling (or even clapping to the rhythm) without any words.
Level up: If they get too good, start humming just the verses but not the chorus—this requires really good listening skills and recall.

113. Be Funny
Can you teach someone how to be funny? Sort of. Some people are naturally so, but the best comedians study their art and practice it extensively. Ask your kids to define what is funny and give examples. Show them clips of videos you find funny ("The pellet with the poison" from *The Court Jester*, the stateroom scene from *A Night at the Opera*, everything in the movie *Airplane!*). Teach them some basic jokes and ask them to tell the jokes to others. They'll get a sense for comic timing. It never occurs to most people

to ask what they find funny or what something funny *is*. Asking such questions leads to interesting discussions.
Level up: Have your kids write a joke, then put on a comedy show when they've developed enough material.

114. Discover Penicillin
Tell the important story of discovering penicillin, which its discoverer, Alexander Fleming, first called "mold juice." In 1928 he came back from a holiday to find that a mold was contaminating some Petri dishes in his lab, and this mold was killing the bacteria in the dish. This was the birth of antibiotics, which are so hugely important to modern medicine. Explain how they are used and make a homemade version—just let something get moldy. It won't be covered in penicillin, per se, but it will hammer home the anecdote.
Level up: Watch a video of how antibiotics kill bacteria under a microscope; make a list of illnesses that come from bacteria and therefore which antibiotics can cure; eat blue cheese to show that mold can be delightful.

115. How Do Vaccines Work?
Like the anecdote about penicillin, the story of Edward Jenner discovering a vaccine for deadly smallpox (he noted that milkmaids, in daily contact with cows, were immune—it was because they caught cowpox, harmless to humans, and getting this illness made them immune to the really bad one) is a fun, memorable story. The concept of intentionally giving yourself a tiny amount of an illness to train your body to resist a big dose of it is mind-blowing. This is ideally done when your kids are off to get a vaccine anyway, to help them understand why it's cool. Each vaccine literally gives them the superpower of being immune to an illness!
Level up: Teach about all the devastating illnesses eliminated thanks to vaccines, to help them become enthusiastic about their jabs; make a list of illnesses that are no longer a threat thanks to vaccines.

116. Why Does Hair Grow?
Hair is there to keep us warm and to provide a cushion (think of hair as a soft helmet). We don't really need either function in the modern era, what with hats and, if you need them, helmets, so now it's more about the look. Show kids follicles on their skin (we're born with around five million of

them). Each can grow a hair. By combining anecdotes with fun facts with a bit of science, the lessons are more fun and better retained.
Level up: Consider various hair types and styles; explain how hair growth formulae work.

117. Make Your Own Tea Bag

How tea steeps is linked to the lessonlet in solubility, but it's one that you can see when the tea is colored. Let it steep in a glass and watch the flavors diffuse into the hot water. Look at the ingredient list in fruit tea and see how many you're familiar with. You can look up those they don't know (hibiscus and rosehip for example).
Level up: Make your own tea—you can get reusable tea bags and loose tea, or dry your own goodies and make your own recipes.

118. Draw Geometric Shapes and Rulers

Use a compass to draw circles and a protractor to draw angles. Name various geometric shapes and show the difference between ovals and circles, acute versus obtuse angles.
Level up: Ditch the protractor and use a ruler to reproduce angles at precise lengths (to encourage your kids to learn to read ruler markings).

119. Read My Lips

Reading lips is an art form—when my mother's hearing grew iffy, but before she got a hearing aid, she had no trouble understanding someone if she could see their lips moving. It can be a game that develops a talent. Mouth words or phrases silently and have your kids guess what you're saying. Then have them do so for you. Keep score if you like.
Level up: Introduce what it would be like to be deaf and have lip reading be critical, to help promote understanding.

120. Name Kings or Presidents

It's an "old school" school exercise, to memorize the names, dates, and important acts of kings and presidents. It's a bit passé. But it can be fun, and memorizing anything is good for the mind. Plus, it can only help in school. So start with a few historical figures with distinctive stories (George Washington with wooden teeth, Richard the Lionheart who appears in the Robin Hood stories) and pepper the anecdotes with some dates, but don't

sweat the strict memorization. What's most important is keeping it fun and interesting—any facts they recall about historical figures are good ones.
Level up: What I just wrote about not sweating the memorization? Level up by sweating it. Focus on memorization more than you had before.

121. How to Read a Menu
One of my books is about my adopted homeland, Slovenia, and there's a section for foreigners on how to read Slovenian menus. Well, for kids anywhere, menus at restaurants require a roadmap. So one day, when you're out at a restaurant anyway, ask to hang onto the menu for the meal and teach them about appetizers, hors d'oeuvres, entrees, sides, desserts, beverages, and tipping.
Level up: Have your kids make a menu of their own imaginary restaurant, then have them be waiters to walk you through the menu.

122. Make Your Own Mayo
We'll put mayo on anything—the favorite Charney condiment. It's very easy to make your own. Mayo is just oil and egg. You can add mix-ins, like garlic, to make aioli.
Level up: Try other "mother sauces" from the French arsenal, like hollandaise or bearnaise.

123. Design a Dinosaur
Consider aspects of various dinosaurs and how they might be combined into your kids' choice of an ultimate dinosaur. The head of a tyrannosaurus with the tail of an ankylosaurus? Here's the trick: the imaginary dinosaur should be physiologically viable (more or less). No tyrannosaur head on a long brachiosaur neck. This lets kids flex their knowledge of dinosaurs and also their logic.
Level up: Draw the new dinosaur and write out its attributes, where it lives, what it eats.

124. Basics of Massage
Learn some massage basics and teach your kids. Practice on each other. Just the simple motions of a shoulder rub can offer a lesson into anatomy (where to massage—muscles, not on bone) and who doesn't like a massage, right?
Level up: Shift to some specialized massage moves, like shiatsu chopping.

125. Identifying Road Signs
Get started early for the driver's test by helping kids learn road signs. They're seeing them constantly as you drive, but it likely never registered to try to "read" them. A stop sign is easy for starters, then work your way up.
Level up: Ask your kid to navigate while you drive, telling you which signs they see and how you should drive accordingly.

126. Evolution of Prehistoric to Modern Animals
In our *Picturepedia* book, there's a section with pictures of a modern elephant and all the past evolutionary increments, dating back to the earliest Ice Age predecessors. You can follow this example with other animals, talk about how and why evolution takes place. Follow this line in other species. Draw each animal and note the differences.
Level up: Follow the same line with human evolution; predict how, over millennia, humans and animals might evolve further.

127. Famous Fabulous Females in History
History should be more "herstory," as the saying goes, as women and their roles are insufficiently highlighted. Throw in mini history lessons about important women and how they contributed to world history. Each one can be a single lessonlet, from Cleopatra to Marie Curie, the list is endless.
Level up: Write a "herstory" of each century, focusing on the contributions of women by making a poster with cutouts or drawings; follow the same format for any other overlooked group.

128. Microscope
It's striking for kids to learn that there is a world so small that they cannot see it with the naked eye. For most kids, bigger is categorized as better/more interesting/more exciting, but the microscopic world can be just as much, if not more so. If you have a microscope, that's a great place to start, or find online images and videos looking through microscopes of varying powers. Preview what they might see, engage while looking and then review what you saw afterward.
Level up: Explain how a microscope works.

129. Museum Walkthrough

As mentioned in one of our chapters, walkthroughs of cultural institutions make for great virtual "outings." Preview what you'll see, engage during the video walkthrough. If it can be controlled (a proper walkthrough in which you decide what to see and where to go, as opposed to somebody's video tours) then let the kids choose. Afterward, review what you saw and discuss what sort of thing you'd like to see next time.

Level up: Make a map of the institution as you go so your kids are following along, mapping the space and marking what they see and where.

130. Weaving Friendship Bracelets

Kids inevitably go through friendship bracelet phases. They make for great, inexpensive gifts for other friends, and here is where you can turn them into a lessonlet. Think about friends, what colors they might like, which friends your kids consider closest, for whom they'd like to make a gift. Talk about what friendship is and means to them. The bracelets are a vehicle for discussing the important theme of friendship.

Level up: There are various weave patterns, some more difficult than others, that kids can graduate to; leading on from the theme of friendship you can talk to them about what love and loyalty mean—talking about "heavy" topics is best done with kids while they're doing something else that doesn't require their full attention, as the discussion becomes less confrontational and more incidental.

131. Tying Shoes

Shoelace tying is a life step lessonlet. A friend tried to teach his kids but couldn't manage—instead, he left them with a YouTube video, and they learned on their own. To each their own method. There are also various techniques: I learned one way while my European wife has a different approach.

Level up: Go for a double knot; use this as a lead to learning various knots.

132. Sewing

Home crafts are practical, fun, and make for good lessonlets. Learning to sew gives kids the superpower to fix ripped clothing or even make clothing

from raw textiles. Teach the basics of sewing, threading needles, not pricking yourself, and the like.
Level up: Teach sewing machine use.

133. Knitting
Knitting is another craft that is fun and relaxing and allows you to create all manner of woolen goods, from scarves to hats to gloves.
Level up: Try other, similar techniques, like crochet; make more elaborate designs, changing yarn colors or introducing patterns.

134. How We See (Vision 101)
What is sight? Ancient Greeks thought that we shot beams out of our eyes and these beams bounced off things we saw and sent information about them back into our eyes. That's not quite how it works, but not so far off. Particularly if anyone in your family has glasses, this is a good topic to explain how we see and what can go wrong, requiring glasses or medical intervention.
Level up: Explain how glasses work and the history of eyeglasses.

135. Dusting for Fingerprints
Let your kids play detective and dust for fingerprints around the house. Any very fine powder (like talcum or cocoa powder) will work, scattered over a surface with a fingerprint (ideally smooth and flat) using a soft brush. The powder should adhere to the lines of the fingerprint, which had residual oil on them from the skin. Then lay any clear tape over the fingerprint. Lay down paper that is a contrasting color to the powder used (if the powder is white, use black paper). Lay the tape flat on the paper and press it down. You should see the fingerprint clearly.
Level up: Learn the history of fingerprint identification and other ways to identify individuals; compare fingerprints blown up and learn what points of comparison criminal investigators look for.

136. Piano Basics
Learning any musical instrument is great for many reasons, and piano is a good one to start with. Learn the basics, playing short songs, like "Jingle Bells" with one finger, then use the finger on the weaker hand, then two hands. There are many good online tutorials or apps that help you learn.

Learn about the history of the instrument and listen to some famous performances of piano pieces. Listen to the same piece performed by different musicians to recognize how a piece can be interpreted.
Level up: Get better and play more complex works; take proper lessons with a good teacher.

137. How to Argue
Your kids will sometimes argue with you, so they might as well do it properly, right? In third grade, we learned a lite version of Cicero's system for making a strong argument. State your thesis, give three reasons supporting it, then repeat the thesis in your conclusion. Have your kids argue in this way. "You want ice cream? Explain to me why." Then they might say, "I want ice cream because it's delicious, and I did the work for school and I'm a very good boy so I deserve it. In conclusion, I want ice cream because it's delicious, I did work for school and I deserve it." Cicero would buy him an ice cream.
Level up: Make more nuanced arguments; add in some counterarguments that an opponent might say to counter what you'd like but preempt them by commenting on them yourself.

138. Make a Lemonade Stand or Bake Sale
A little capitalism makes a good lesson. Have your kids set up a lemonade stand or bake sale. They should make whatever they'll sell. Calculate how much the ingredients are and how much each portion should be sold for to make a profit. Be sure to include the time they took to make it, which should be covered by the profit margin. Proto economics.
Level up: Have your kids imagine they're the manager of a stand with employees—how should the business plan be changed to cover payment to employees and something for the manager? This is a chance to talk about fair management and fair prices for customers.

139. Make Candles
You can make your own candles with wax and a wick. Melt the wax, mix in fragrance if you like and coloring, pour it into a container and place the wick in the middle. Let it harden, and you've got a homemade candle.
Level up: Make dipped candles—one step trickier but still nice and easy.

140. Write, Address, and Post a Letter
We passed a phone booth, and I had to explain to my kids what it was—a piece of high technology that they'll never have to use. Letters haven't quite gone the way of the phone booth, but your kids are unlikely to handwrite and post letters unless you go out of your way to encourage it. Whether it's to a friend or Aunt Gertrude or Santa, give them the experience of writing a letter, then explain how postage works and what happens to the letter on its way to its destination.
Level up: See if a friend or family member would become a pen pal, starting a handwritten letter correspondence over an extended period of time.

141. Super Scientists and Their Successes
Pick a scientific breakthrough and tell its story. Each one is a narrative of triumph after constant failure and they make for good anecdotes that, in turn, make the science easier to remember. Explain why it is important, and once the basic story is covered, introduce the scientist and how they changed the world.
Level up: Narrate the story of a phenomenon that involved many scientists over a long period of time, for instance the development of vaccines or anesthetic.

142. Make Preserves and Seal Them Hermetically
Making preserves is great for the winter, and homemade goodies always taste better (or at least we assume they *should*, so we decide they do). Take berries, fresh or frozen, and let them simmer with a sweetener and gelatin. Make your own recipes.
Level up: Don't just eat the preserves fresh, but you can seal them and teach kids about hermetic sealing and help them do it (under supervision, as there will be boiling water involved).

143. Make Slippers Out of Felt
Slovenians wear slippers at all times indoors. This was new to me, as an American used to wearing outdoor, muddy shoes throughout the house. Slippers are, generally, a better way forward, especially if you're the one who has to vacuum each week. Make your own with felt. There are simple instructions online, and you need nothing more than felt and a needle and thread (though they'll last longer if a parent helps using a sewing machine).

Level up: Make slippers out of other materials, like textile or leather; make needlepoint decorations on the slippers.

144. Learn Magic Tricks

Sleight of hand is like superpowers without the magic—just practice is required. Learn basic magic tricks, many of which are simply about distracting the audience, so they don't follow the "trick" part of your magic trick and focus elsewhere.

Level up: Magic tricks are suited to lots of levels up, so you can get as complex and elaborate as you like; Penn and Teller have a series in which amateur magicians try to fool them and they try to deconstruct how a trick was pulled off—it's fun to watch and suits the lessonlet.

145. Telescope and Binoculars

Zooming in to get a better look at things far away sounds like a superpower, and with a bit of tech, we can harness it. Pick the same target at a distance and look at it with the naked eye, with binoculars and with a more powerful telescope, if you can, to see the difference (or find a test example online).
Level up: Explain how binoculars and telescopes work.

146. Acupressure

Reflexology and acupressure are ancient healing practices that have a basic concept—press on parts of the body to feel good and heal other parts. It's like a magic trick and one that requires mapping zones of the body, but the pressure of which even a kid could apply. Teach your kids some basics. One of the easiest and immediately applicable is the acupressure point three finger widths beneath the sternum. Pressing hard there fends off nausea.
Level up: Pick a section of the body and memorize the zones and pressure points there and their effects—after a few such sessions, you'll have the whole body covered.

147 & 148 & 149. Snorkeling/Scuba Diving/Free Diving

These three ways of seeing the underwater world can each provide a lessonlet. Since they're related, they are good to cover in a cluster. Snorkeling is something you can try on holiday or in a tub. Free diving will have to wait but a basic, supervised game of dipping your head underwater and looking around is a start. Check out snorkel, scuba diving and free diving videos.

They can be beautiful and mesmerizing. When it comes to scuba diving, discuss the equipment and the potential dangers (like the bends).
Level up: Practice some of the techniques yourself when circumstances allow; explore what undersea life you could see by visiting different sites around the world, to hammer home the diversity of aquatic life and geography.

150. How Feathers Work
Feathers are super light, push air away to help with flight, keep birds warm and wick away water to keep them dry. Amazing attributes. When you find a feather on a walk one day, use it as a chance to talk about this.
Level up: Check out different types of feathers; compare feathers of flightless birds (like an ostrich) to birds of flight.

151. Working Out
Proper workouts shouldn't come until kids are older, and the use of weights isn't recommended until after puberty. But you can teach about how to keep yourself healthy and fit anytime. Show exercises that promote aerobic vs. anaerobic workouts, which use your own body weight, not free weights. Running, jogging, skipping rope, crunches, pushups, pullups, swimming are all good for any age. Knowing how and why is good at any age and then they can put this knowledge to use later on.
Level up: Look at some vital statistics at rest and when exercising—what happens to heart rate, blood pressure, blood oxygen levels.

152. Make a (Non-Tiny) Book
Make a book with your kids. You can go simple—colored, heavier paper for the binding and normal paper for the inside, stapled together or fastened with an elastic. Talk about the story you'll write with your kids or let them do it all themselves and have them read you their story. Talk about the history of books, the printing press invention, and what books are really for (storing knowledge and making it available to others).
Level up: Make a sturdier book with a firmer binding sewn into place.

153. Make a Flipbook Cartoon
To understand how cartoons used to be made (before the digital revolution), make a flipbook cartoon. In the outside corner of a booklet made of equally

sized pieces of paper (smaller and square works best) stapled together, make a series of drawings (stick figures are fine). Each drawing should show the figure in an incrementally different pose. There should be at least ten images, and more is better. Then very quickly flip through the book, beginning to end, letting the pages fly out from under your thumb. In the speed of viewing, our minds skip over the in-between bits and focus on the images, which appear to move due to the rapidity of the shifting pages. Filming this is how the earliest cartoons were made.
Level up: Have your kids make their own flipbook cartoons to tell a whole story; film the flipping and speed up the recording so it moves more seamlessly and looks truly animated.

154. Design Your Own Superhero
In my youth I spent a lot of time reading the origins and details about Marvel superheroes (I had the complete *Marvel Universe* series with biographies and info on every hero and villain in the Marvel Comics pantheon). I also would design my own, including their costumes, superpowers, weaknesses and origins. Have your kids invent their own and think about what goes into designing a character. The question of what superpower they should have is just the start.
Level up: Give the characters three-dimensionality by fleshing out their background.

155 & 156. Horse Riding/Horse Care
Take your kids horseback riding and learn about grooming, how horses behave, and how you should behave around them. What do they like to eat? What are some potential health problems that they might have?
Level up: Give your kids some lessons so they can trot and even gallop; map out what it would take to keep a horse as a pet, the budget and space needed.

157 & 158. Make a Bird Feeder/Learn What Birds Eat
You can make a birdhouse or feeder out of balsa wood or something stronger. Design it together with your kid, tailor-made for local birds. Look up which birds live near you and what they like to eat.
Level up: Plan what food you'll give them and, if it's a house, how to make an entryway big enough for the birds but that will keep out squirrels.

159. Paper Airplane Architecture
There are scores of ways to make paper airplanes. It's its own category of origami. Learn some variants and see which fly farthest.
Level up: Introduce the idea of aerodynamism and how gliders fly.

160. Learn Three Column Capitals
Get your Vitruvius on and learn to identify the three main types of classical column capitals: Doric, Ionic, and Corinthian. Draw and label them. All of a sudden you'll be able to name just about every column capital you see the world over, as they are inevitably one of these three types labeled by the ancient Roman architect, Vitruvius.
Level up: Learn some other classical architectural terms, like fluted columns, buttresses, architraves, and barrel vaults—draw each to secure them more easily in the mind.

161. Learn to Say Hello
How many languages can you learn to say "hello" in? The more the merrier, and this is a happy word to choose. Upgrade with more languages, first spoken, then written out. Writing out "hello" in other alphabets is particularly fun.
Level up: Follow the same pattern for other happy words, like "love."

162. Identify Continents
Look at a world map or globe and memorize the names and locations of the continents. See how many countries your kids can name in each.
Level up: Shift from continent spotting to country spotting based on the location on a world map, then level up even further with just the shape of the country (without its context on a world map) to make things trickier.

163. Capital Cities
Begin with the capital of your country (or state). Describe what happens at a capital city, what the government consists of and what decisions it makes. Show a picture of the capital building. Learn some of the facts of your capital (population, iconic elements).
Level up: Expand to capitals of other countries; quiz with flashcards or images online.

164. Octopus vs. Squid

Comparing similar things—whether sea creatures or anything else—is a good exercise in observation and theory. Observation can sometimes mislead—in having tentacles, octopi and squid have superficial similarities but are different in the details. So while finding similarities is one aspect, understanding that things that look similar can actually be very different is also useful. Draw a squid and an octopus side by side and focus on what they have in common and how they differ.

Level up: Extend this to any two other foci (dogs vs. wolves, roses vs. hyacinths, bees vs. wasps); get deeper into the biology if the basics are well understood.

165. Write a Song

Inviting your kids to write their own song is actually a big, inviting, multilayered project. First, break down pop songs into component parts. An intro, verses, choruses, and a bridge. Invite them to make up a tune, then add words to it, then repeat one turn for the verses and one for the chorus. It's creative but also helps them understand music through deconstruction.

Level up: Perform the song; write an album's worth and record the whole album.

166. Learn Mythological Creatures

Famous monsters of myth, from basic tropes like dragons and unicorns to more sophisticated, like manticores and harpies. There are many approaches: illustrated books of myths, encyclopedias (like the *Encyclopedia of Things That Never Were* mentioned earlier), or movies (like *The Last Unicorn*, which introduces in a beautiful cartoon a variety of such creatures). Each one has an origin myth from which they emerged, and these should be read, then perhaps have your kids draw their interpretation of the creature. Because they are borne of classical literature and oral tradition learning them adds to the cultural touchstones in your kids' arsenal.

Level up: Invent your own myth, including one or more creatures; invent a new mythological creature.

167. Transplant a Plant Clipping and Grow It

You can plant a garden, and that's one form of multifaceted lessonlet. But the act of helping a plant to grow can be simplified down to its most basic form: a cutting placed in water. Take the base of a scallion, for instance. The part that you normally throw away, the base beneath the white bulb that has some roots growing from it, can be placed in a glass of water and it will slowly regrow into a whole, green-topped scallion. This can be used to teach about how plants grow and about regeneration. Many plants can follow this model—you can then place them in soil or just keep using the glass and water approach, where the growth is slow but visible each step of the way.

Level up: Let your kids try this out with any plant or vegetable they're interested in and experiment, perhaps with many at once lined up each in its own glass, to see which grow and how quickly.

168. Adopt a Succulent

This category of dessert plants, many of them cacti, are the easiest to grow and toughest to kill. They can take neglect and most do not need active watering but absorb enough moisture from the air to do just fine. They're an ideal first plant to give a kid and make their responsibility. We even named our first cacti (Spike is a good option). They can help give kids a sense of responsibility and show that they can care for a living thing and maintain it.

Level up: Expand to an indoor garden of potted succulents, and work up to more intricate ones, learning the differences between them.

169. Potential Energy vs. Kinetic

I can barely remember physics class, and I was terrible at it, but I do like the super simplistic lesson of potential vs. kinetic energy. Potential energy is most easily explained when the potential force is gravity. An object (a pillow, for instance) when held in your outstretched arm has potential energy to fall to the floor at a rate of 9.8 meters per second. That potential becomes kinetic once you drop it. That's about as much physics as I can easily handle, but it's a good start.

Level up: Calculate potential and kinetic energy based on the mass of objects falling; go more complex with things that don't just freely fall but have other factors, like an arrow drawn on a taut bowstring or a bowling ball atop a slope.

170. Test Your Reflexes
Reflexes can be developed with training and that training is usually fun. The simple game of one player holding their hands outstretched, palms up, and the other trying to slap their palms before the first player pulls them away is one option. You can also demonstrate involuntary reflexes, like breathing or blinking if something flashes past your face.
Level up: Ask kids to list which reflexes are involuntary and train their speed in voluntary reflexes.

171. Mammals vs. Eggs
Help your kids learn to categorize mammals, which give birth to live young, versus egg-laying animals, like fish, reptiles, amphibians, birds, and insects. You can take the "Name Ten" approach (they should name ten of each) or use flashcards or have kids draw animals in each category.
Level up: Move on to various egg types, incubation periods, and newborn development in mammals.

172. Cloud Spotting
Lie on the grass with your kids and check out the clouds in the sky. Can they spot a nimbus or a stratus cloud? What about the more complex options like nimbostratus? Have your kids draw or photograph each type over many days and write them out. There are a finite number so you can learn them all.
Level up: Keep a journal of which clouds they've seen and which they should keep an eye out for; talk about the physics of clouds and their movement.

173. Catalogue Shopping with a Fixed Budget
I have a strange love for print catalogues. I enjoy browsing them and thinking about things I might buy but never will. I get excited about the local supermarket catalogue in the post. But now my kids think they're fun, too, and so we made a game of having a fixed imaginary budget and I ask them what they'd buy. They have to subtract the cost of each item from the budget to be sure they have enough left. We've done it with school supplies and groceries, but you could try it with anything.
Level up: Give special assignments, like shopping for ten meals' worth of groceries, so they need to calculate not just what they'd like to get but what is needed for specific recipes within the umbrella of a fixed budget.

174. Math Olympics

Make a game show format math competition, with questions of various values, all geared toward the level of your kids. You can borrow the questions from their textbook, no harm in that. Include a buzzer and time limit and points and real rewards (candy, ice cream, going to the movies).
Level up: This is easily leveled up with more complex mathematics; use the same format for other disciplines of study.

175. Clean the House

Sounds like fun, right? Kids like to help and to be with you and can approach work as a fun activity. But it's also useful for them to learn why and how a house gets dirty and what components there are to cleaning it. Sweeping, mopping, dusting, scrubbing the bathrooms, taking out the trash, recycling. Lay out the various chores and take turns involving them in each. You can set informal timers to make sure they do it long enough by playing songs they like in the background (e.g., vacuum your bedroom for the duration of the first two songs in the *Frozen 2* soundtrack). Be supportive about their intent to help—the results, at this point, aren't important.
Level up: Give them complete ownership of one whole room or one whole category of cleaning (vacuuming, for instance).

176. Check Your Own Moles

This is an important aspect of skin health and no one will be as observant and hands-on as you about your own body. Get your kids to know where they have moles and photograph them holding a ruler alongside, so you can monitor the size. Do this every few months. Explain why this is important (as well as seeing a dermatologist for a general checkup at least once a year). Tell them you've forgotten where their moles are and see their delight in being able to guide you to them.
Level up: This lessonlet is a portal to general awareness of the body and health, which will serve them in good stead, so shift to other aspects to keep track of (like teeth or nails).

177. Types of Teeth

Speaking of teeth, when your kids' start falling out it's a great chance to explain what teeth are, what they're made of, the difference between baby teeth and permanent, the number of teeth, the types of teeth and what they do, and why cleaning them is important.

Level up: Talk through your next visit to the dentist as a preview so it will be interesting and not scary for the kids—if they know what to expect and what each step of this visit is for, the visit is easier for all.

178 & 179. Caramelizing Food/Making Caramel

Illustrate how applying heat to food brings out its natural sweetness with onions. Sautee them and taste at each step, from raw to beautifully caramelized. Then show where the term comes from by caramelizing sugar to make . . . well, caramel.

Level up: Go deeper into the chemistry about how heat brings out the sugar inherent in food; use a blowtorch to caramelize the top of a flan. Kids think blowtorches are badass.

180. Is It Legal?

Explain what laws are and why they are important to follow. Start with just one, for instance that you're not allowed to steal. Let your kids explain why. You can use role-playing ("How would you feel if someone came in and took your stuffed stegosaurus without asking and never gave it back?") If that feels understood you can move on to others. It's good for kids to know what the law is, at this point for moral reasons, and also to know how and why breaking the law is punished.

Level up: You can get more specific and/or esoteric with laws; pose situations and let your kids "choose their own adventures" to do what's legal in a situation that you can make complicated.

181. Grow an Avocado at Home

This feels like a magic trick. Take the pit of an avocado, pierce it with toothpicks at three points around the bottom hemisphere and use the toothpicks to suspend it over a glass filled with water so that the water touches the bottom of the pit. Then watch it grow. It needs about six weeks, then you can transfer it to a pot and you have yourself an avocado plant.

Level up: This activity can be a chance to talk about "healthy fats" of which avocado is perhaps the king.

182. Make Your Own Butter
Watch an episode of *Little House on the Prairie* and point out the inevitable butter churn in the background. Full-fat milk churned turns into whipped cream and then into butter. This can be done at home. If you overwhip whipped cream the air that you whipped in starts to come out and it deflates. The fat separates out into little blobs. Keep churning or whisking and you'll be left with fat (the butter) and a liquid (buttermilk). Pour out the buttermilk (use it for baking by adding a bit of vinegar or lemon juice to it, so it reacts when baking soda is added) and rinse and squeeze out the solid-y flecks in very cold water to get rid of remaining buttermilk (this will make it last longer). Then press it into a paddy of butter. Wrap it in cling film and put it in the fridge.
Level up: Make flavored butter by mixing in herbs; use this as a point of departure for a physics of food lesson.

183. Make Eggs Five Ways
How do you like your eggs? There are numerous options for eggs as the focal point of a meal (let alone as an additional ingredient) but introduce your kids to five for starters. Take five eggs and make each one in a different way: scrambled, omelet, hardboiled, poached, fried. Explain the techniques, what to look for, some tricks (a drop of vinegar in the simmering water for a poached egg). Then do a taste test. Which method do they like best?
Level up: Explore more methods for this, the most complete single ingredient in terms of what it gives your body.

184-188. Which Are Poisonous? (Mushrooms/Snakes/Frogs/Spiders/Berries)
This cluster of lessonlets is based on the same potentially very helpful principle: distinguishing which types of X are poisonous, and which are safe. Choose your category and either use flashcards or images in a book or online. Have your kids draw the various options, especially the poisonous ones and highlight distinctive physical attributes that can help them remember and distinguish.
Level up: Do speed rounds of flashcard quizzes so kids practice quick, reflexive responses and internalize correct answers.

189. Learn a Fancy New Word
Nothing's cuter than a little kid with a big vocabulary. I love that my kids use brachiate in general conversation (moving by swinging, a la Tarzan), a word my parents had never heard before. Pick a new, mostly useless but fun "fancy" word a day. How about gubernatorial or antidisestablishmentarianism? Wow their friends and confuse their teachers!
Level up: Teach idiomatic phrases that no kid their age should know (when my kids put in elaborate preparation and then nothing impressive results in it, we say "that was much ado about nothing").

190. Jeopardy
Set up an at-home version of Jeopardy, with or without having to form your answers as questions. Make categories and values for a set of questions and either prewrite the questions or improvise. Your kids have to "buzz in," by raising their hand or ringing a bell. This is really a vehicle for quizzing on anything you hope your kids are learning, perfect for revising for exams.
Level up: Let your kids write the questions to try to stump each other and you.

191. Boil an Egg
How do you like your eggs boiled? To demonstrate the effect of heating an egg, place four or five eggs in boiling water and cook them for varying amounts of time, from too short to be really cooked to soft-boiled (about six minutes) to hardboiled (about eight minutes) to boiled for too long (ten to twelve). Then crack them open and note the differences. Let your kids then choose which level is their favorite to eat (we like seven minutes).
Level up: Under supervision, let your kids make you boiled eggs to your preference and see how accurate they are in achieving it.

192. How Do Volcanoes Work?
Something about the heat, destruction and force of an eruption is mesmerizing for kids, so turn it into a geologic lesson. Watch a video about volcanoes, draw a volcano and a cross-section of the earth, with kids coloring in the magma at the earth's core. Talk about plate tectonics and, as a bonus, watch an episode of *Floor Is Lava*.

Level up: Discuss or show documentaries on the destructive results of volcanic explosions, like the extinction of the dinosaurs or the covering of Pompeii.

193. Float Ping-Pong Balls on a Hairdryer

Air pressure and resistance lessons can make a fun game in which kids have to balance a floating ping-pong ball in the air by holding a hairdryer beneath it. You can also go horizontal and make marks on the floor as targets, then get kids to try to get the ping-pong ball to roll onto the mark using a hairdryer.

Level up: Get a pair of hairdryers and ping-pong balls and throw down with your kid to see who can keep the balls in the air longer.

194. Liquids with Different Densities

Liquids look like, well, liquids to kids, so it's eye-opening to see that they can have different densities. This is easiest to demonstrate with oil and water, which will not mix. You can try out various liquids in water and other liquids to see whether they mix or stay separate.

Level up: You can make your own lava lamp at home.

195. Test Gravity

By dropping things of various masses from the same height, you can test gravity. First tell them the likely apocryphal Isaac Newton story of an apple falling from a tree under which he was relaxing. It's good for them to know fun facts about Newton and the very basic gravitation acceleration of 9.8 meters per second squared. Have kids choose a wide variety of things that will not cause too much destruction (dice, a feather, a pillow, a tennis ball, a ping-pong ball) and have them drop each from the same height. Explain why some hit the ground more quickly even though they all technically fall according to the same set rate.

Level up: Older kids with a bit of math under their belts can predict how quickly things will fall based on the 9.8 meters per second rate.

196. Make a Tutorial Video for Other Children

The sign of really understanding a concept is if you can teach it to others. In this lessonlet, have your kids make a tutorial video for other children. It can be on anything they like or recently feel that they grasp. It can be another

lessonlet or how to make your bed, whatever suits. Film them. So often I'll incorporate watching a tutorial video into a lessonlet that it's high time my kids made some in return.
Level up: Post the video online and show your kids any positive responses to it.

197 & 198. Climbing Trees/Climbing Rocks

Climbing is fun but it also is a sport and an art form. There's strategy involved and physical strength and balance, all of which can be developed. In either of these lessonlets, first let your kids climb freely on trees or rocks, but then give them some tips, like feeling for footholds at each new step to be sure they'll hold or using chalk dust to give fingers better grip. You can watch some impressive free climbing videos for inspiration.
Level up: Take it up a notch by visiting professional courses for climbing (with harnesses) or doing a climbing class in a gym.

199 & 200. Spot the Zodiac in the Sky/Learn the Zodiac Signs

The Zodiac has a magical, mystical quality about it, and many are animal forms, so kids think of this like learning a magic trick. There are good apps to help spot signs in the night sky, and it's a bit like "connect the dots." You can expand to other constellations in a separate lessonlet, but for now concentrate on the zodiac signs in the sky and how they are meant to relate to birthdays and personality types. Yours and your kids are the best points of departure. They can then feel a personal link to their Zodiac sign and can draw it.
Level up: Figure out the signs of friends and family and discuss whether they possess the personalities associated traditionally with those born under each sign.

201 & 202. Start a Fire/Cook Over an Open Flame

Starting a fire is a primeval act that links to our ancestors dating back millennia. And yet almost no one today knows how to do it without a lighter or matches. Teach kids fire safety as you go and how to build up a good fire and maintain it with tinder and dry wood. There are various survivalist tricks to starting a fire (with a flint firestick or, if you want to get fancy, with a bow drill). Try them all. Then let your kids cook with you over open flame. Roasting hot dogs and marshmallows is a good place to start,

and then let them assist with a proper barbecue grill of various meats and veg.
Level up: Do a camping overnight with them and let them lead everything, especially the fire making and food roasting.

203. No-Bake Desserts
A handful of these lessonlets involve baking, but there's a world of no-bake desserts that are delicious and easy. Simply mixing ingredients and doing nothing else provides an immediate satisfaction as kids can skip the parental guidance step of handling the application of heat in an oven or stovetop. No bake cheesecake and tiramisu are perhaps the most obvious choices, but the raw food movement has resulted in recipes for all manner of goodies.
Level up: Since even younger kids can mix ingredients (and there's no need to heat them) let them make a dessert all alone for the family to enjoy.

204 & 205. Solve Riddles/Invent Riddles
Why is a raven like a writing desk? It isn't, which makes this famous riddle from *Alice in Wonderland* one of the worst—it's unsolvable because the inventor never came up with an answer. But riddles, from easy to complex, are essentially logic puzzle games and kids enjoy them. Make the exercise more of a historical lesson by introducing famous riddles, like the riddle of the Sphinx: What walks on four legs in the morning, two legs in the afternoon, and three legs at night? Throw in the Riddler from Batman (preferably the super cheesy Adam West TV version) and you combine the puzzle solving with a historical flashback.
Level up: Shift from easier to more complex riddles; invent solvable riddles and test family members.

206. Build a Dam
There's great satisfaction and numerous learning opportunities in building something together with children (or with anyone, for that matter). Normally this involves Legos or the like, but it takes on a new scale when it is a full-sized structure. It gets even better when what you build has a visible, immediate effect in altering the world as a child sees it. Find a body of water that is not long across, like a stream or small pond. Let your kids pick stones or pieces of wood, only natural materials found on-site, and let

them choose where to place them to block the water. Be sure to remove the dam afterward so as not to interfere with natural flows.
Level up: Plan out the dam and draw it up ahead of time; integrate some physics and teach about flow and hydrodynamics.

207. Spot the Difference in Nature
This can be a life saver. Distinguish differences between similar-looking wild things. Trees, grasses, but also mushrooms and berries. Distinguish the grass that comprises most of your lawn from weeds and invasive grasses. And berries that look similar, like red currant (yummy) vs. dwarf honeysuckle (do not eat!)
Level up: Begin with side-by-side photos but move on to finding specimens outdoors on hikes.

208. Learn Do Re Mi
To teach Do Re Mi, I enlisted the help of Julie Andrews. We found a charming clip from *The Sound of Music* and let the song be our guide to start learning music.
Level up: Sing Do Re Mi without the song (a cappella—it's trickier, just like it's trickier to say the alphabet without singing the Alphabet Song); do it backwards (Do Ti La . . .); sing it in various octaves.

209. Blind Testing: Scents
Continuing the blind testing theme, turn to scents. Choose a selection of scented things (cinnamon, lavender, vanilla, orange). For beginners, show them the options, have them take a deep sniff and commit them to memory. Then put on a blindfold and ask them to name which they are smelling as you present them, one at a time. At a higher level, don't show your kids the options—they have to just guess.
Level up: Choose things with mixed scents (oatmeal cookies, for example, which combine cinnamon, brown sugar and oatmeal) to make things trickier; let your kids prepare a scent test for you.

210. Blind Testing: Touch
Covering the senses, turn to touch. A blind test of touch is just as fun. Pick a selection of items with different, distinctive consistencies: maybe an orange, an apple, a key, a fork, a leather wallet. This is about the feel of

material and also the shape of objects. Blindfold the kids and hand them one thing at a time. At a higher level, don't show your kids the options—they have to just guess.
Level up: Incorporate more than one of the same object (like two forks, each of different shapes).

211. Blind Testing: Musical Instruments
Help learn the sound of instruments and their proper names by playing the sound of instruments one at a time (on YouTube or if you have a synthesizer with this feature). Then have your kids close their eyes and name which instruments you play for them.
Level up: Play a piece of music featuring multiple instruments (a quartet, for example) and ask them to name all the instruments present and playing in the same piece.

212. Learn the Orchestra
Orchestras generally follow a formula when it comes to seating arrangements. Like the Periodic Table, this can be memorized. Watch an orchestral concert or attend one in person. While watching, point out the performers of each instrument and help your kids remember them. Then draw out an orchestra on a sheet of paper and have your kids indicate where each instrument is positioned.
Level up: Ask your kids to draw the instrument on the correct place in the orchestra chart.

213. Ferment at Home
It's a la mode to ferment, from NOMA in Copenhagen to the kimchi of South Korea. It's one of the most ancient preservation methods and makes food taste better. You can make many such dishes at home safely and easily. We live in the land of sauerkraut so that's where we started, but you can also easily make mixed pickled vegetables. There's something nest-like, homey and satisfying about preparing stores of delicious food for the winter months, and it's great to get kids involved.
Level up: Make your own yogurt by adding some purchased yogurt to fresh milk and letting it work its magic; kimchi is a step more complex, as it doesn't just pickle but uses lacto-fermentation and you can throw in spice.

214. Make an Itch-Soothing Serum
There are a number of homemade remedies for itches. The next time you get a mosquito bite or the like, try all three to see which works best. Rub the itch with the inside of a banana skin. Or with the underside of a basil leaf. Or with a cotton pad dipped in cooled black tea.
Level up: Design your own anti-itch serum based on these components.

215. Glass Scale
Learn the musical scale using glasses of water. Line up eight glasses and fill them with increasing levels of water. When you tap each with a spoon it will ring with a tone. The first is "Do" and then on you go: Re, Mi, Fa, So, La, Ti and Do again. The water amount alters the tone when you tap it with the spoon.
Level up: Play a tune on the glasses of water.

216. Spelling Treasure Hunt
Hide letters around the house (they could be from Scrabble or handwritten and cut out, whatever is easiest). The first person to find letters that can spell a real word wins.
Level up: Start with three-letter words and level up to longer ones.

217. Balancing Games
Walk an imaginary line on the floor. Walk on a string on the floor. Walk on the edge of a curb outdoors. Hop on one foot. Games that promote balance are fun and good for coordination, but you can also use them to teach about balance and distribution of weight.
Level up: Incorporate offset weight that kids have to compensate for (like give them a lightly filled backpack that they have to keep on one shoulder).

218. Track and Field
Do some homemade versions of track and field events, particularly the running. Let kids use a stopwatch to learn about seconds and milliseconds. Have them map their own track for the sixty-yard dash, to learn about distance. Then see how quickly they run and beat their own time.
Level up: Add in some mathematics by helping older kids calculate how quickly they run an average yard in the sixty-yard dash based on their best time.

219. Jumping

Kids jump for fun and the phrase "jump for joy" is right on. But jumping can be a lessonlet if you talk about propulsion, momentum (why they might fall forward when they land), distribution of weight (it feels better to land on two feet than on one). Try standing jumps and running jumps. Mark jump lengths and try to make new records.

Level up: Add in some mathematics by helping older kids calculate the average length of multiple jumps.

220. Popcorn

Popcorn is like a magic trick, but why limit it to the inside of a bag, where you can't see it? Well, the reason is that it will otherwise explode all over your kitchen. But you might want to try because there is no clearer demonstration of the power of heat to totally change the consistency of something. Pop in a glass-covered saucepan and watch the hard kernels transform into a delicious treat.

Level up: Take one batch of cooked popcorn and make it into three taste varieties (salted, buttered and caramel) to demonstrate how adding a single additional ingredient can totally change the flavor profile.

221. Heat Converting Matter

As with popcorn, it's a scientific magic trick to transmute one thing into something that appears entirely different. Begin with a simple demonstration of turning water into steam. Put cored apples into a saucepan, cover and heat and in about twenty minutes you'll have apple sauce. Heat sugar in a pan, stirring, and you have caramel.

Level up: Demonstrate the Maillard effect caramelizing meat when it touches a hot pan.

222. Review Films

Kids don't assume that their opinion matters. Not enough, anyway. So help them understand the value of their opinion by asking them to review something they watched, read or did. Take a movie. You'll watch movies anyway, so try having them review it. You can even post the review online. This will make your kids feel proud but also encourage them to think critically.

Level up: Start a series of review and help your kids write them out. A child review blogger is a cool thing.

223. Make Ice Cream at Home

The best ice creams are made with special machines, but you can make a solid, tasty option at home which differs only in texture from the professional level, just by using a Ziplock bag. You need ice, sugar, salt, milk, and flavoring (vanilla is the most basic). Teach about how salt added to ice lowers the freezing point. Water normally freezes at 32°F, but if there's a 20 percent solution of salt it freezes at 2°F. That's why salt is scattered on icy roads in winter. The ice will melt because of the salt unless the temperature is lower than 2°F. Mix 1 cup of milk, ½ teaspoon vanilla, and 1½ tablespoons of sugar in a Ziplock bag. Mix 3 cups of ice and 1/3 cup of coarse salt in a gallon-sized Ziplock bag. Place the smaller bag of ingredients inside the larger one. Shakes them violently for five minutes (kids love this part). The liquid in the smaller bag will have hardened. Let the bag sit for five more minutes, nestling the smaller back inside the ice in the larger bag. Then it's ready to serve!

Level up: If you have an ice cream machine you can go pro, otherwise experiment with different flavors and mix-ins.

224. Make a Slushy at Home

You've spotted a trend correctly. There are quite a few "make X at home" lessonlets here. And with good reason. These are easy, fun and taking ingredients and putting them together to make something delicious—especially something delicious that feels like you should only be able to get it at a restaurant—really is a superpower. Now we're onto slushies, which are surely only available at 7-11 and similar 24-hour convenience stores, right? Au contraire, mon frère. As with the make-your-own ice cream lessonlet, the trick here is lowering the freezing temperature of ice by adding salt. Pick your favorite drink. Pour it into a smaller plastic bag. Put salt and ice in a larger plastic bag (so you've got about 20 percent salt solution). This lowers the freezing temperature by 30°. Put the smaller bag with the drink inside the larger bag. Shake for five minutes. The smaller bag now contains your slushy. Watch out for head freeze.

Level up: Set up a slushy stand or shop for your friends and neighbors—make a menu and take orders as you go.

225. How to Melt Ice
Here's the puzzle for your kids. Given a limited amount of time and patience, how can you get a sphere of ice to melt, other than just leaving it alone for hours? See your kids problem-solve and realize that heat will speed melting. To do this, take a balloon and drop something fun inside. It could be a small plastic toy or a well-wrapped candy perhaps. Then fill the balloon with water, tie it tight and put it in the freezer. When frozen, cut the balloon away and you'll have a sphere of ice with whatever you put inside in the middle. Set your kids the task of releasing what's inside.
Level up: Give them a time limit; make a bunch of balloons and they need to free the inside of them all in a set amount of time, perhaps with limited tools of your choice available.

226. Make It Rain in a Jar
The lesson here is about what rain is and how it happens. The sun heats water on Earth. This turns the water into steam which rises into the sky. Clouds are comprised of this steam, water vapor, coalescing in the sky. Once the warm air in the sky cannot absorb any more water vapor it becomes saturated and begins to cool down. This results in condensation, which turns the water vapor into liquid water droplets that gravity causes to fall as rain. The game to demonstrate this uses shaving cream, food coloring, and a jar or glass vase. Fill the vase with water. Add a thin layer of shaving cream to the top. That's the cloud. Add drops of food coloring to the "cloud." At first nothing will happen, but when enough drops of food coloring—the water vapor—load up the cloud then they will break through and fall through the water as lovely "tentacles" of color—rainfall.
Level up: Have your kid teach you about rain doing this experiment themselves and narrating.

227. Frisbee Golf
Step one is teaching kids to throw a frisbee. You can add in the physics lesson of how frisbees fly (the curved lip pushes air downward to keep it afloat). Once they get the hang of it you can play frisbee golf. I played this at boarding school (go Choate!), picking targets across campus and trying to land the frisbee next to them in as few throws as possible. You can go big as we did or start small around your yard. This teaches control when throwing.

Level up: Have your kids make their own frisbee golf course, picking the "par" or how many throws should be needed.

228. Jump Rope
This is an old-school kids' game that teaches body control and coordination. It can also offer a lesson on momentum, keeping the rope swinging by applying continuous pressure. See how many jumps your kids can do without stopping the rope.
Level up: Try to go double Dutch with two jump ropes each wielded by a friend on either side of the jumper.

229. Bug Hunt
Make a scavenger hunt out of collecting bugs in your yard or the woods. You can either "collect" them by taking a digital photo or by actually placing the bugs in a glass jar. Whoever finds the most bugs wins. Then look up which bugs you've caught and learn about them.
Level up: Look up which bugs live around you and make a checklist of which you hope to find and where they're most likely to be (in fallen trees, in puddles, etc.).

230. Soft Fencing
If you have floatation "noodles" that kids use in pools (or something else long and soft) then you can teach a version of fencing that won't hurt anything or anyone. Watch some fencing videos and learn the basic moves. Then try them out using the noodles instead of foils.
Level up: Learn the names of specific positions and moves and try to choreograph a fencing match that you found a video of online.

231. Building Stability
Use Jenga blocks or other wooden blocks to create a tower. See how high you can make it without it falling. This teaches basic structural engineering.
Level up: Remove blocks, as in the game Jenga, trying to avoid the structure collapsing.

232. Suction
Give your kids twenty M&Ms or Skittles or some other similar small candy. Give them a straw each and a bowl. Without touching the candy with their

fingers, just using the suction of the straw, they have to move the candy from the tabletop into the bowl. Explain how suction works and how it can be applied in engineering in real life.
Level up: Set a timer and have the kids race to put the candy in the bowls in a set amount of time.

233. Phases of the Moon
This can be an extended, month-long lessonlet. Start on a new moon and check out the moon each night for a month. Have your kid draw it each night and name the phases. You can also do this with a moon phase watch. Talk about what the moon is, where it is, how it actually affects things on Earth (like tide). Watch a video of a moon landing.
Level up: Do a pretend moon walk with your kids, imagining the rocket launch, the space flight, the landing and bouncing on the low-gravity surface of the moon.

234. Planet vs. Satellite vs. Star vs. Plane
On a clear evening, look up at the night sky (preferably from a remote spot, away from electric lights). Look for planets (the brightest star-like thingies), stars and slow-moving satellites and fast-moving planes. Can they distinguish them visually? What does each do and how high above the Earth is each likely to be?
Level up: Use a telescope; use a night sky app to help identify and name planets and stars in the sky.

235. Semaphore Code
Semaphore Code feels arcane to non-sailors but it has its place in history and is a simple visual language that can be learned. Talk about what it is, why it was used, and learn some basic moves.
Level up: Learn more so you can actually "speak" in semaphore code.

236. Special Events in the Night Sky
Keep an eye on the cosmological calendar for special events in the night sky, like a comet or blood moon. Take these as opportunities for lessonlets on what is happening, why, and a chance to observe it firsthand, without equipment.
Level up: Watch some videos or professional images from NASA or the like.

237. Nautical Terminology

Draw a picture of a boat viewed from above and label the nautical terms for the sides of it (starboard, port) and front (bow) and back (stern). Learn vocabulary terms of sailing, like leagues (*20,000 Leagues Under the Sea*) and the ever-popular-with-children "poop deck."
Level up: Go into more detail, with terms like "leeward" vs. "windward," "ballast," "bearing" and more; go sailing and put the terms to use.

238. Learn Exotic Colors

Learning basic colors is something everyone at kindergarten will do. The rainbow colors, the primary colors. But there is a world of others that have fancy names that can be fun to learn and the try to reproduce with watercolor. Mauve, chartreuse, indigo, maroon, cobalt, marigold, burnt umber, navy, turquoise, and more.
Level up: Make an enormous, oversized color wheel packed with these extra colors, all labelled; make a special wheel for each color spectrum (one for blues, one for greens, one for yellows, etc.).

239. Make a Color Wheel

Learning the color spectrum, which colors are complementary, is standard for introductory art classes and design classes. They're also fun to paint, so pull out your watercolors and make a color wheel (using the aforementioned compass to make the inner and outer lines of the wheels).
Level up: Encourage your kids to memorize the color wheel and quiz them on which colors are complementary.

240. Maze Navigation

Mazes are a frequent element of kids' workbooks and activity books. Learn a bit about their history, different shapes, hedgerow mazes. You can read them the myth of Theseus and the Minotaur, with its famous labyrinth. They can play Labyrinth, the ball bearing rolling game. Mazes are easiest to solve by going backward, from finish to start, so that's a good trick for them to learn.
Level up: Have them design their own maze for parents to solve.

241. Recreate a Scene from a Film
The idea of acting takes some abstract thinking. People pretend to be someone they are not. Kids do this, of course, pretending to be unicorns or She-Ra, Princess of Power, they just don't call it acting. But you can help your kids learn by encouraging them to reenact a favorite scene from a favorite film. They can perform it for the grownups, with costumes and scenography. You can make a video of it so they can see themselves in action.
Level up: Have your kids memorize the real dialogue to be as accurate as possible in the recreation.

242. Introduce Black and White Films
As discussed in a previous chapter, it's easiest to introduce black and white classic films through short clips on YouTube. A single sequence at a time is easily digestible and after stringing together a few scenes you've dipped deeply into the full film. I remember loving *Abbott and Costello Meet Frankenstein* in my youth, but I couldn't find the whole movie. I showed the girls a few scenes, each of which they liked. When I finally got a DVD of the movie, they enjoyed the pleasurable familiarity of having seen certain scenes and were happy to watch the whole thing.
Level up: Go with more sophisticated films aimed at older viewers step by step. Abbott and Costello movies are very kid-friendly, but you can move up to early musical comedies or light mysteries (I loved the *Thin Man* movies, for instance, or *Charlie Chan*) as your kids grow and grow in patience and interest.

243. Non-Narrative Elements in Film
We watch films for stories and characters, but when you study film, there are a lot of other details. Encourage kids to notice other aspects like lighting (shadows particularly), music (scary music or happy music), camera angles (bird's-eye-view).
Level up: Watch a film on mute—it encourages studying what you see. It's good to do this with films your kids have already seen, and they'll start to see films in a new way, deconstructing them.

244. Learn Camera Angles
Continuing the theme of how to watch films from a more professional standpoint, spend a lessonlet on camera angles. Bird's-eye view, wide shot,

closeup, low angle looking up (à la Hitchcock), panning shot, and so on. Each one is part of the filmmaking vocabulary and helps kids see the film not as a passive entertainment to be enjoyed but also as an artwork created through different video recordings from different angles.

Level up: Have your kids take videos from all the angles you've covered using a phone or digital camera.

245. Show Early Slapstick Silent Films

Laurel and Hardy, Buster Keaton, Charlie Chaplin, and the Keystone Cops are all among the earliest silent film stars. They rely on slapstick, physical humor that anyone can relate to. And they're brilliant. Give your kids a touch of film history, either just individual scenes (Buster Keaton's clock scene, Laurel and Hardy wrestling a piano, Charlie Chaplin eating a shoe), or whole movies.

Level up: Watch *Hugo*, a magical children's film about the earliest silent films to inspire curiosity in your kids to watch them.

246. Design Your Ideal Meal

What would your kids choose for their ideal meal? An appetizer, entrée, and dessert. Draw the ideal meal and then cook it together.

Level up: What ingredients would they need to prepare this ideal meal? Make a shopping list, go shopping together so kids can see what goes into preparing food, and talk about the price of ingredients so they understand the cost of eating.

247. Make a Menu for Your Own Restaurant

The components of most menus include appetizers, entrees, side dishes, desserts, and drinks. What would your kids choose for their ideal restaurant? Have them make a menu and put in items they'd like to offer. Decorate the menu and, if you like, add prices and then invite family and friends to an imaginary restaurant experience.

Level up: Decorate a room in the house as if it's your restaurant, set the table, and have someone be the pretend chef and someone else a waiter.

248. Learn Basic Massage

Everyone likes a massage, and you can teach your kids the basics—you and siblings will benefit. Choose easy motions and keep massages short. This is a lesson that's a gift that keeps on giving.

Level up: Try other types of massage beyond traditional Swedish, for instance throw in some Shiatsu moves like chopping with two hands rapidly to loosen a muscle.

249. Learn Basic Reflexology

Healing through foot massage is an ancient art. Give it a go by finding a foot acupressure chart and massaging your kids' feet; have them massage yours too. See if you or they can feel anything special when special parts of the foot are pressed.

Level up: Reproduce the foot chart on your own foot, letting your kids draw the sections with a safe, washable marker.

250. Play Costume

Kids love dressing up, so make a thoughtful game by looking up the history of costume. What did people wear in different eras or in different professions? Then make a scavenger hunt to find items to wear to mirror some of the historical costumes found in books or online, take photos and have a fashion show.

Level up: Have your kids draw a photo of them in the costume noting elements of it that are distinctive (knee-high boots and a bandana for a pirate, for instance) so you begin a costume drawing album.

251. How Music Is Saved and Played

The other day I found myself explaining what a cassette was. It's a technology my kids will never see or use, but it was critical to my youth. Make a history lesson out of introducing them to different music technologies: records, cassettes, 8-tracks, minidiscs, CDs, and now digital.

Level up: Listen to the same song in various formats (available online) to note the differences.

252. Group Family Dancing

Individual dance moves are good and we've mentioned them, but nothing gets the family going like a group dance. Learn the moves together and

bust them. The Bunny Hop, the Hand Jive, the Electric Slide, La Macarena. Learning choreography promotes memory and coordination and there's likely a cultural historical story behind each dance craze to mention.
Level up: Have a "dance off" competition to see who most closely mimics the proper moves; invent your own choreography.

253. The Opposites Game
Ask your kids to tell you the opposite of . . . anything you like. It stretches vocabulary and imagination, and it's a spoken problem-solving game. "What's the opposite of subtle?" I ask. Izabella says "Strong." That's a point. We're not after dictionary definitions, just to see if the kids get the concept. You can start with simpler things: "What's the opposite of tall?" Short or small. Keep score if you like or just ask randomly here and there.
Level up: Go with more complex ideas ("What's the opposite of an overcast sky?" "A sunny sky."); look for a definition closer to the dictionary; ask for synonyms of opposites.

254. The Synonym Game
Your kids can turn into mini, walking thesauruses (sounds like a type of dinosaur, right?) Ask for other ways to say the same thing. In English, with our vast lexicon, there's a diversity of options. An average American adult has a vocabulary of 42,000–48,000 words, but we only use around 5,000 words in daily conversation. But if you want to get fancy, there are around 300,000 words in the English language. "What's another way to say happy?" (Euphoric, delighted, content, jubilant, effervescent . . .) "What's another way to say red?" (Crimson, scarlet, maroon). Don't be a stickler—if the answer gets the gist of what you're after, go with it. We know that maroon has more brown in it than "red" but it's still in the red continuum. "Content" is less happy than "happy" but it's all good.
Level up: Be a stickler and point out the differences in responses that aren't direct synonyms; ask for two synonyms for each word.

255. Name That Planet
Like memorizing flags or animals or dinosaurs, recognizing planets and some of the planet's characteristics is the sort of exercise likely to be done in school, but just as interesting at home. The act of drawing and writing out helps commit things to memory, so it's good to have your kids draw their

own rendition of each planet, to draw out our solar system, and to note some fun facts about each. You can run a pop quiz by pointing to a drawing and asking which planet it is or make a blank drawing of our solar system and they have to insert the planets in the correct places.
Level up: Take Styrofoam balls and make 3D models of the planets and hang them from the ceiling via a mobile for a 3D solar system model.

256. Songs with Moves

Some songs, particularly for children, have movements associated with them. The "Hand Jive" is one, but "She'll Be Coming Around the Mountain When She comes" and "B-I-N-G-O" do likewise. Find your choice of songs that have interpretive motions (not necessarily dances, that's a different lessonlet) and do them along with your kids.
Level up: Let your kids make up their own hand choreography to a favorite song that doesn't otherwise have any.

257. Save Dead Bread

When bread is stale it's "dead" and should be discarded, right? Not so! That's just the starting point for transforming it into various goodies. This teaches using as much as possible, not being wasteful with ingredients, and creativity. You can make French toast, Panzanella, stuffing, bread dumplings, bread pudding, etcetera.
Level up: Instead of following a recipe, invent your own together with your kids.

258 & 259. A Jar Full of Estimates and Categorizations

Keep a jar full of something in abundance. Buttons, coins, candies, whatever. This is practical, but also becomes a fount of lessonlets. Make a competition to estimate how many, say, buttons are in the jar. Eyeballing quantities can be useful. Then remove the buttons, or whatever you have, and place them in order of size—smallest to largest or the other way around. Use them to make letters, words or shapes. If your jar contains various things, a sort of catchall container, then have your kids divide the contents by category or use.
Level up: Go bigger than a jar and use the same lessonlets on a closet, a cupboard drawer, or a whole room. How many items are there? How would you categorize them or put them in order?

260. Annoying Insect Traps

Skip this one if the idea bothers you, but many are familiar with traps for bugs that you'd rather not have around the family (flies, mosquitoes, slugs, wasps). This can be a learning opportunity, studying what attracts these insects and how to either repel them or trap and kill them. Kids find fascinating the simplest wasp trap, an empty soda bottle with a little soda or juice or sugar water at the bottom, just hanging from a tree. Wasps find their way in but can't figure out how to exit.

Level up: Let kids invent their own experimental traps—including making blueprint-like drawings—and see if they work; experiment with different bait (set up four soda bottles, for instance, one with a bit of soda, one with a bit of orange juice, one with sugar water, one with Diet Dr. Pepper and see which "wins" by attracting the most "guests"—this is a lite version of a proper science experiment.

261. Drawing Diary

Keeping a written diary is not for everyone and it requires proficient writing. Younger kids can keep a drawing diary instead. It can be a designated blank book, it could be drawing on calendar squares, whatever suits. They can draw what they did that day or just make a free drawing. It's a lovely souvenir and you can see the development in drawing ability over time.

Level up: Have your kids draw something specific from each day so it really functions as a visual memory tool; try assigning your kids the same thing to draw (a horse, for instance) once a month for a year and see how their sophistication develops.

262. Name That Tune

With songs your kids know, you can play Name That Tune by whistling, humming or clapping in their rhythm and the rest of you have to guess which song they have in mind.

Level up: Look up the original story of songs and relate them as a history lesson for each song they get right; some will have a memorable or powerful story behind them (like "Amazing Grace").

263. Natural Dyes

My parents used to have tie-dye parties—my father wore a tie-dye cummerbund at his wedding. Tie-dye may be a bit late 1960s, but it's still

fun and looks like a magic trick to kids. Explain how it works, then let your kids pick something white (T-shirt, bandana, cummerbund), pick the dye colors, and make their own. You can also dye other things, like rag paper, using onion skin, beet juice or tea.
Level up: Have your kids predict what a tie-dye project will come out like, based on which colors are used and where rubber bands are placed.

264. Empathy Visualization
Cultivating empathy is hard to do in an elegant way but try this: ask your kids to close their eyes and imagine what it would be like to be blind or deaf or not to be able to walk. It's a balance, as you don't want to upset them, but you want them to understand that there are conditions or handicaps that exist and we should be sympathetic and sensitive to them, and grateful for what we have.
Level up: Watch a film that has a handicapped character and afterward talk about what it was like for them.

265. Senseless
Play a game in which you eliminate one of your senses and see how it changes perception. For example, try eating a bite of something and then eat the same thing while holding your nose. Listen to music normally and then with your eyes closed. Talk about the five senses and how they interact with each other.
Level up: Invent a multisensory experience, for example what would your kids recommend eating when listening to a favorite song, or smelling while looking at a favorite picture?

266. Weights and Measures
Kitchen tools can be introduced as lessonlets. A kitchen scale, for instance, is a chance to explain how scales work and how we use them, but it can also be a guessing game. Test how much certain things weigh, to get a sense, and then guess the weight of other things. Measure out a cup of flour with a cup measure, then ask your kids to use a teaspoon to spoon out a cup's worth of flour into a bowl—then test if they eyeballed the amount correctly.
Level up: Talk about relative measures, for instance ounces to pints, or liters to gallons.

267. Play Balderdash

This is a board game you can buy but also something you can do for fun, with or without a board and pieces. Write a bunch of words on scraps of paper and place them in a bag or bowl. Each player reaches in and pulls out a word. They have to speak in such a way that the other players guess the word, but they cannot say the word in question nor any of its direct synonyms. So for "noon" you could not say "twelve o'clock" but might say "the time of day when gunfighters would duel in the Wild West." This makes kids think outside the box and on their toes.

Level up: Make the words as complex as your kids can handle, expanding their vocabulary as you go.

268. Pictionary

As with Balderdash, this is a board game, but you can play it without the official game. Write a bunch of words on scraps of paper and place them in a bag or bowl. Each player reaches in and pulls out a word. The player must draw the word in such a way that other players can guess it.

Level up: Make the words more complex or try idioms; add a timer to up the pressure.

269. Charades

Charades plus Pictionary plus Balderdash combine in a popular German boardgame, Activity, from which these three ideas hail. We make our own words that suit the age of our kids (the set we have is for adults and is really quite tricky). In charades you have to silently act out, interpret and mime the word in question so that the other players guess it.

Level up: Include specific people you know of whom you'll do impressions; add a timer.

270. Learn Your Bones

Find or draw a picture of a human skeleton and start to learn the bones. You can begin with the song "Dem Bones": The leg bone's connected to the knee bone…" and then move on to more specifics (as there's actually no such thing as a "leg bone," but that'll do for little kids).

Level up: Buy a plastic set or cut out bones from paper, then arrange them in proper order to form a skeleton (you could also do this outdoors using gathered twigs instead of bones, laying them on the ground in a large scale); learn the bones of an animal.

271. Plant Your Own Garden
In the family garden or a window box, let the kids choose a plant to call their own. They can name it, and it is theirs to care for. They learn responsibility, see the growth process, can harvest its fruits (for example, for a basil plant or tomato), and you can teach them about how plants grow.
Level up: Give them a whole section of the garden to design and plant themselves or just care for.

272. Swim Strokes
Watch some professional or Olympic swimming and note the different strokes. Next time you're at a pool, try to teach them specific strokes. If they're enrolled in a swimming class (this is required where we live in Slovenia) then they might have basics of breaststroke and freestyle, but you can introduce others. Talk about the physics of swimming, why fins make it easier, what professional swimmers do better than amateurs.
Level up: Move from swimming to diving.

273 & 274. Learn to Run and Learn to Ski
Running comes naturally, right? I thought so, too, until a friend who is a professional running coach explained otherwise. Most people run incorrectly and that can lead to injury. The best trick he taught me was two key thoughts: first, think to yourself when you run "I am tall." This encourages you to extend your back vertically and have better posture. Second, try to keep your feet on the ground as little as possible. This promotes running the way you would barefoot, which is most natural and healthiest. So have your kids run but help them do so healthfully. Talk about how humans evolved to run barefoot well and try different running distances (sixty-yard dash, a mile). Take the same principle and apply it to skiing (or cross-country skiing). Humans have not evolved to ski, but the idea of encouraging proper form still holds.
Level up: Keep track of times for various distances every few months to see improvement; take videos of running (or skiing) to analyze together afterward.

275. Become a Comedian

The art of being funny will be a lifelong benefit. How do you get there? Well, jokes are usually the least successful way to be funny, but they're the easiest thing to try proactively, and it's a start. Tell your kid a joke and have them tell it to others. Develop a small arsenal of jokes (good, bad, cheesy, it's all good). Have your kid put on a mini standup show (performing for an audience of any sort is good for self-confidence).

Level up: Have your kids write some of their own jokes; make a video of your kid's standup performance.

276. Image Software

Our children live in a digital, computer-savvy era. Start them early with basics of image adjustment software. This could be a simple drawing or photo retouching app or program, or it could be something more elaborate, like Photoshop. It will be a play tool at first, a game, but that's how they'll learn it best.

Level up: Give them assignments, for example to turn a color photo into black and white or to cut out one of the figures in a photo.

277. Breeds

It's one thing to learn to recognize animals, but it's another level to distinguish and name various breeds of the same animal species. Start with easy ones, such as dogs: spotting a German Shepherd, a Chihuahua, a Bulldog, and a Peruvian Hairless (that's our dog) is pretty straightforward. Show pictures of videos of each breed and ask your kids to name the breed. Watching a dog show is a fun way to do this.

Level up: You can add more breeds or learn characteristics of the breeds you know; learn various types of other, more exotic animals (amphibians, snakes, frogs).

278. Professions

It sounds funny, but like spotting breeds or flags or musical instruments, you can have your kids learn to spot people dressed for various professions. We use a visual dictionary to do this. Does someone dressed as a butcher look different from someone dressed as a doctor, even if they both wear white? This lets your kids become miniature Sherlock Holmeses, analyzing what they see for information. You can explain what different professions

do and ask which ones sound interesting for your kids to try when they're grown-ups.
Level up: Have your kids play pretending to be each profession and see how well they understand what that profession does.

279. How We Heal
The human body has the superpower of healing itself, ridding itself of harmful bacteria and viruses, of skin miraculously swallowing up cuts and becoming whole again. Explain these processes, especially when your kid is healing (recovering from a flu, with a scab over a cut).
Level up: Talk about more complex and, at this point, theoretical illnesses and how the body tries to fight them off, and how medicines and therapies help this.

280. Balancing Act
I'm bad at balancing. I look at a skateboard and fall over. Better if your kids don't. Have them practice balance by walking on curbs or boards. Talk about our sense of balance, how our inner ear helps, how weight should be evenly distributed. A seesaw is a good place to illustrate how weights can be balanced.
Level up: Move on to moving balancing exercises, like skateboarding.

281. Survivalist
Shows hosted by the likes of Bear Grylls and Ed Stafford are fascinating for kids and adults. There are practical lessons to be learned about survival in the wilderness, each one a lessonlet granting a superpower. Watch an episode and then learn to actually do what you see. Starting a fire with a flint looks easy on TV but is *way* harder in person (who knows how many takes they needed to film it).
Level up: Spend an overnight with your kid in the forest putting into practice various survival lessonlets you've learned together.

282 & 283 & 284. Creatures We Couldn't Live Without (Worms/Ants/Bees)
Buzzy, crawly creatures are either gross or annoying or something you should flee from because they can sting, right? That's what most kids would say, so pointing out how valuable they are is helpful. Without many of them, particularly worms, ants, and bees, our entire planet would cease

to function. Spend a lessonlet on each, including a documentary on the creature in question. Then find them in the garden and observe them. What do they eat, how do they move, why are they so important to the environment?

Level up: Go the extra mile with an ant farm, a worm farm, or visit a local beekeeper.

285. Make Your Own Popsicles

There are so many store-bought goodies that you can easily make at home. It's economical and educational. Popsicles are a no-brainer. Just buy a popsicle mold once and you're covered. Pour in any liquid (fruit juice is best), with nothing else required, and let it freeze. Use this as a chance to talk about freezing temperatures and how the form of matter can shift depending on the temperature around it.

Level up: Make more complex popsicles, even savory ones or "cocktail" popsicles with various juices and goodies, like raspberries, buried in them.

286. Make Your Own Dried Fruit

My mother has "too much" fruit in the summer and you can only eat so much of it. So the rest is sliced into strips and laid out inside the windshield of her car in the summer sun. She jokes that her car is the world's biggest and most expensive dehydrator, but it works just as well as a purchased dehydrator. The dried fruit lasts for ages and the act of drying sweetens it.

Level up: Dry other goods, like tomatoes or even strips of meat.

287. Make Your Own Fruit Rollups

You only need three ingredients to make one of my favorite childhood snacks, fruit rollups (a.k.a. fruit leather). Pick any fruit or combination. Puree it with lemon juice and (optional) a sweetener, like honey or agave syrup. Then lay it out very thin on a baking tray (put down wax paper first) and bake it at a very low temperature (around 140°C) until it is dried (about six hours) and takes on that nostalgic texture. Then use scissors to slice into panes of fruit and eat!

Level up: Let your kids make cutout shapes from the fruit leather and encourage them to play with their food.

288. Analyze Money (Who's on a Fiver)

Money is beautiful, literally. It is covered in ornate designs and particular iconography. Wherever you live, whatever your currency, turn an analysis of the aesthetic of money into a lessonlet. For US dollars, which president is on which bill, and what are some fun facts about their presidency? Which building is depicted on the back? What's the deal with the eye in the triangle? We handle money so often without thinking twice about it, but it's worth examining.

Level up: Explore foreign currencies.

289. Iconography 101

I'm a professor of art history and my favorite course to teach is for younger or beginner students learning iconography, the study of symbols in art. Which saint is represented by two keys? What does a dog represent in an Old Master portrait? Basic iconography is a series of visual equivalents: If you see X, it represents Y. Because they are visually based they're easier to remember and open up a whole world of visual arts for future enjoyment. Use flashcards or a slide show to test and have your kids draw key icons to help remember them.

Level up: Visit an art museum and learn on-site or quiz your kids on-site, asking them for help in interpreting the art.

290. Regrow Veggies from Scraps

The ultimate money saver and organic recycling endeavor, there are many veggies you can regrow from the scraps you might think to discard. Potatoes, leeks, scallions, onions, celery, fennel, carrots, turnips, parsnips, beets, lettuce, bok choi, kale, cabbage, and herbs like cilantro and mint all work. When a potato grows "eyes" slice this section off, let it dry overnight, then plant it in the soil with eyes facing down. Cut half a sweet potato with "eyes" growing on it and place it eyes down in a glass of water. It will grow roots out the bottom and sprouts out the top. The sprouts can be planted in soil to grow new potatoes. Scallions are even easier—just put the base with some roots in a glass of water and the new, yummy green part will start to grow up out of it. (See more ideas at ruralsprout.com)

Level up: Make a whole garden out of recycled bits.

291. Capillary Action in Plants

The ability to soak up a liquid is called capillary action. The easiest way to illustrate it is to use a sponge or paper towel to absorb liquid. This is how plants "drink." Explaining it to kids is most conveniently done when they (or you) spill a liquid and then you (or even better, they) clean it up. It illustrates, in less than a minute, the way watering soil around plants provides fuel for the plant itself. This is an example of how to throw in a lessonlet in the course of daily life.

Level up: Expand the vocabulary and talk about cohesion (when chewing gum sticks to your shoe), adhesion (when water leeches up from the edge of a towel higher onto the towel's surface) and surface tension (an insect standing atop water instead of floating in it).

292. Ways to Fall Asleep

Some nights we'll fall right asleep, others we'll toss and turn. Teaching kids how and why we sleep is a great chance to learn and can also be practical, as there are numerous tricks to help you fall asleep if it's not coming naturally. Counting backward from one hundred, counting sheep, thinking about a favorite song, listening to relaxing music, using an aromatherapy pillow or essential oil of lavender are just the start.

Level up: Check out a video of brain waves during sleep and get more technical in your explanation, including sleep cycles (which are roughly ninety minutes long, so we feel more refreshed if we wake after six or seven and half hours of sleep than at an interval not divisible by ninety minutes).

293. What Are Dreams?

Moving on from falling asleep, talk about what dreams are, when they come (during the rapid eye movement phase of sleep), and why scientists believe we have them (no one knows for sure). You can introduce basic dream analysis and ask your kids to tell you when they remember their dreams and whether they ever have recurring ones.

Level up: Introduce Freud and Jung, with dream analysis and archetypes in dreams.

294. Two-Ingredient Cooking

Cooking projects can be great fun for kids but the younger ones have limited patience. Mixing eight ingredients might lose them, but two? Anyone's up

for that. There's a world of two-ingredient recipes, and my favorite is this: peanut butter and an egg. Mix them together into a dough, plop them on a baking sheet in dollops, and bake them into super simple cookies.
Level up: Invent your own two-ingredient recipes by thinking of taste combinations that would work well, savory and sweet.

295. What Are Allergies?
There's a good chance you or your kid will have allergies of one form or another. I used to have none and grew up with cats, but now I'm allergic to them, so these things can even come on later in life. Explain what allergies are, why it's an autoimmune problem (your body attacking something that it doesn't need to attack), and how medicines can help. Go into greater detail about anything a family member is allergic to. Talk also about the reaction to the allergy, from annoying symptoms to severe, and what to do if someone comes into contact with the allergen.
Level up: Go deeper into the science; take your kid for an allergy test (it involves light pricking but is fascinating as you immediately see results of different allergens dropped onto a grid on your arm).

296. Food Allergies and Intolerances
From allergies to pollen and dander shift to food allergies and intolerances. Learning about how much of the world is intolerant to certain foods (lactose, gluten) makes kids more tolerant. This hits home best if a family member has such an intolerance or allergy, but it can also be simply theoretical.
Level up: What is the body doing (or not doing) that results in this? Which foods have the allergen in them?

297. Being Polite
What would Ms. Manners do? Each family will have their own definition of being polite but teaching your preferred approach to your kids is something you'll want to do anyway. Roleplay with your kids: in this situation, what is the polite thing to do? Whether it's saying "please pass the ketchup" or helping a little old lady cross the road, roleplaying conversations will lead to mirrored behavior in life. You can test with narrating behaviors and asking, "was that polite?"

Level up: Present more complicated, nuanced scenarios and ask what the polite thing to do would be (rather than stating what happened and asking whether it was polite).

298. Bake Bread in a Can

You can bake bread in, like, normal vessels, like a loaf pan or a Dutch oven or on a baking stone. But kids think it's weird and cool to bake it in a can, the sort of forty-eight-ounce can that might contain juice or a lot of white beans (as in the one we grabbed). The metal can super-heats and stimulates the rising bread. So make any bread recipe, knead it, and stuff it into the can about one-third of the way up (it will rise). Be sure to remove the label or it will burn up in the oven.

Level up: Use one bread dough base and divide it over several cans, each with different mix-ins of your kids choice (like nuts or seeds or honey and oats) to try a variety of breads in one bake.

299 & 300. Design a Tree House/Design a Deluxe Birdhouse

What would your kids' dream tree house look like? What would be inside? How about a birdhouse that would be perfect for the birds of your area? Draw up blueprints and talk through the details of what your kid would include. Have your kid scout for a good tree to use (choosing one sturdy enough). Learn about the preferences of local birds to know what sort of food to leave for them and when to expect birds in various seasons.

Level up: Actually build the tree house (a model of it using balsa wood or, if you can, the tree house itself); build the birdhouse and see how it works.

301. Birdwatching

Study up on which birds are in your region at various times of year. Put out food for them if that seems doable. Invest in a pair of binoculars. Learn the names of the birds, what they look like, and some fun facts about them. Then, over the course of the year, try to check off of a list all the birds that you see. This is a long-term lessonlet with many smaller lessons within.

Level up: Go on birdwatching expeditions to proactively seek out birds on your list, rather than passively waiting to see who shows up outside your window.

302. Parents' Pick of Nostalgic Games

Parents, it's totally cool (as outlined in a chapter) to try to brainwash your kids into loving what you loved when you were their age. Your enthusiasm will be contagious, and your kids will want to please you and give what you loved the benefit of the doubt (until they're teenagers, of course, but we'll wait to cover that in a different book). So make lists of your old favorites, in this case, games and board games (Clue, Life, Candyland, Othello, Battleship, Operation) and play them with your kids. These games are evergreen and are likely to be just as popular with your brood as they were for you.

Level up: Have family board game tournament days when the weather is inclement and play your way through a stack of boardgames while eating snacks that are bad for you.

303. Parents' Pick of Nostalgic Cartoons

As with the aforementioned games, try cartoons as well. My dad loved *Beany and Cecil*; my wife grew up with some Yugoslav classic cartoons; I loved *Scooby-Doo*, *GI Joe*, *Transformers*, *He-Man*, and *Thundercats*. Again, your enthusiasm really encourages your kids to follow suit. Old episodes are often found on YouTube—we just ran into *Fractured Fairy Tales* from *The Rocky and Bullwinkle Show*, and it was a big hit.

Level up: Let each member of the extended family recommend a different cartoon and then have a classic cartoon marathon, popcorn included.

304. Interviews

Have your kids interview someone—you, a friend, a relative, or make an imaginary set of interview questions for a celebrity or even fictional character. Thinking up good interview questions is an art form and prompts your kids to probe deeper, analyze what they already know and search things they'd like to learn.

Level up: Set up your kid to conduct an interview with someone they haven't met (maybe just one of your friends or colleagues) to give them the experience of meeting someone they don't know at all and starting to interview them from scratch; have them later write up their interview as a profile of the person.

305. Vital Statistics

I learned this term based on a play on it in *Asterix*, where the name of the village chief is Vitalstatistix. Still it's good for your kids to know their own basic facts: height, weight, gender, hair and eye color, shoes size, blood type, and so on. It's up to you which you include, but knowing them is as useful as knowing your home phone number. Each one is a lessonlet opportunity. What is weight, and how is it measured? Why are there blood types, and why is knowing yours important?

Level up: You can get into more complex vital statistics, like average blood pressure or glucose levels to fill out the picture of your kids' own health and body.

306. Memorize Numbers

When I was a kid, I had dozens of phone numbers memorized. My own home, my parents at work, my parents' friends, my nanny's. Now I barely know my wife's number, because the little computers we carry in our pockets with us (a.k.a. smartphones) remember everything for us. But memorizing some numbers is good and a safety benefit. Your kids should memorize their own address and the phone numbers of each parent. Memorizing things promotes memory (obvious but worth repeating), and this is a good life skill.

Level up: Expand your child's mental rolodex and try to have them memorize ten numbers, then more.

307. What to Do in an Emergency

Speaking of memorizing numbers, it's useful to drill your kids in what to do if there's an emergency. They should know what number to call (911 in the United States or 113 in Europe). They should also be taught what an emergency might look like. You might instruct them to first call a relative and only call the authorities if a relative can't be reached. Whatever seems right to you, but better that they know this and internalize it in a calm moment than, heaven forbid, have to figure it out in the midst of a real emergency. Making plans, repeating them, drilling them is useful.

Level up: For older kids you can roleplay various emergency situations and what they should do in them; you can teach your kids some basic CPR or fire extinguishing techniques so they don't just call for help but can possibly help themselves.

308. Card Games

Playing cards offer endless gaming possibilities with lessonlets aplenty. "War" teaches hierarchies (which card is more valuable). Blackjack, also known as 21, teaches basic math and, if you like, statistics (the chances of the card a player wants showing up in the deck). "Spit" teaches fast reflexes. Teach the history of playing cards and why they have suits and face cards. It's also good for teaching sportsmanship, winning elegantly, and losing with grace.

Level up: More complex games like Gin Rummy or Poker, games with chips, exotic card games like Tarok (a European favorite that Americans rarely have heard of).

309. Learn a Musical Instrument

You've learned about musical instruments and orchestras. Now let your kid pick an instrument that intrigues them (or that you happen to have at home) and try to learn all about it in depth. Take a piano, for instance. How does it work? What is the history of the piano? What are some historical piano compositions or performances to listen to? Who are some famous pianists? What styles of music suit the instrument?

Level up: Have your kid take lessons in the instrument, in person or using an app or videos, and try to get good at it.

310. Set the Table

This can be a daily activity (that sounds better than "chore" doesn't it?) that your kid can help with and make a lesson of it. Each day tell your kid what's for lunch and have them set the table for the correct number of people in order to have flatware and silverware for all and for the meal in question.

Level up: Tell your kid what you'll be making for a meal, show them the recipe, and ask them to pull out all you'll need to make it, from ingredients to implements, vessels, and cookware.

311. Doing the Right Thing

In *Frozen 2* (which should be on your watch list) there's a theme of, when in doubt, just focus on doing "the next right thing." Help your kids with morality lessons by describing situations to them and asking what they think would be the right thing, the moral thing, to do? You can use examples you encounter in movies, in stories or in real life.

Level up: Go a bit more abstract and ask your kid what's something nice they could do in a given situation you describe (for example, "Your sister has a sore throat and is home from school in bed. What would be a nice thing you could do for her?" and they might say "Make her tea and bring her lozenges and put on a movie").

312. Teach Your Friends
They've taught you in past lessonlets. Now have your kid make a plan to teach something to their friends and encourage them to do it on their own, without you supervising, and then ask them how it went. This helps kids feel like they are more grown-up and a leader among their peers.
Level up: Choose more elaborate things, like teaching their friends a game they don't yet know, including various rules.

313. Invent Your Own Lessonlet
Now that your kids have played Lesson Games with you so many times, it's their turn to get creative. Have your kid invent their own lessonlet based on this formula they will by now have experienced. What superpowers do they lack that they'd like to acquire? How might they go about learning them with your help?
Level up: Find an activity (a film, a trip, a book) that could contain multiple lessonlets (like our *Harry Potter* example) and see how many lessonlets your kids could draw from them.

Suggested Further Reading

This book does not have a traditional bibliography as it is not a researched, academic work but one designed by me based on my own parenting strategies. I'm sure that I got inspiration for the ideas from various sources, but they arrived organically, without my proactive research. In lieu of a traditional bibliography, then, I'm pleased to offer a concise list for suggested further reading.

Druckerman, Pamela. *Bringing Up Bébé: One American Mother Discovers the Wisdom of French Parenting.* New York: Penguin Press, 2012.

Dweck, Carol S. *Mindset: The New Psychology of Success.* New York: Ballantine Books, 2006.

Faber, Adele, and Elaine Mazlish. *How to Talk So Kids Will Listen and Listen So Kids Will Talk.* New York: Scribner, 2012 (originally published in 1980).

Faber, Adele, and Elaine Mazlish. *How to Talk So Little Kids Will Listen: A Survival Guide to Life with Children Ages 2–7.* New York: Scribner, 2017.

Gottman, John, and Joan Declaire. *Raising an Emotionally Intelligent Child: The Heart of Parenting.* New York: Simon & Schuster, 1997.

Grose, Michael. *Spoonfed Generation: How to Raise Independent Children.* Sydney: Penguin Life, 2017.

Grose, Michael. *Why First-Borns Rule the World and Last-Borns Want to Change It: The Science of Sibling Personality.* Sydney: Random House Australia, 2003.

Juul, Jesper. *Your Competent Child: Toward New Basic Values for the Family.* New York: Farrar, Straus and Giroux, 2001.

Kabat-Zinn, Myla, and Jon Kabat-Zinn. *Everyday Blessings: The Inner Work of Mindful Parenting.* New York: Hachette, 2014.

Markham, Laura. *Peaceful Parent, Happy Kids: How to Stop Yelling and Start Connecting.* New York: Perigee, 2012.

Markham, Laura. *Peaceful Parent, Happy Siblings: How to Stop the Fighting and Raise Friends for Life.* New York: Perigee, 2015.

Montessori, Maria. *The Absorbent Mind.* New York: Holt Paperbacks, 1995 (originally published in 1949).

Mrgole, Albert, and Lea Mrgole. *Connect with Your Teen: A Guide for Con-*

scious Parenting. Ljubljana: Cangura, 2016.

Nelson, Jane. *Positive Discipline: The Classic Guide to Helping Children Develop Self-Discipline, Responsibility, Cooperation, and Problem-Solving Skills.* New York: Ballantine Books, 2006.

Siegel, Daniel J., and Tina Payne Bryson. *No-Drama Discipline: The Whole-Brain Way to Calm the Chaos and Nurture Your Child's Developing Mind.* New York: Bantam, 2014.

Siegel, Daniel J., and Tina Payne Bryson. *The Whole-Brain Child: 12 Revolutionary Strategies to Nurture Your Child's Developing Mind.* New York: Bantam, 2011.

Skenazy, Lenore. *Free-Range Kids: How Parents and Teachers Can Let Go and Let Grow.* Hoboken, NJ: Wiley, 2010.

About the Author

Dr. Noah Charney is the internationally best-selling author of more than twenty-five books, translated into fourteen languages, including *The Collector of Lives: Giorgio Vasari and the Invention of Art*, which was nominated for the 2017 Pulitzer Prize in Biography, and *Museum of Lost Art*, which was the finalist for the 2018 Digital Book World Award. He is a professor of art history specializing in art crime and teaches for the Smithsonian, the National Gallery UK, and Yale University online. He is also the founder of ARCA, the Association for Research into Crimes against Art, the first research group in this field (www.artcrimeresearch.org). He has written often for major magazines and newspapers, including the *Guardian* and the *Washington Post*, and writes for the TED platform. He is also a TV and radio presenter, with programs for the BBC and The Great Courses, among others, and is an award-winning podcast host. He lives in Slovenia with his wife, children, and their hairless dog, Hubert van Eyck, where he is also Ambassador of Tourism (believe it or not). Learn more at www.noahcharney.com.